October 15—17, 2009
Minneapolis, MN

Creating a New Craft Culture

/ American Craft Council Conference 2009

Editors/ Jenny Gill, Monica Hampton
Copy Editor/ Belinda Lanks
Design/ Rational Beauty: Jeanette Abbink,
Natasha Chandani

Edited transcripts from the American Craft
Council's 2009 conference "Creating a New
Craft Culture" have been published as a visual
and verbal record of the event. For audio podcasts (including all Q&A sessions), photos
from the conference, and continuing conversation, visit the "Creating a New Craft Culture" website: www.craftcouncil.org/
conference09.

ISBN 978 – 1– 4507 – 0392 – 5

Published by American Craft Council
72 Spring Street, 6th floor
New York, NY 10012-4109
www.craftcouncil.org

A note to the reader:
Whenever possible, we have included images
taken from the presentations to illustrate the
conference transcripts. Where specific images are referenced in the text, you will find
a blue circled letter corresponding to that
image. Please note that additional images not
included in this book are referenced in the
transcript and that image placement does not
correspond to directionals in the text (for
example, "on the right" or "on the left"),
which refer to on-site slide presentations.

Table of Contents

Creating a New Craft Culture / American Craft Council

We are pleased to present to you the publication of the American Craft Council's 11th national conference, "Creating a New Craft Culture," held on October 15–17, 2009, in Minneapolis, Minnesota.

This publication is a comprehensive transcription of what was presented at the conference, along with an introductory essay by the conference presenter and craft scholar Sandra Alfoldy. What we cannot document is the sense of community, energy, and enthusiasm that was pervasive among the more than 300 individuals who attended this conference not only from around the United States but from Canada, New Zealand, Scotland, and England. Attendees represented a range of professions, including architects, designers, collectors, educators, writers, museum professionals, makers, retailers, and students. The high level of discussion that took place at "Creating a New Craft Culture," both inside and outside of the conference program, served as a true testament to the interest and need for ongoing dialogue around critical issues related to the field.

It has been more than 50 years since our first conference and, while the world is a different place than it was back then, issues of transition and change remain a constant. The words of welcome from Mrs. Aileen Osborn Webb, the founder of the American Craft Council and godmother of the modern American craft movement, called on makers from across the country to come together in Asilomar, California, in 1957 in much the same way her words call on us today:

The aim of our conference is to afford participants the chance to meet, communicate and cooperate in solving problems; to formulate, through discussion and interchange of ideas, a basic understanding of the place of the craftsman in our contemporary society—the philosophical and sociological role of the crafts, the need of a creative and experimental approach to design and the craftsman's practical problems of production, marketing and industrial affiliation.[1]

Greatly influenced and shaped by the responses and outcomes gathered after our 2006 conference in Houston, this year's conference was designed to leave participants thinking about the larger community of craft in a new way. We wanted to explore not only the act of making but the concept—how shaping and creating something with your hands adeptly addresses the rapidly changing world and craft's role in it. Additionally, we wanted to offer a program that would challenge, educate, and inspire our audiences to view their personal community through the lens of the wider craft world, broadening their view of how craft intersects with current political, social, cultural, and marketplace trends.

A series of critical questions around the notion of craft, with a shift in focus from thinking about the objects to investigating what is at the core of being a maker, led us to our conference themes: "Craft and the Individual," "Craft and the Community," and "Craft and the Marketplace."

1/ Mrs. Vanderbilt Webb, "Craftsmen Today," in *Asilomar: First Annual Conference of American Craftsmen* (New York: American Craftsmen's Council, 1957), 5.

Our first day, dedicated to the individual and community, encouraged people to think about how craft is impacting the world at large through the individual. Conference speakers and artists—including the sociologist Dr. Richard Sennett, Sandra Alfoldy of the Nova Scotia College of Art & Design, Natalie Chanin of Alabama Chanin, and the filmmaker of *Handmade Nation*, Faythe Levine—all reflected on the ethical and political choices that create communities of people who choose to make their living by making things by hand or teaching those ideas to others.

Our second day focused on the individual and the community's relationship to the marketplace. This session explored the forever dynamic and changing marketplace for craft. Conference speakers—including *The New York Times Magazine* columnist Rob Walker, Lisa Bayne of the Artful Home, Maria Thomas of Etsy, Julie Lasky of Design Observer, Robin Petravic of Heath Ceramics, and the ceramic-arts writer Garth Clark—explored where, and what, the marketplace for craft is, as well as the vastly different approaches for how people sell their work today to survive in this fast-paced global environment.

The American Craft Council relishes our role as the only national organization to represent and champion all craft media, and we can think of no better purpose than to gather thought leaders, practitioners, participants, admirers, teachers, and students to examine our world. Past conferences have played a role in changing the way we think about craft.

With that, we would like to extend our heartfelt thanks to the people, organizations, and institutions whose patronage and support have helped make this conference and this subsequent publication possible. Chief among them is Andrew Glasgow, our former executive director. We thank him for all he has done for the Council, this conference, and the craft field. We also wish to thank the members of the American Craft Council board of trustees and the local and national members of the "Creating a New Craft Culture" conference committee. Without continued support such as theirs, initiatives such as this would not be possible.

We hope readers of this publication will gain a sense of understanding about the field of craft at this moment in time and that the thinking and discussions that took place in Minneapolis will help to stimulate continued dialogue and collaboration among the diverse craft communities, creating a sense of shared excitement, community, and passion within our audiences.

We look forward to championing craft in the coming years of continued transition. +

Lani Duke /
Board Chair
American Craft Council

Susan Cummins /
Chair, Conference Committee
American Craft Council

Top to bottom, left to right: Lani Duke, Monica Hampton, Richard Sennett, Elissa Auther, Sandra Alfoldy, Claudia Crisan, Tom Patti, Michael Sherrill, Adam Lerner, Jennifer Komar Olivarez, Kristin Tombers, Natalie Chanin, Faythe Levine, Rob Walker, Namita Gupta Wiggers, Lisa Bayne, Amy Shaw, Maria Thomas, Julie Lasky, Robin Petravic, Lydia Matthews, Garth Clark, Sonya Clark, Stefano Catalani, Andy Brayman, Garth Johnson, Jean McLaughlin, Lacey Jane Roberts, and Brent Skidmore.

These transcriptions and final text presentations are a companion to our website, which contains downloadable podcasts, full Q&A sessions following presentations, images of the conference, and ongoing blog dialogues among readers. For more information, please go to www.craftcouncil.org/conference09.

What Would Mrs. Vanderbilt Webb Think? The American Craft Council in Its Season of Change / Sandra Alfoldy

1/ Jay Doblin, "The Position of Crafts in America Today," in *Asilomar: First Annual Conference of American Craftsmen* (New York: American Craftsmen's Council, 1957), 51. http://www.craftcouncil.org/html/council/index_books.php?book=1&page=1&title=title_1957_june.
2/ Paul Cummings, oral history interview with Mrs. Vanderbilt Webb, May 7–June 9, 1970, 3. Archives of American Art, Smithsonian Institution, Washington, D.C., mq24004. Eleanor Roosevelt played a role in Webb's later interest in social assistance through the crafts, as Roosevelt and her friends Marion Dickerman and Nancy Cook had generated the idea of Val-Kill Industries

"You craftsmen have the wonderful opportunity to make a tremendous contribution to the culture, comfort, and happiness of America, to build a sound basis for your crafts, if you can resolve some of the practical problems and aesthetic drives."
/ Jay Doblin , industrial designer, 1957 [1]

Continuing its rich tradition of organizing conferences, the American Craft Council hosted "Creating a New Craft Culture" in Minneapolis, Minnesota, from October 15–17, 2009. Conferences are funny things in that they quickly develop a tone or feeling that is shared by many of the attendees. This mood is difficult, if not impossible, to capture in the published conference proceedings, and often readers who did not have the opportunity to attend are left with a neutral impression of the event. As soon as delegates gathered in Minneapolis, an electric atmosphere emerged. This was helped along by pre-conference discussions called "convenings," which united craftspeople, academics, curators, administrators, collectors, editors and writers, and American Craft Council board members in identifying issues and successes in areas that affect the crafts, such as education, museums, the marketplace, and writing/media. The energy generated by these unscripted meetings spilled over and influenced the entire conference. However, beneath the surface of excitement there was some stress. It became clear that rather than just presenting an idea-generating exercise, the American Craft Council was seeking some help with future directions.

Now this is not to suggest that this was a negative thing. The American Craft Council was built on the needs and desires of craftspeople and has successfully tuned into these demands, creating infrastructures to support artists for more than 60 years. Initially, this was done with the guidance of Aileen Osborn Webb , also known as Mrs. Vanderbilt Webb, who spearheaded the formation of the Council in 1943. She was active in politics from an early age and, around 1912, served as vice president of the Women's Democratic Committee in Putnam County, New York, where she hosted a Democratic picnic that featured a speech delivered by Eleanor Roosevelt—"the first political speech that Eleanor Roosevelt ever made." [2] Webb became involved with the crafts in 1929, when she and her friends Nancy Campbell and Ernestine Baker established Putnam County Products in Garrison, New York, to market local crafts during the Great Depression. [3] She recalled that they expected the local people to arrive ready to sell string beans and eggs and were instead delighted when the women produced needlecrafts and the men woodwork, demonstrating "the latent art consciousness in people." [4] For Webb, the crafts were unique in their ability to tap into this consciousness.

Mrs. Vanderbilt Webb consistently emphasized the ability of crafts to communicate across language, geographical, and cultural barriers. The American Craftsmen's Council held its first conference in 1957 in Asilomar, California, a pivotal event, as described by Lydia Matthews, dean and professor at Parsons the New School of Design: "Asilomar, California, 1957. That phrase is shorthand in some circles for a remarkable gathering of minds and makers whose dialogues shaped the professionalization of American craft during the postwar years." [5] This conference was one of the projects Webb supported, and her introductory remarks focused on the need for improved communications: "The simple thing which we are offering you here is the possibility of communicating, one with another... to afford participants from all over the United States the chance to meet, communicate, and cooperate in solving problems." [6] The 2009 "Creating a New Craft Culture" conference shared this emphasis, with Susan Cummins, chair of the conference committee, and Andrew Glasgow, executive director of the American Craft Council, placing Webb's quote on the front page of the conference booklet. Cummins and Glasgow urged participants to "view their personal community through the lens of the wider craft world, broadening their view of how craft intersects with current political, social, cultural, and marketplace trends," [7] highlighting parallels with the 1957 Asilomar conference, which sought to recognize the socioeconomic implications of craft.

in 1927. Val-Kill was an Arts and Crafts colony producing Colonial Revival crafts inspired by Roosevelt's "cottage" located on her Springwood, New York, estate near the Val-Kill stream.
3/ Aileen Osborn Webb, *Almost a Century*, unpublished autobiography in American Craft Council archives, 69.
4/ Ibid., 68.

5/ Lydia Matthews, "Expanding Networks and Professional Proposals: Shaping the Future of Craft in an Age of Wicked Problems," in *Shaping the Future of Craft: 2006 National Leadership Conference* (New York: American Craft Council, 2007), 13.
6/ Mrs. Vanderbilt Webb, "Craftsmen Today," in *Asilomar*, 5.

7/ Susan Cummins and Andrew Glasgow, "Welcome," in "Creating a New Craft Culture" participant booklet, October 15–17, 2009.

In order to understand the impact of 2009's "Creating a New Craft Culture," this essay will compare and contrast seven major themes that emerged from the event with similar ideas presented at 1957's "Craftsmen Today" conference: the marketplace/economic realities, education/communication, cross-disciplinarity, new materials/new technologies, professionalism, gender, and spirituality/lifestyle. Despite more than 50 years of growth and development, the crafts continue to focus on these areas—some formally, as part of the conference program, and some informally, in the form of questions and debates that emerged following formal presentations. Given the enormous changes that are impacting the American Craft Council, most notably the resignation of Andrew Glasgow as executive director and the announcement that the Council's offices and administration will be moving from New York City to Minneapolis in 2010, it is timely to connect our current perspectives and concerns with those that helped to shape and build the American Craft Council.

Marketplace/ Economic Realities

"I feel that a tremendous amount of people are being taught to be craftsmen, and that something has to be done with them. The rate of proliferation is about the same as rabbits." Michael Higgins , glass artist, 1957[8]

The American Craft Council was formed to create improved markets for craftspeople. As much as Council conferences are about the exchange of ideas, the financial survival of craftspeople is the only way to ensure the development of craft discourse. It is all very well and good to pontificate on the deep meaning of the crafts when one is a regularly paid professor, curator, or arts administrator, but it is an entirely different thing when the ability to have time to shape your ideas surrounding craft depends on earning enough through selling your art to cover your expenses. How fortunate, then, that

given the economic recession of 2008–9, a crowd of more than 300 was still able to gather in Minneapolis to share information and debate concepts. There was a sense that it was still too early to tell if the new Obama administration was going to have a positive impact, and the political conversation of craft largely focused on the recession, with general agreement (an observation gathered through informal discussion) that sales by individual craft artists had dropped and that everyone was impacted by lower market earnings that affected the philanthropy of individuals as well as museum, art-gallery, and craft-organization endowments. In spite of this, *The New York Times* and other media have noted a movement toward the handmade, an observation that began just prior to the economic downturn. Craft sales may have dropped, but not only are they holding up better than expected, their resilience is attracting media attention.

Asger Fischer , from the Danish Society of Art and Craft and Industry (Den Permanente), gave a keynote paper in 1957 that chided American craftspeople for being too concerned with money, stating that this is what prevented them from being as successful as their Scandinavian counterparts: "In one way it's very difficult for me because I come from a little country, and here you are a huge country and you are talking more about money and business than we do in our country inside arts and crafts. I think there is a sort of danger if you get on a too economic state in life, in doing business you may lose some of your face as an artist."[9] The emphasis on the marketplace at craft conferences has a long history. As Susan Cummins reminds us, "Craftsman as business person is a strong tradition which is unlike the artist or designer."[10] However, in 2009, the discussion was less about money and more about the marketplace. It is assumed that craftspeople now receive some training in how to run a business as part of their undergraduate education, so sessions like 1957's "The Small Business Man," which featured such basic market information as how to price your work and the difference between commissioning and wholesaling your work, are no longer present

8/ Michael Higgins, "How I Became a Designer of Glass," in *Asilomar*, 121.

9/ Asger Fischer, "Discussion—The Small Business Man," in *Asilomar*, 131.

10/ Susan Cummins, email communication, November 27, 2009.

at the American Craft Council conferences (much to Fischer's relief, I'm sure).

Instead, thought-provoking views of the marketplace are put forward. This was evident in Robin Petravic's "Story of Heath Ceramics." Petravic, a product designer who has consulted for major companies as well as managed the design and engineering teams at LightSurf Technologies, purchased Heath Ceramics in 2003 with his wife, the industrial designer Catherine Bailey. Petravic's story provided insight into what sustains a successful craft business, as Heath Ceramics was established in 1948 and still thrives today.

become rather blurry. Just as craft is in flux, so is the marketplace, and shifting perceptions on ethical consumerism are working in craft's favor.

Lydia Matthews's presentation, "New Models of Marketplace," used contemporary craft and design projects to demonstrate that craft need not feel threatened by today's economic uncertainties. She argued that sustainable systems and their interconnected lifestyle ideas provide new opportunities for the crafts but that craftspeople must be willing to embrace the changes wrought by young entrepreneurs. Craft artists are not as interested

"In today's fast-paced, economically uncertain, and increasingly computerized world, the crafts continue to grow and flourish, despite what would naturally seem to be insurmountable obstacles."

It became clear from Petravic's presentation that his experience in design as well as new technologies provided the impetus for Heath Ceramics to not only stay in business but to flourish during these difficult economic times. In 1957, at "Craftsmen Today," Edith Heath , the company's founder, presented an overview of how she established Heath Ceramics, building from producing dinnerware with just herself and one assistant to a staff of 23. Heath concluded her paper by asking, "Is what we make mundane? To me, it is like good food, well-made, with a subtle flavor. Is this art? Time will tell."[11] And time has proven that good craftsmanship, excellent design, and demand for the product create art.

By dint of not being directly involved in the crafts, the journalist and writer Rob Walker delivered a powerful presentation titled "Handmade 2.0." Walker is known for his deconstructions of the marketplace, and he put his finger on the pulse of craft today by reminding the audience that we are experiencing an exciting moment when the crafts have great potential to expand into the consumer market. He did issue a sardonic reminder, however, that the line between independent craftspeople and big-box stores can

in past histories of the marketplace as what is happening today, and they recognize that the market is constantly shifting. Therefore, the discussion of economic realities at "Creating a New Craft Culture" followed Walker's and Matthews's lead and focused on predicting future trends and directions. It is interesting that the environment and sustainability have continued to be a theme in the discussion of craft since the founding of the Society for the Protection of Ancient Buildings by William Morris and Philip Webb in 1877. At Asilomar, the ceramist F. Carlton Ball  spoke of the opportunity for crafts to play a role in "the socio-economic future of small towns." "In many parts of the country," he said, "man has over-exploited the land, taken away the mineral wealth or destroyed the fertility and wasted natural resources."[12] Craft, according to Ball, would be the solution: Moving craftspeople into these rural areas would rejuvenate them through creation rather than destruction. A similar level of romanticization of craft's role in economic and environmental sustainability exists today, only at the 2009 conference, it was channeled through its connection with the already established desires of eco-friendly consumers.

11/ Edith Heath, "A Small Business in Ceramics," in *Asilomar*, 127.
12/ F. Carlton Ball, "Ceramics—A Socio-Economic Outlook," in *Asilomar*, 14.

Natalie Chanin's "The Marketplace and the Personal: A Story of Thread" personalized these broader ideas of community and sustainability. Chanin spoke about her return in 2000 to her hometown in Alabama, where she reached out to local makers to establish Alabama Chanin, a business dedicated to slow design and environmental sustainability. Chanin emphasized the importance of connecting consumers to the individual artisan through her company motto, "grown-to-sewn in the U.S.A.," a political statement that strongly resonates in this time of economic recession.

No one, either today or in the past, has undertaken a sustained discussion of the contradictory nature of craft in relation to the perception of its being an eco-friendly endeavor. Revealing the true cost of craft production in terms of the environment would be counterproductive to marketing the image of the sustainability-minded craftsperson. However, students are not under any illusions. A large number of undergraduate and graduate students in the crafts were present in Minneapolis and provided excellent insights into the concerns of emerging craftspeople. Although conversations with these students revealed they are creating dynamic and innovative work, many with sustainability at the heart of their projects remain anxious about the viability of supporting themselves in the marketplace.

Education / Communication

"Man cannot exist for and by himself, nor can the craftsman. The very fact we are here proves that we feel a need for improved means of communication with others."
Karl Laurell , designer and weaver, 1957[13]

It was wonderful to hear some participants swooning over their interactions with Faythe Levine, the director of the documentary *Handmade Nation*, and Richard Sennett, author of *The Craftsman*. We attend conferences to gain proximity to those whose voices we want to hear, whether they are established "stars" in our profession or new acquaintances. Apart from the networking and socializing that goes on, conferences serve as important testing grounds for students to see what areas capture their interest, or whether they want to remain involved in the field.

It was possible to witness this internal and external dialogue during "Creating a New Craft Culture," particularly through the question-and-answer periods when microphones were passed to audience members. The polite crowd revealed itself to be teeming with insights and opposing positions. The spontaneity afforded by person-to-person interaction inspired Sonya Clark, the chair of craft and material studies at Virginia Commonwealth University, to initiate a participant survey covering a wide range of questions that emerged during the conference. This was very appropriate, as Clark's presentation, "Craft as Subject, Verb, and Object," emphasized craft as a call to action, and she relied on the survey's results to highlight key directions in the field, including a passionate appeal to the academic community to recognize the importance of continuing to support the crafts. Indeed, the college and university system plays a central role in determining craft's future. During the educators/academia convenings roundtable prior to the official start of the conference, it became clear that, despite the challenges faced by craft as a result of what Lydia Matthews calls the "excis[ing of] the word 'craft' from the public titles of colleges and art galleries,"[14] craft has established itself as an invaluable part of many academic programs. Although almost all the participants on the panel were administrators, a level of fear was evident—fear that, despite the inroads made by craft in the academic community, it remains vulnerable, as institutions make drastic cuts to programming. It also appears that art schools are beginning to think of craft programming outside traditional institutional methods, or, as Susan Cummins observed, "Craft is not only invaluable in academic situations, but young people are looking for experiential learning, and some art schools are beginning to understand that."[15] Matthews's and Sonya Clark's presentations underscored the importance of craft representing itself as

13/ Karl Laurell, "Textiles—The Socio-Economic Outlook," in *Asilomar*, 35.
14/ Matthews, "Expanding Networks and Professional Proposals," 13.
15/ Susan Cummins, email communication, November 27, 2009.

invaluable to higher education. Although the survey results Clark gathered were disparate and not entirely easy to read as a cohesive whole, her presentation established that deep pride in the materials and meanings of craft still exists.[16] Her message provides an interesting counterpoint to the position taken by the writer Garth Clark.

Clark has become known as a critic of the craft movement, which he views as outmoded and headed for its own demise. His lecture, "Palace and Cottage," critiqued craft's willingness to become a hybrid practice with design and the fine arts, something he calls a "corruption of identity." This corruption results in the diminished power of craft and weakens the ability of craft to survive in perilous times. Although great controversy has surrounded Clark's presentations in the past, his message this time did not seem to provoke hostility or resentment from the audience. Instead, people were thoughtful about what this idea of hybridity really means for the crafts. Is it about increasing communication with artists working outside the crafts? And if so, is this shifting identity necessarily bad? Many of the students at the conference were not shocked by this idea; instead, they made it apparent that while they feel a personal affinity for the crafts and are willing to dedicate their careers to its materials and ideals, they are not always willing to call themselves craftspeople, nor are they worried about crossing boundaries.

Cross-Disciplinarity

"We must look not only outside our culture but outside our medium also… these provide our inspiration."
Jack Lenor Larsen , textile designer and weaver, 1957[17]

When the American Craft Council held its first conference in 1957, "cross-disciplinarity" was not an academic buzzword. It was simply remarkable that craftspeople working in ceramics, textiles, metal, wood, glass, and enamel came together to share ideas. To some, this was seen as what might be considered a boundary-crossing activity. The design historian Dr. Karl With  argued that soon the crafts would have to work with other disciplines and that this was a positive step: "I see a trend toward the collaboration of the trained craftsman, designer, artist, engineer, and architect. Craftsmen and craftsmanship have found a new and tremendous territory for activity."[18]

At the 2009 Minneapolis conference, it was evident that crossing disciplines is a common activity in the crafts and that this openness has led to some exciting breakthroughs in terms of where and how craft is accepted. The American Craft Council has kept a delicate balance between the delineated materials of craft and the infusion of new disciplines. At "Creating a New Craft Culture," delegates spanned the spectrum in terms of how they defined their practice. While Garth Clark reminded participants of the dangers existing at the edges, some of the most interesting dialogues opened up in the spaces between craft and other areas, most notably food. Claudia Crisan, the co-owner of a small bakery and edible-art gallery in Albany, New York, and Kristin Tombers, the butcher and owner of Minneapolis's Clancey's Meats and Fish, highlighted the connections between craft and food. For Crisan, the beauty and impermanence of her sugar sculptures and jewelry provoke ideas of the body and temporality. Crisan brought a tray of luminescent, colorful sugar jewels to give to the audience following her panel talk, and this offering created a visceral reaction among audience members lucky enough to select a pin. In a fascinating bit of theater, the large crowd refused to simply grab the works, opting instead to set up the tray so everyone could have the opportunity to admire and photograph Crisan's pieces. Only then did an orderly frenzy of jewelry selection begin. Tombers was paired with Jennifer Komar Olivarez, a curator at the Minneapolis Institute of Art, in a session called "Mixed Taste: Tag-Team Lectures," which brought together Olivarez's overview of Prairie School Architecture and Tombers's description of meat fabrication. Although the gaps between the two areas were pronounced at times,

16/ The American Craft Council hopes to conduct a follow-up and more in-depth survey based on Sonya Clark's initiative.
17/ Jack Lenor Larsen, "Discussion—The Socio-Economic Outlook in Textiles," in *Asilomar*, 37.
18/ Dr. Karl With, "The Future of the Craftsman," in *Asilomar*, 7.

certain thematic overlaps emerged, such as a reverence for materials, careful consumption, and thoughtful creation.

The Slow Food movement and craft have been linked for well over a decade, but the inclusion of food-related crafts and processes at "Creating a New Craft Culture" was new and seemingly successful. In her assessment of the Council's 2006 "Shaping the Future of Craft" conference, Lydia Matthews addressed the issue of cross-disciplinarity: "Craft can no longer be regarded or justified as its own closed system. It does not seem fruitful to talk about 'the crafts' as an amalgam of medium-specific practices (clay, textiles, wood, metals, etc.) supported by their attendant communities. Rather, it is time to address 'craft' as an active verb and an expansive cultural terrain that is now moving beyond prescribed disciplines."[19] Although this is certainly true, there was a growing conviction in 2009 that the urge to dismiss crafts as a relevant collection of established materials contained as many dangers as advantages, particularly given the state of unrest within the Council. Perhaps Garth Clark's paper, in its critique of the craft movement's aspiration to cross over into the art market, serves as a timely reminder that some self-definition is necessary to ensure that the crafts remain cohesive. Even as new materials and new technologies bombard the field, there is a strong sense that something called craft remains.

New Materials / New Technologies

"Concentrating on new materials can turn into a handicap… leading the craftsman away from creative thinking and into the realm of the new and novel."
Anni Albers , weaver and author, 1957[20]

Craft can be fickle, shifting its devotions. At Asilomar, enameling was its own category, with specialists prophesying enormous growth and development for the material. Jackson Woolley , the panel chairman of the enameling discussion, recognized that

"many of the problems of the enamellist are paralleled by those faced by workers in glass. Both crafts must find ways to remain vital and flexible, attuned to modern vision, habits, economies, and architecture."[21] Of course, we know which of these materials went on to enjoy greater popular success.

For centuries, craftspeople working with established materials and techniques have been divided between those who embrace and those who resist new materials and technologies. With the advent of accessible computer technologies in the early 1990s, this separation became more pronounced. Computers and the Internet are now accepted as part of most craft practices, but not all. During the 2009 panel discussion "Craft in the 21st Century: Identity, Choice, Meaning," the glass artist Tom Patti stated that he does not employ computers and feels that the loss of hands-on contact would be detrimental to his work. Claudia Crisan strongly disagreed, arguing that, for her, a computer is simply another tool that she employs in the creation of her designs.

While the computer discussion and debates have subsided in the craft world, the contrast between the slow, deliberate, and hands-on approaches to craft and the rapid, virtual methods of computer software is being better analyzed. The sociologist Richard Sennett addressed this in his keynote presentation, "The Craftsman in Society." Sennett drew a metaphorical link between the head and hand as represented by computer programming. He compared the idea of open-source software available to anyone, which gives rise to collaborative applications such as Wikipedia, to a community of craftspeople with skills passed down from master to apprentice. According to Sennett, the computer-programming community is currently in crisis, with breakaway groups wanting to apply editorial standards to overcome the problem of quality that comes with open access. This was an effective analogy to draw between the fields of craft and computer programming; in both, new materials and technologies have led to debates over quality and loss of skill. Sennett referred to the "craftsman's awareness" and argued that the dialectic of the machine re-

19/ Matthews, "Expanding Networks and Professional Proposals," 15.
20/ Anni Albers, "Discussion—The Socio-Economic Outlook in
Textiles," in *Asilomar*, 36.
21/ Jackson Woolley, "Enamels—The Socio-Economic Outlook," in *Asilomar*, 23.

moves the need for tacit understanding but that smart machines force users to become craftspeople. It was a provocative and strangely reassuring interpretation of the fraught relationship between craft and new technologies.

The panel session "Riding the 'Long Tail': Marketing Craft on the Internet" provided excellent examples of the effective marketing of craft online, but most interesting was the way the message was delivered. The underlying assumption of the discussion was that the Web is a positive force that enables craft to reach a global audience. This

of comments from Richard Sennett regarding his confusion over the role of instrument makers within studio crafts (remarks made during an open discussion period that revealed that he was not a studio craft insider), there was no rehashing of the now exhausted art-versus-craft debate. There was no "us" versus "them" with regard to disciplines such as design, industry, and architecture. The topic was simply a nonstarter. It was wonderful to see that the energy wasted on these discussions can now be directed toward more fruitful explorations of issues affecting craft.

This is the area where the most startling

"One striking similarity between professional studio crafts-people who occupy the inner sanctum of the contemporary craft movement and DIY-ers is their dedication to the lifestyle and values of craft, however they define them."

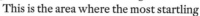

was a refreshing tone and contrasted greatly with previous debates over the Internet's impact on craft. One thing remains as true today as in 1957: Despite our increasing comfort with new technologies and materials, "more and more remarkable advances are being made than one can follow."[22] But in order to be taken seriously as a professional craftsperson in 2009, a Web presence is mandatory.

Professionalism

"It is quite wrong for anyone to assume the title of designer-craftsman. This title has to be earned and received from society in recognition of our work."
Victor Ries Ⓛ, metalsmith, 1957[23]

The recognition of craft as a profession is one area in which the field has come a long way. Whereas at Asilomar, outside experts were brought in to give firm directions on how craft should proceed, in 2009, they were called in to talk about how their areas of expertise might enhance craft. How refreshing it was that, with the exception of a couple

changes have occurred for craft since 1957. At Asilomar, Dr. Karl With's "The Future of the Craftsman" keynote address not only started by defining what craft is not (it is *not* art, it is *not* industry), he further reduced the scope of craft, stating, "The most important criteria for any craft object is—does it function?"[24] The speakers and panelists in Minneapolis shared the assumption that the crafts under discussion were necessarily professional, but beyond that, the definition was blown wide open. Utilitarian, conceptual, small or large scale, media-specific or media-crossing, the scope of craft has grown enormously. Julie Lasky, a design writer and editor, presented "Men in White," an exploration of design's willingness to adopt the dress, language, and social codes of other creative industries in order to permeate boundaries. Her lecture was timely, as craft is growing increasingly adept at being a "submerged creative identity," as Lasky describes it. This subversive submerging can succeed only if it is undertaken by a fully professionalized field, so rather than worrying that craft's cross-disciplinary tendencies are a sign of weakness, they should be read as symbols of strength. The audience opinions appeared mixed as

22/ Lawrence Peabody, "Wood—The Socio-Economic Outlook," in *Asilomar*, 38.
23/ Victor Ries, "Metals—The Socio-Economic Outlook," in *Asilomar*, 31.

24/ With, "The Future of the Craftsman," 7.

to the role traditional studio craft continues to play today, although everyone assumed that the different iterations of craft activity were all professional—with one major exception: DIY.

Gender

"So don't you ever, man, tell me it cannot be done."
Marguerite Wildenhain Ⓜ, ceramic artist, 1957[25]

In 1957, Marguerite Wildenhain took exception to the ceramist F. Carlton Ball's remark that "it's practically impossible for a craftsman to earn his living at doing craft."[26] She pointed out that since 1925 she had earned her income from her pottery, "and I'm a woman by myself."[27] Wildenhain was exceptional as a single woman who established herself as a professional in a male-dominated field, so her feisty objections to remarks that reduced her success make perfect sense. During the Asilomar conference, gendered comments were made, but, with the exception of Wildenhain, not by women; they came from men who were anxious that hobbyists and dilettantes would hinder attempts to professionalize craft. The enamellist Jackson Woolley worried that the involvement of amateurs would "result in a cheapening of the craft."[28] The metalsmith Arthur J. Pulos Ⓝ said, "I suspect the dilettante who effortlessly and without conscience turns from one craft to another."[29]

Of course, Woolley, Pulos, and others were not talking exclusively about women,[30] but the word "dilettante" is implicitly gendered. And gender remains an issue, albeit an unspoken one. (But it must be noted that in 2009 the term "craftsman" is still in common usage in the United States, while one would be pilloried for using that label in the United Kingdom, Canada, or Australia.) Following Elissa Auther's paper, "Lifestyle and Livelihood in Craft Culture," an audience member asked about the impact of the feminist movement of the 1960s and 1970s on the back-to-the-land craft activity Auther so beautifully evoked. Auther's response was surprisingly vague. Faythe Levine's talk, "A Handmade Nation," which outlined lessons learned as the director of the documentary *Handmade Nation*, glossed over the obvious female constituency. When Catherine Whalen, of the Bard Graduate Center, asked Levine her views on the feminist revival of craft practices implicit in her work, they were dismissed as outside the realm of discussion.

And yet all this vagueness cannot conceal the fact that gender is still a concern. When an image of Martha Stewart was shown during the "Craft in the 21st Century: Identity, Choice, Meaning" panel, it provoked a tremendous response. Some, including a young stay-at-home mother who pursues her craft as a "DIY-er," jumped up during the question period to say how excited she was to see Martha Stewart as part of the discussion. Others, such as the venerable Helen Drutt, who has made remarkable contributions to advancing the contemporary craft movement, were appalled that Martha Stewart was even part of the conversation.

However, the DIY movement has so permeated popular culture (the December 2009 issue of *O: The Oprah Magazine* features a DIY crafter from the Renegade Craft fairs) that we would be remiss if we did not address the impact of the DIY culture on public perceptions of professional craft. DIY participants are largely young women, so are we reverting to outdated and gendered ideas of hobbyists and dilettantes when we dismiss the impact of this demographic on future directions for craft? And why is it that some of these young women are not tuned into their feminist predecessors? How many of them know the story of Wildenhain's struggles and successes, or of Mrs. Vanderbilt Webb's determination to make life better for the craftspeople of America? One striking similarity between professional studio craftspeople who occupy the inner sanctum of the contemporary craft movement and DIY-ers is their dedication to the lifestyle and values of craft, however they define them.

Ⓝ

25/ Marguerite Wildenhain, "Discussion—The Socio-Economic Outlook in Ceramics," in *Asilomar*, 21.
26/ F. Carlton Ball, "Discussion—The Socio-Economic Outlook in Ceramics," in *Asilomar*, 21.
27/ Ibid.
28/ Woolley, "Enamels—The Socio-Economic Outlook," 23.
29/ Arthur J. Pulos, "Metals—The Socio-Economic Outlook," in *Asilomar*, 29.
30/ In fact, the well-known metalsmith John Paul Miller confessed that he "began his work as a type of 'how-to-do-it' craftsman." Quoted in ibid., 32.

Lifestyle / Spirituality

"Here is a human being faced with a raw material. What he does with this stuff, how it is shaped, drawn, colored, formed leads me to believe, in all seriousness, that each one of us is given the opportunity of a divine spark…cloaked in the term we know as craftsmanship."
Virgil Cantini , enamellist, 1957[31]

When more than 450 craftspeople, teachers, and collectors gathered in Asilomar for the American Craft Council's first conference, they hoped to generate a new era for the crafts. The ceramist F. Carlton Ball waxed poetic about the future "Golden Age of craft activity, one with a new outlook, new aims where the soul of each man is the important product and the craft work only the reflection of the craftsman's soul."[32] Lifestyle was an essential component of the event, as reflected in the conference's California surroundings, which were described by Lydia Matthews as a retreat on the "majestic Pacific coastline [with] gorgeous and understated craftsman-style wooden buildings."[33]

Although the 2009 conference was held in a generic hotel conference room, attention to lifestyle was still in evidence, from the creative crafts on display on attendees' attire (you have to love the profusion of amazing jewelry and textiles at an American Craft Council gathering) to the overview of "Lifestyle and Livelihood in Craft Culture," provided by Elissa Auther, which demonstrated the close relationship between alternative lifestyles and the rise of the contemporary craft movement. Faythe Levine's synopsis of the DIY superstars featured in her film further reinforced the fact that alternative lifestyles still move people to create crafts. Sometimes it is done as overt politics, such as when the group Knitta performs its late-night knitted interventions on city streets, or through more subtle expressions, such as when someone is moved by a desire to help the environment by living sustainably.

The ceramist Michael Sherrill quietly inspired the audience with his strength of conviction that creating a life supported through the crafts is still viable despite economic fluctuations. Why? Because craftspeople would not be happy doing anything else. Richard Sennett's paper was filled with almost spiritual examples of the grace and meaning that making objects by hand invests in the lives of craftspeople and their fans. In today's fast-paced, economically uncertain, and increasingly computerized world, the crafts continue to grow and flourish, despite what would naturally seem to be insurmountable obstacles. Of course, given the demographic attending the conference, it appeared that the contemporary craft movement remains largely a white, middle-class enterprise. Perhaps future conferences will explore if that is indeed the reality.

2010 and Beyond

It is too early to answer the biggest question that arose from the conference: What is the new craft culture? Susan Cummins, chair of the Conference Committee, wonders, "Is it really just the same as it was in the past, only more so? Or are we evolving toward something we can't quite see yet?"[34] And what would Mrs. Vanderbilt Webb think? Would she take solace in the fact that the community she helped foster continues to grow in strength? Would the persistent conversations about the marketplace, lifestyle, and education encourage her, or would she hope to see them resolved by now? We will never know, but there is one thing we can be certain of following the 2009 American Craft Council conference: Mrs. Webb would want this communication to continue. It was her life's work, and we owe it to her to carry through her vision of a flourishing professional craft field. Just as Asilomar provides a wonderful counterpoint for contextualizing the issues facing the crafts today, may the American Craft Council thrive long into the future to ensure that the 2009 "Creating a New Craft Culture" conference plays an equally important role. ✦

31/ Virgil Cantini, "Enamels—The Socio-Economic Outlook," in *Asilomar*, 26.
32/ Ball, "Discussion—The Socio-Economic Outlook in Ceramics," 16.
33/ Matthews, "Expanding Networks and Professional Proposals," 13.
34/ Susan Cummins, email communication, November 27, 2009.

"Craftsmanship appears to the man or woman who dwells in quick results to be a marginal activity." / Richard Sennett

Day 1
Friday, October 16, 2009
9:45—10:45 am
Lifestyle and Livelihood in
Craft Culture
See page 34

William Morris, wallpaper
designed for St. James's
palace, c. 1880.

Day 1
Friday, October 16, 2009
11 am—12 pm
Craft in the 21st Century
See page 48

Michael Sherrill,
Julesvernium–Seaflower
(detail), 2008, silica,
bronze, Moretti glass,
porcelain, mokume.

Entryway sidelight,
Purcell-Cutts House,
Purcell and Elmslie,
Minneapolis, MN, 1913

Day 1
Friday, October 16, 2009
4—4:30 pm
The Marketplace
and the Personal
See page 76

Abbie's flower appliqué
coat, from Alabama
Chanin's spring 2010
collection.

"Craftifesto," written
by Cinnamon Cooper and
Amy Carlton and illustrated
by Kate Bingaman-Burt.

The Craftsman in Society / Richard Sennett

Thank you for inviting me. I'm really pleased to be here to speak to you on a subject that for most of the audiences I speak to is something that seems rather strange to them: Why craftsmanship, and why does it matter? You'll have to forgive me if I speak a little slowly; I'm a night person, so I'm at the end of something rather than at the beginning.

What I'm going to talk to you about today is another way of looking at craft, which doesn't contradict at all the relationship between craft and art but is an extension of what we mean by craft into the technical world, because technicians, in ways that I hope to describe to you, both in the laboratory and in computing, also think of themselves as craftsmen. In fact, there is a new group that's just been founded of computer programmers called Craft in Code. So I want to talk to you about the expanding horizons of craft and what kind of obstacles these expanding horizons encounter. I'm very long-winded, so I'll time myself.

If we think about the traditional image of a craftsman, we can summon to mind, for instance, if we were peering through a window into a carpenter's shop, we'd see inside an elderly man surrounded by his apprentices and his tools. Order reigns within, parts of chairs are neatly clamped together, there's a fresh smell of wood shavings that fills the room. This is an image that all of us have from our own practice, and we know that its social problem is that this shop is menaced by a furniture factory down the road.

Another dimension of craft, however, would be found if we went into a modern laboratory like the laboratories I know from MIT, where I've taught off and on over the years. You might see a young lab technician frowning at a table, as I have, on which six dead rabbits are splayed on their backs, their bellies slit open. She is frowning because something has gone wrong with the injection she has given them, and she is trying to figure out if she did the procedure wrong or if there is something wrong with the procedure. In other words, she's trying to make sense of technique, and that's a craftsman's absorption.

When we use the term "craftsman," we mean that both of these people are dedicated to doing good work for their own sake. This is a practical activity, but their labor is not simply a means to another end. A carpenter might make more furniture if he worked faster, the technician might make do in the lab by passing the problem back to her boss. When we talk about craftsmanship, we are talking about people who don't take those shortcuts.

Craftsmanship is really poorly understood, in my view, when it is equated only with manual skill of the carpenter's sort, and that's really what I want to unpack for you today. Maybe looking at some words will help us in this. German employs the word *handwerk*, and French the word "artisanal" to evoke the craftsman's labors. But in English we are much more inclusive. Craft includes the word "statecraft," for instance; or in Russian the word for craftsmanship is *mastersvo*, which applies to a doctor as much as to a potter.

The reason this matters, that I'm making such a big deal of this, is that the big problem we face in modern society is how to connect, as it were, the head and the hand. That is, to understand that mental activity has some of the properties and should be measured by some of the standards that apply to our domain, which is the domain of manual craftsmanship. And just the other way around, that many of the things that we are doing that we think of as manual activities are, as you know well, highly intelligent. So what I've been trying to do in my work is understand this relationship between head and hand.

I'm going to give you an example of this in a field where you think this would be absolutely absurd—computer programming. It's something I'm quite interested in. I'm going to describe to you a computer program that may seem to you so far away from lathe work that it doesn't bear comparison, but, in fact, it does. I'm going to describe to you the Linux system.

Linux is a code, which I won't explain to you, but I'll give you a quickie description. The thing about it is that it's a public craft. The underlying software kernel in Linux code is available to anyone; it can be employed and adapted by anyone, and people donate time to improve it. I'm a part of a circle of people in a chat room who make up one little part of this phenomenon. Linux contrasts to the code used in Microsoft, whose secrets, until recently, were hoarded as the intellectual property of one company. In one current,

> "[Workers] are under enormous time pressure to deliver goods in a short time. The result of this is that craftsmanship in the terms that we think about—doing it slow, taking care, and looking for what might *become* out of what *is*—becomes economically dysfunctional."

popular Linux application—Wikipedia, which I'm sure you have all used—the code kernel makes possible an encyclopedia to which anybody can contribute (unfortunately). [Laughter]

When established in the 1990s, Linux sought to recover some of the adventure of the early days of computing in the 1970s. During these two decades, the software industry had morphed within its brief life into a few dominant firms, buying up or squeezing out smaller competitors. In the process, the monopolies seemed to churn out evermore mediocre work. That's what prompted Linux to come into being.

Technically, open-source software follows the standards of what's called the Open Source Initiative, but the brute label "free software" doesn't quite capture how resources are used in Linux. Eric Raymond usefully distinguishes between two types of free software: the "cathedral" model, in which a closed group of programmers develop the code and then make it available to anyone (they are the bishops distributing the code to others), and the "bazaar" model, in which anyone can participate via the Internet to produce code. Now Linux draws on craftsmen in an electronic bazaar. The kernel was developed by Linus Torvalds, who in the early 1990s acted on Raymond's belief that engineers write like this: "Given enough eyeballs, all bugs are shallow." Which is engineer-speak for: If enough people participate in the code-writing bazaar, the problems of writing good code can be solved more easily than in the cathedral, and certainly more easily than in proprietary commercial software.[1]

1/ See Eric S. Raymond, *The Cathedral and the Bazaar: Musings on Linux and Open Source by an Accidental Revolutionary* (Cambridge, Mass.: O'Reilly Linux, 1999).

This is then a community of craftsmen focused on achieving quality, on doing good work, which is our primordial mark of identity. In the traditional world, say, of the potter, standards for doing good work were set by the community, skills passed down from generation to generation. The transmission from master to apprentice creates a community. In Linux, however, this chance mission—this community made by passing down your skills, having the skills slowly, slowly mature—is facing a kind of crisis.

The programming community is grappling with how to reconcile quality and open access. Great problem—quality and democracy. In the Wikipedia application, for instance, many of the entries are biased, scurrilous, or just plain wrong. A breakaway group now wants to apply editing standards (and I'm part of that group), acting on an impulse that runs smack up against the movement's desire to be an open community. The editor "elitists" don't dispute the technical proficiency of their adversaries. This isn't a debate about that. All the professional parties in this conflict feel passionately about maintaining quality. The quality is equally strong in the generative realm of Linux programming. Its members are grappling with a structural problem: How can quality of knowledge coexist with free and equal exchange within in a community?

We'd err to imagine that because traditional craft communities pass on skills seemingly more slowly from generation to generation, the skills they pass down have been rigidly fixed. Not at all. I'll give you an example of ancient pottery making. It changed radically when the rotating stone disk holding a lump of clay came into use. New ways of drawing up the clay then ensued. But this change appeared slow to us because it took about two or three generations to effect itself, whereas in Linux the process of skill evolution speeds up; change occurs almost daily. I've frequently had the experience of opening up one of the chat rooms and going, "Huh?" because I've been away for two or three days, and, in the meantime, things have moved on.

Again, we might think that a good craftsman, be she a cook or a programmer, cares only about solving problems, about solutions that end a task, about closure. And in this way, we would not credit the work that all craftsmen actually do. In the Linux network, when people squash one "bug," they frequently see new possibilities open up for the use of the code. The code is constantly evolving; it's not a finished object, not a product in that sense. In other words, in all craftwork there is a deep relationship between problem solving and problem finding. The techniques we have are not techniques of closure. Closure occurs, of course; we want to solve problems. But if we are good craftsmen, whether we are working with clay or computer code, we want to see what opens up as a result of solving a problem.

Therefore, rather than contrasting the head and the hand in terms of craft, we'd do better to see that many of the skills that we learn with our hands are also skills we have to use in our heads. We would do better to contrast Linux programmers, for instance, to a different modern tribe—those bureaucrats unwilling to make a move until all the goals, procedures, and desired results for a policy have been mapped in advance. This is a closed knowledge system. In the history of handcrafts, closed knowledge systems have tended to have very short life spans. The anthropologist André Leroi-Gourhan contrasts, for instance, the open, evolving, difficult but long-lasting craft of metal knife making in pre-classical Greece to the craft of wooden knife making. Wooden knife making is simpler; you can solve all of its problems fairly easily. But the knives were still abandoned because they lacked potential.[2] This is, to me, a kind of fundamental issue not only in the past but in the present. The real preference, the real conflict that we are seeing in the modern world is between the desire for solutions and the desire for craft. The desire for solutions is a bureaucratic pressure, which erodes the essential, exploratory character of craftsmanship. Every solution, difficult as it may be to use or understand, is something that opens up more than it closes down.

The Linux community might have served the mid-20th-century sociologist C. Wright Mills in his effort to define the character of the craftsman. You should really name an award in his honor. He was the first sociologist to really take craftsmanship seriously. He taught in New York. He was quite leftwing and so didn't get much recognition in his own time. But he thought craftsmen were the most dignified figures in the labor movement. He writes, "The laborer with a sense of craft becomes engaged in the work in and for itself; the satisfactions of working are their own reward; the details of daily labor are connected in the worker's mind to the end product; the worker can control his or her own actions at work; skill develops within the work process; the work is connected to the freedom to experiment; finally, family, community, and politics are measured by the standards of inner satisfaction, coherence, and experiment in craft labor."[3]

There's probably no better statement of the craft ideal, but if this description seems implausibly idealistic, rather than reject it, we might ask instead why craftsmanship is so unusual—even the craftsmanship of Linux programming. Why is it that mediocrity tends to dominate over quality? The question is a modern version of Plato's ancient worry. The Linux programmers are certainly grappling with fundamental issues like collaboration, the necessary relation of problem solving to problem finding, and the impersonal nature of standards. Yet this community seems special, if not marginal. Some cluster of social forces must be pushing craftsmanship aside.

In the second part of this talk, I want to explain why I think modern capitalism stacks the cards against you, whether you are a potter, a lab technician, or a Linux programmer who's really absorbed in your work, trying to get it right rather than deliver a product that's closed and finished. Some of this story I tell at much greater length in a book of mine called *The Corrosion of Character*, a very cheap book. [Laughter] It's about the labor process, published about ten years ago. Now this is just my argument—and I may be totally wrong about this—but to understand why quality is not preferred in the modern economy, we need to reckon some ways in which the work world itself has changed. We know that the corporate system that once organized careers

2/ See André Leroi-Gourhan, *Milieu et techniques*, vol. 2 (Paris: Albin-Michel, 1945), 606–24.
3/ C. Wright Mills, *White Collar: The* *American Middle Classes* (New York: Oxford University Press, 1951), 220–23.

long term is now a maze of fragmented jobs. The idea of being an apprentice to someone, the model of lifelong careers (say, if you were in finance and spending a period of time as a journeyman and then becoming yourself a master) is as much as gone in the financial world. It's been gone for a generation.

In principle, many "new economy" firms subscribe to the doctrines of teamwork and cooperation. But, unlike the actual practices of Nokia or Motorola, which are craft-based enterprises, these principles are a charade. In the studies that my team and I did for *Corrosion of Character*, we found that people made a show of friendliness and cooperation under the watchful eyes of boss minders, rather than in good firms such as Nokia, where workers challenged and disputed their superiors. We found in other research that people seldom identified as friends the people that they worked with in

"Craftsmanship appears to the man or woman who dwells in quick results to be a marginal activity."

teams. This was a big shift from the social world of craftsmen, in which (as you probably know only too well) your friendship circle is the people that you are also in shop with. That's not true in the modern business world.

Some of the people we interviewed were energized by this individualized and competitive world, but more were depressed by it—and for a particular reason. And this is that the structure of rewards didn't work well for them.

The new economy has broken two traditional forms of rewarding work. Prosperous companies are intended, traditionally, to reward employees who work hard, at all levels. However, in this new economy, the wealth share of middle-level employees has stagnated over the past generation, even during the boom and while the wealth of those at the top ballooned. One measure is that in 1974 the chief executive officer of a large American corporation earned 30 times as much as a median-level white-collar employee, whereas in 2004 the CEO earned 350 to 400 times as much. In these 30 years, real-dollar earnings at the median point have risen only 4 percent.

I just cite this statistic to illustrate my point that in the practical world of reward for work, financial rewards have not really been forthcoming to people for working hard, loyalty to the company, or long-term service. But more especially, and here is where we come to our own concerns, the rewards for quality in work are disappearing in the modern workplace—particularly in the kind of workplace that's orientated toward very short-term task labor and in which the workers are employees who will be with the company for two or three years and then move on.

The idea of delivering quality, in the sense of delivering something that is full of promise, becomes less important than delivering results. And that's a fundamental characteristic change in the modern work world… that you have to take on board.

I can't name names because I've been sued once for this, but in a very large computer corporation located north of California [laughter], if some-body comes to a team manager and says, "I've found something, but I don't know what it's about," the team manager is going to say, "We are under a lot of pressure to deliver a version of this unnamed software package, and we can't waste time on this." And what happens in this unnamed company is that the people who have that kind of craftsman's awareness tend to leave. They go to a company I can name, Google, where if you come to team managers and say, "I don't know what to make of this, but it's interesting," you're rewarded.

What happens at the unnamed company happens even more strongly when you look at the world of financial services. People want closure, and the reason for that is not that they are stupid but that they are under enormous

> "What that should lead us to be thinking about socially is what's wrong with a world that's organized to discriminate against people for being good craftsmen."

time pressure to deliver goods in a short-term economy. The result of this is that craftsmanship in the terms that we think about—doing it slow, taking care, and looking for what might *become* out of what *is*—becomes economi-cally dysfunctional.

This is a huge change in the modern economy. It's often said about craftwork of the manual sort that it is old-fashioned in the sense that craft care, slowness, and so on, all belong to a vanished age. The reality is that if you take this more expanded trajectory of what we mean by craft—craftwork of the most advanced sort, the kind of craftwork that we see going on among computer programmers—you see that it is also dysfunctional. What that should lead us to think about socially is what's wrong with a world that's organized to discriminate against people for being good craftsmen.

You can spin this out in many, many ways. I'm just going to give you one more example. You can see this in education in the use of standardized tests. I don't know if any of you have ever taken the SATs or any standard-ized test that follows the same procedure. The trick to taking a test like that is getting as many questions right as possible in the shortest space of time. What is fatal is for somebody to stop over a question, a particular question, and say, "That's interesting." Or even more, to consider whether the wrong answer is really more interesting than the right answer.

Well, that's craftsmanship in learning, right? You stop, you dwell, you want to see what's really there. The wrong answer is something that's suggestive, just the way it is to many programmers of the unnamed company north of California. But it's penalized, and evidently there is now a huge de-bate in the testing community, because what I'm describing to you is so self-evident, about how to actually reward people who have a more craftlike and less product-oriented relationship to the content of what they are learning.

How do you recognize that and see it? Well, for a very long time we haven't. So the dimensions of what I'm describing to you are pervasive in modern society. The reason we don't reward craftsmanship is because we don't reward quality in the sense that you and I know it. That's quite a damn-ing state of affairs.

I want to end this talk because I've tried to sort of stretch you a little to think about craftsmanship as something that belongs to *now*, rather than just *then*, in terms of technology—to talk a little about craftsmanship in the kind of dialectic of the machine. We often think about building up skill, which is slow and experimental, as something that we have to experience within ourselves. The search for quality and the ability to understand how a process is put together is something that is within us. No code book can ever write it down. That's true even in programming: The code books that tell you what to do are often as mystifying for programmers as they are for the general public because there's a lot of tacit and experiential knowledge that tells you that between step B and step C there's actually another thing you need to do that the programmer takes for granted. You all know this if you've ever done do-it-yourself kits, which rigidly edit out that kind of taken-for-granted knowledge. That's what I would call subjective knowledge, not in the sense that it's emotional or passionate knowledge, but it's something in you.

It seems that machines remove that need for tacit understanding; once a machine is programmed to do an operation, there is no subjective relationship to the machine itself. I think this notion that the machine is going to eliminate this kind of subjective experience of the user is, in the technology world, a great misuse of machinery. The mechanical equates an ordinary language with repetitions of a kind of static sort. But thanks to the revolution of microcomputing, modern machinery is not static. Through feedback loops, machines can learn from their own experience. They can begin to have, I hate to say a subjective life, but they can have an inner life.

Yet machinery is misused when it deprives people of learning through

"The modern machine's threat to developing skill has, I think, a different character. It's a character not built into the machine but into our misuse of it."

that subjective experience themselves. The smart machine can separate human mental understanding from hands-on learning. When this occurs, conceptual human powers suffer.

I want to explain this problem of what happens when we stop having a hands-on subjective relationship to machines to you, because it's more complicated and, I would say, more pressing than we often think about. Since the Industrial Revolution of the 18th century, the machine has seemed to threaten the work of the artisan-craftsman. The threat appeared physical; industrial machines never tired, they did the same work hour after hour without complaining. The modern machine's threat to developing skill has, as I say, a different character. It's a character not built into the machine but into our misuse of it.

An example of this misuse occurs in CAD, which, as you know, is computer-aided design, the software tool that allows engineers to design physical objects and architects to generate images of buildings on-screen. The technology traces back to the work of Ivan Sutherland, an engineer at the Massachusetts Institute of Technology, who in 1963 figured out how a user could interact graphically with a computer. The modern material world could not exist without that graphic interface—or, indeed, without the marvels of CAD.

It enables instant modeling of products, from screws to automobiles; precisely specifies their engineering; and commands their actual production.

In architectural work, however, this necessary technology also poses dangers of misuse. The designer establishes on-screen a series of points; the algorithms of the program connect the points as a line in two or three dimensions. Computer-aided design has become nearly universal in architecture offices because it is swift and precise. Among its virtues is the ability to rotate images so that the designer can see the house or office building from many points of view. Unlike a physical model, the screen model can be quickly lengthened, shrunk, or broken into parts. Sophisticated applications of CAD model the effects on a structure of the changing play of light, wind, or seasonal temperature. But the person watching the computer monitor doesn't do any of that. He is a passive witness to the machine doing this.

Traditionally, architects have experimented and analyzed solid buildings in two ways: through thinking and drawing in plan and section. Computer-aided design permits many other forms of analysis, such as taking a mental journey, on-screen, through the building's airflows. But this is not the journey of an actual body. What CAD has done is disembodied the experience of design and rendered the designer a kind of spectator to an actor who is not him or herself.

When CAD first entered architectural teaching, replacing drawing by hand, a young architect at MIT observed that "when you draw a site, when you put in the counter lines and the trees, it becomes ingrained in your mind. You come to know the site in a way that is not possible with the computer... You get to know a terrain by tracing it and retracing it, not by letting the

"The real conflict that we are seeing in the modern world is between the desire for solutions and the desire for craft. The desire for solutions is a bureaucratic pressure that erodes the essential exploratory character of craftsmanship. Every solution, difficult as it may be to use or understand, is something that opens up more than it closes down."

computer 'regenerate' it for you."[4] This is not nostalgia; her observation addresses what gets lost mentally when screen work replaces physical drawing. As in all other visual practices, architectural sketches are often pictures of possibility; in the process of crystallizing and refining them by hand, the designer proceeds just as a tennis player or musician does, by getting deeply involved in the practice and maturing their thinking by drawing it. The site, as this architect observed, "becomes ingrained in the mind."

This is why high-tech architects like Renzo Piano will explain their

4/ Sherry Turkle, *Life on the Screen: Identity in the Age of the Internet* (New York: Simon & Schuster, 1995), 64, 281 [note 20].

own working process thus: "You start by sketching, then you do a drawing, then you make a model, and then you go to the computer, then you go to reality—you go to the site—and then you go back to drawing. You build up a kind of circularity between drawing and making and then back again."[5] About repetition and practice Piano observes, "This is very typical of the craftsman's approach. You think and you do at the same time. You draw and you make. Drawing… is revisited. You do it, you redo it, and you redo it again."[6] This attaching, circular metamorphosis can be aborted by CAD. Once points are plotted on-screen, the algorithms do the drawing, and, as I've said, misuse occurs if the process is a closed system, a static means and ends. It delivers a product rather than engaging the maker in "circularity," which is the point I am trying to make. The physicist Victor Weisskopf once said to his MIT students who worked exclusively with computerized experiment, "When you show me that result, the computer understands the answer, but I don't think you understand the answer."[7] I think this says it all.

Now for me, as somebody who is really interested in technology and work, this is the greatest promise of manual craftsmanship and the greatest challenge that it brings us. Because so far we've used technology in what I would say is both an uncraftsmanlike and unintelligent way. We've used it to remove ourselves from the process of making, as evinced by CAD and the very marginal status that Linux has in the high-tech community. You see this in the traditional world of craftsmen as the relationship, say, of that chair carpenter to a chair manufacturer. Craftsmanship appears to the man or woman who dwells in quick results to be a marginal activity.

To me this seems wrong. The real promise of craftsmanship is also political, which is to say that we need a different way of working so that people slow down, dwell on problems, look for possibilities. In getting things right, they want to see what else they can do. We need to remove craftsmanship from the mentality of products, which is a capitalist mentality, and take it into the realm of work process, which might politically involve another kind of social order.

Just to conclude, what I've tried to convey to you is that craft is very new as well as very old. Its principles fly in the face of the way in which we currently organize work, which tends to disembody us from using the extraordinary machinery we have and indeed prevents us from thinking like craftsmen.

Thank you very much for your attention. ✦

5/ Quoted in Edward Robbins, *Why Architects Draw* (Cambridge, Mass.: MIT Press, 1994), 126.
6/ Ibid.
7/ Quoted in Sherry Turkle, "Seeing Through Computers: Education in a Culture of Simulation (Advantages and Disadvantages of Computer Simulation)," *American Prospect* (March–April 1997): 81.

Lifestyle and Livelihood in Craft Culture / Elissa Auther

Thank you for having me here—it's wonderful. Thank you for that introduction.

My subject today is lifestyle and livelihood in craft culture, specifically the way the two concepts have been amplified, experienced, and practiced since the 1960s. In addition to discussing the history of the relationship of lifestyle to livelihood, I will also consider its implications for the contemporary moment, and how questions of identity, community, and authenticity in craft culture are shaped through and against the marketplace.

The two images I'm beginning with function as a visual plan of my talk. On the left side is a group shot of the members of the Baulines Craftsman's Guild Ⓐ, a countercultural association of craftspeople established in 1972 in Northern California. You see the members here gathered in front of Alexandra Jacopetti's fiberwork known as *Macramé Park*. The Baulines Craftsman's Guild stands as an ideal example in my presentation of the collapse of boundaries between work, craft, and politics as expressed as lifestyle. A driving force behind this type of integrated life was the countercultural, especially the movement's anti-capitalist and anti-consumerist beliefs that circled around craft in the 1960s and 1970s.

On the right is a contemporary photo of the retail clothier Brooklyn Industries' slogan: "Live, work, create." Ⓑ It is stenciled on the side of one of their stores. With this example we see a co-optation of a central concept of the craft lifestyle—its integration of work and life—deployed as a marketing or branding strategy. Toward the end of my presentation I'll address this phenomenon and the response to it within craft culture.

As a prelude to this, I'd like to clarify how I'll be using the terms "lifestyle" and "livelihood." And then I will briefly discuss the historical background to the intertwining of the two in craft culture. By "lifestyle" I mean a "style of life as a source of social identity."[1] Often the term is reduced to mean merely a pattern of consumption, like the example of Brooklyn Industries, and I'll return to that issue later in my talk. But for the most part, I am going to emphasize lifestyle as a reflexive practice, that is, an active project defined by personal choice.

To engage lifestyle as a reflexive practice of identity is to understand it as individualistic and inventive. The sociologist Sam Binkley, in his wonderful study on this topic, *Getting Loose: Lifestyle Consumption in the 1970s*, emphasizes the inventive aspect of lifestyle when he describes its relationship to identity as a "[feat] of narrative."[2] So as opposed to a situation in which identity is derived from a stable social, cultural, or institutional authority—like class membership or religious belief—in the reflexive model of identity it is understood as a form of "artistry."[3]

By "livelihood" I also refer to a means of living, but in this case more strictly confined to how one earns money. Within craft culture, livelihood, like lifestyle, is often understood as a mode of self-expression. I'll return to that point toward the end of my talk as well.

Top left to right:
The Baulines Craftsman's Guild, photographed in front of Alexandra Jacopetti's fiberwork *Macramé Park*.

The side of the Brooklyn Industries building in Park Slope, Brooklyn.

Day 1 / Lifestyle and Livelihood in Craft Culture / Elissa Auther

1/ The phrase belongs to Sam Binkley, whose study on lifestyle consumption of the 1970s I am drawing upon here. See *Getting Loose: Lifestyle Consumption in the 1970s*

(Durham and London: Duke University Press, 2007), 59.
2/ Ibid., 61.
3/ Ibid., 14.

Top left to right:
William Morris, photographed by Emery Walker, c. 1875.

William Morris, wallpaper designed for St. James's palace, c. 1880.

Morris & Co. textile printing at Merton Abbey, c. 1890.

Below:
Portrait of John Ruskin by William Gershom Collingwood, 1897.

Now I want to move on to a little bit of historical background. In craft culture, it is difficult to pull apart lifestyle and livelihood because they have been intertwined in some form since the 19th century, although the term "lifestyle" and the concept of creating one's life as a form of artistry would not be articulated as such until the late 20th century. It's with the rise of the Arts and Crafts movement in England in the 19th century that one can detect the core elements of what came to be known as the "craftsman ideal," which is the term that precedes the appearance of "craft lifestyle." The craftsman ideal is characterized by the desire for the intertwining of art and life, or more specifically, craft and work. This intertwining of art and life was viewed as a return to a precapitalist context in which work, creative practice, and everyday life had not yet been divided from each other or compartmentalized as they came to be under industrialization.

The Arts and Crafts movement, as I'm sure you are all aware, rose in reaction to the industrial revolution in Britain, and leaders of the movement, such as William Morris , argued that the division of labor within the workplace alienated workers from their own nature, destroying their pleasure in labor and, as a result, quality and pride in workmanship. For Morris and other leaders of the movement, the conditions of industrial production undermined the wholeness of the human being. Morris, as we know, advocated a return to handicraft that reunited the designer and the craftsman with every stage of production. This return, he believed, would restore the dignity of labor, improve the quality of goods that were available to consumers, and address the myriad social problems associated with the exploitation of workers under wage labor.

The call for a return to craft as a form of meaningful work that would promote the integrity and moral health of workers and culture as a whole was also articulated by John Ruskin , whose writings were an inspiration to the advocates of the Arts and Crafts movement. Ruskin had the following to say about the role craft could play in the restoration of the value of labor and, by extension, the whole individual: "It is only by labor that thought can be made healthy and only by thought that labor can be made happy, and the two cannot be separated with impunity. It would be well if all of us were good handicraft men, and the dishonor of manual labor be done away with all together."[4]

In the philosophies of Morris and Ruskin, you see the source of the beloved equation within craft culture between craft or creative labor and the well-being of the laborer or the maker. In the American context, the model of the Roycroft Workshops, which was an Arts and Crafts–era enterprise in East Aurora, New York, similarly advocated a theory of craft as meaningful work that promotes joy and personal revitalization. Indeed, one of their mottos insisted that "The love you liberate in your work is the love you keep."[5]

Before moving forward, let's review the core elements of the craftsman ideal that were established in the late 19th century. First, craft is identified in opposition to the prevailing economic system and labor

[4] John Ruskin, as quoted by Eileen Boris, *Art and Labor: Ruskin, Morris, and the Craftsman Ideal in America* (Philadelphia: Temple University Press, 1986), 5.

[5] This motivational message is inscribed on a door in the Roycroft campus's historic inn, which was originally its print shop.

conditions. Out of this eventually comes an aversion to materialism and thoughtless consumption (this becomes key in the mid 20th century). Second, there is an anti-establishment stance associated with craft that emphasizes a "desire for autonomy and self-sufficiency in relation to work."[6] Third, craft is posited as a conscious choice, a way of life meant to restore something that has been taken away, namely, honesty, goodness, and morality in work. Thus, as a practice, craft is considered restorative. It is spoken about as a search for wholeness or for personal meaning. Finally, there is an emphasis on work, both as a "process of discovery and as an inward development."[7]

Taken together, these points add up to a position that idealized the integration of work, craft, and life. Underscoring this equation is a definition of craft shaped against prevailing market conditions, working conditions, and patterns of consumption. These characteristics have formed the basis of a craft philosophy that has maintained significant coherency, from the Arts and Crafts movement, to the early 20th century, to the counterculture of the 1960s and beyond.

With regard to time constraints, I'm gong to move straight into the mid 20th century and talk about the integration of art and life for the postwar generation. Let's begin with additional examples that foreground craft as a conscious choice, an alternative to mainstream market practices, and as a path toward self-realization.

My first examples come from the writings of the woodworker George Nakashima , who often spoke about his commitment to the integration of craft practice and life. "Our purpose as a family was to integrate work and life," he stated, and "It seems to me that one of the most important aspects of design is integration, not only the relationship of design to the processes of manufacture, but also to life itself and the creation of an environment."[8] In both of these statements, design or craft is viewed as the basis for a total way of life, one that helps the individual toward a better existence.

On your right is an iconic image of Nakashima in front of the great Jomon cedar of

Top to bottom:
George Nakashima and the great Jomon cedar of Yakushima, Japan, 1982.

Interior of the showroom at the Nakashima compound in New Hope, Pennsylvania.

George Nakashima, table and chairs, photographed for Knoll Associates.

6/ Mary Douglas, *The Craftsman as Yeoman: Myth and Cultural Identity in American Craft* (Deer Isle: Haystack Mountain School of Crafts, 1994), 12.

7/ Ibid.
8/ George Nakashima, "Presentation at the New York Herald Tribune Forum," typescript, October 19, 1953, George Nakashima Papers, Archives of American Art, Smithsonian Institution, Washington, D.C. Reprinted in *Choosing Craft: The Artist's Viewpoint*, eds. Vicki Halper and Diane Douglas (Chapel Hill: University of North Carolina Press, 2009), 8.

Top left to right:
Marguerite Wildenhain's
pottery, photographed
in the artist's studio by
Otto Hagel.

Marguerite Wildenhain,
photographed by Otto
Hagel.

Yakushima, Japan, in 1982. It is one of many photos that thematize his love of nature and show him physically connected to trees or wood through touch. You see another example on the left with Nakashima grasping a wood plank in his studio.

Photographs like this one and others that place craft objects in nature—like these photos from the California Design catalogs of 1965 and 1971—emphasize another aspect of the craftsman ideal discussed in detail by Mary Douglas, that of the "craftsperson's cosmic sense of belonging, of having an understanding of the world beyond oneself."[9] This cosmic sense of belonging is another way that Nakashima, as well as other craftspeople, expressed the desire for an integrated life through craft practice.

In the post–World War II generation, Marguerite Wildenhain's [F] writings on the subject of the integration of work, craft, and life are especially good examples of the craftsman ideal put into action. As many of you know, Wildenhain was the founding member of Pond Farm Workshops, and she conducted highly experimental summer pottery courses on the property located in Northern California, from 1949 to 1980. On your left is one of the buildings on the Pond Farm property, and on your right are two examples of Wildenhain speaking with her students around the property.

About Pond Farm, Wildenhain declared, "Pond Farm is not a school, it is actually a way of life."[10] In essence, she is saying craft is a way of life. And the way of life, students discovered, was quite radical. For in-

9/ Douglas, *The Craftsman as Yeoman*, 7. Douglas also discusses the practice of photographing works of craft in natural settings in this study.
10/ Marguerite Wildenhain, *The Invisible Core: A Potter's Life and Thoughts* (Palo Alto, CA: Pacific Books, 1973), 145. Jenni Sorkin is completing a doctoral dissertation titled *Live Form: Gender and the Performance of Craft, 1940–1970*, that considers the confluence of gender, craft pedagogy, and artistic labor among women ceramists in the postwar era. Marguerite Wildenhain is one her subjects.

stance, students threw forms eight hours a day but took nothing with them when they left. This was Wildenhain's way of purging her students of the desire to produce finished pots, redirecting that energy toward a focus on process and experience that was meant to transform the student.

For Wildenhain, like others of her generation, the unity of work, craft, and life that she strove for was rooted in a moral principle. She wrote, "When more men and women are willing to live with one basic idea in mind—the unity of work and life, based on an ethical conviction—we shall have a chance for a valid human civilization."[11] She extends her thinking about the crafts lifestyle as an ethical practice in this statement about the pot: "The pot is absolutely the image of the maker who makes it... if that man is nothing... that pot... will also be nothing. For the secret of making a good pot... lies in an honest and decent and ethically convinced man."[12] For Wildenhain, craft had a noble purpose. She uses the language of work ethic, which initiates a concern with quality and integrity, and equates craft with natural or honest labor.

The potter M. C. Richards Ⓖ also embraced the connection between craft and a value-centered lifestyle. In her case, she used the terms "wholeness" and "centering" to express it. The following quote comes from her well-known book *Centering in Pottery, Poetry, and the Person*: "I, like everyone I know, am instinctively motivated toward symbols of wholeness... as a kind of inner equilibrium.... In wholeness I sense an integration of those characteristics which are uniquely ME, and those interests which I share with the rest of mankind."[13]

In the book, Richards goes on to describe centering as an overcoming of boundaries that commonly separate the mind from the hand, art from labor, or, in a summary her own words, the artist and the homemaker, the teacher or the poet, and the craftsman and the intellectual.[14] Like Wildenhain, the emphasis throughout Richards's *Centering in Pottery* is on the work, both as a process of discovery and as inward development.

In these three cases I've just presented, the philosophies of Nakashima, Wildenhain,

Left:
M. C. Richards.

Below:
Mugs by M. C. Richards.

11/ Marguerite Wildenhain, *The Pottery of Marguerite Wildenhain* (Raleigh: North Carolina Museum of Art, 1968), 5.
12/ Marguerite Wildenhain, "Media

Needs," in *The Craftsman's World* (New York: American Craftsman's Council, 1959), 167. As quoted in *Choosing Craft*, 11.
13/ Mary Caroline

Richards, *Centering in Pottery, Poetry, and the Person* (Middletown, Conn.: Wesleyan University Press, 1962, revised 1989). Reprinted in *Choosing Craft*, 12.

14/ Ibid., 13.

and Richards, craft is posited as a form of natural work that mends the divide between regular work, craft practice, and everyday life, otherwise ordering one's day in the service of capital.

In the 1960s in the U.S., a new generation of craftspeople came to the fore. Many shared with the previous generation a desire for independence and freedom from corporate life and held similar attitudes toward work and self-discovery. Among other links that demonstrate the continuity between these two generations was the popularity of Richards's *Centering in Pottery*, which became a bible of sorts for the younger generation seeking self-realization through craft practice. There were also established figures, such as the woodworker Art Carpenter, whose anti-establishment worldview functioned as a living link between the craftsman ideal and that of a younger generation energized by the counterculture and emerging as craftspeople in the '60s and '70s.

About the connection Carpenter had to the younger generation, he stated, "I was a flower child before there were flower children…. I have a fundamental belief–the more independent people there are, who are not

reconceptualization takes place in a social context that emerged in the 1960s in which every aspect of one's life could involve, for the first time on a wide scale, aesthetic choice. Associated with this modern formation is the expectation for one to approach choices about one's life as a form of artistry. Craft plays a visible role in this experience, and its tremendous expansion in the period is connected in part to this phenomenon.

The woodworker Tom D'Onofrio was one such member of the younger generation choosing craft in the 1960s, a choice that was motivated by a personal politics inflected by the countercultural values of freedom, self-determination, direct experience, and meaningful work. These values breathed new life into craft's historical connections to the concept of natural, noble work and its associations with independence from the mainstream market. What resulted was an unprecedented integration of workmanship and lifestyle. D'Onofrio really put it best himself when he stated, "To become a master craftsman is really to become an enlightened human being, whereby all of life is an artistic expression."[16] In other words, your life is a work of art. This quote comes from D'Onofrio's 1976

"Craft's identity, its communities, and its styles are, and continue to be, shaped through and against the marketplace."

connected with any organization, the better society is…. Independence of thought requires independence of economics."[15]

Carpenter's reference to the counterculture–the flower child in this quote–and his emphasis on independence from institutions and the mainstream economy bring us to a transformative moment in the evolution of the craftsman ideal. What I'm talking about here is the amplification of the unity of work, craft, and life so central to the tremendous expansion of craft culture (especially in the U.S. but other places as well) in the 1960s and 1970s. This amplification was powered by the counterculture.

What we see under the influence of the counterculture is the craftsman ideal being identified and embraced as a lifestyle. This

master's thesis titled *Craftsmanship and the Quest for Self-Discovery*, which considered ways of improving society through craft, inflected by his embrace of the counterculture, especially its anti-consumerist ethos and emphasis on authentic identity.

The Baulines Craftsman's Guild, which D'Onofrio initiated in 1972, put his ideas into action. The Guild, as it was called, was meant to operate as a traditional structure of apprenticeship, and he gathered local craftspeople, including Carpenter (who was his mentor), from the Bolinas area to take on apprentices. On the right-hand side you see the flyer announcing the first round of apprenticeships from 1972 and 1973, which includes a short description of the program. It reads: "Based on the craft guilds of old"–and you'll notice

15/ Arthur Espenet Carpenter, as quoted by Rick Mastelli, "Art Carpenter: The Independent Spirit of the Baulines Craftsman's Guild," *Fine Woodworking*

37 (December 1982): 65. Reprinted in *Choosing Craft*, 21.
16/ Thomas J. D'Onofrio, *Craftsmanship and the Quest for Self-Discovery*, M.A. thesis,

University of California, Berkeley, 1976, i.

there's a woodcut of a medieval workshop at the top of the flyer– "The Guild... presents an opportunity for students to work with a master craftsman, and learn not only the processes of turning raw materials into products, but equally as important, to learn how to earn one's livelihood."[17]

The idea that one would achieve economic self-sufficiency or autonomy outside the mainstream economy was a goal of The Guild, but it was not always realized, of course.

And this is probably a good moment to emphasize that the decision to turn to craft full-time was rarely articulated by D'Onofrio and his cohorts in the late 1960s or early 1970s as a career move, as we might talk about it today. Rather, it was more often talked about as a lifestyle change, in the sense that it was motivated by the desire to recuperate a way of life perceived as being destroyed by wage labor or corporate culture.

For instance, one member, Al Garvey, saw his Guild activities not as a commercial enterprise but as a contribution to a local, communal lifestyle. He said, "I never made a business out of anything I've done, but we got along in great style on almost nothing. We were all just a bunch of anarchists, but we were willing to break our necks to help each other out. It was like an Amish community. A lot of people helped me; I helped a lot of people. That was the idea of the Guild."[18]

The Baulines Craftsman's Guild was unique in terms of its structure, but there were many other arrangements in the period offering direct hands-on experiences, revolving around craft and couched in the language of lifestyle. I will point to just two examples. Although not a guild, Paolo Soleri's radical architectural sites, Cosanti and Arcosanti ⓘ, in Arizona, similarly offered direct hands-on training to individuals interested in making a lifestyle change that centered, especially in the case of Arcosanti, on ecologically sustainable living and creative artisanry. What I'm showing you here on the right are two shots from an earlier established site, Cosanti, also built by Soleri and architectural apprentices. You see on the bottom right a ceramics area devoted to making what are known as Cosanti Bells, and in the other image, an entryway

Left top to bottom: Cosanti, located in Paradise Valley, Arizona, is the residence and sculpture studio of Paolo Soleri and his staff.

Cosanti entryway.

Arcosanti, an experimental-living community in Arizona, designed by Paolo Soleri and the Cosanti Foundation.

17/ Tom D'Onofrio, flyer for 1972–1973 Baulines Craftsman's Guild.
18/ Al Garvey, as quoted by Glenn Adamson, "California Dreaming," in *Furniture Studio: The Heart of the Functional Arts*, eds. John Kelsey and Rick Mastelli (Free Union, VA: The Furniture Society, 1999), 32–42.

into Cosanti showing its beautiful earth-cast architecture. This additional image is a detail of a poster announcing a "silt-pile workshop." This particular workshop was sponsored by Arizona State University, so it was open to students but also to other members of the public who wanted to participate in the construction of these buildings or participate in the production of ceramics.

Arcosanti, a much larger site about an hour out of Phoenix, included a "craft apse," where the Cosanti Bells continue to be made to this day. On the right-hand side you see a variety of shots of the architecture of the site circa 1974. Arcosanti, and to a certain extent Cosanti, were communal living arrangements that were meant to meet all the social and economic needs of its residents. Together, residents constructed these compounds and engaged in various forms of craft.

You see a similar emphasis on the integration of work and craft expressed as lifestyle in the founding gatherings of Pilchuck Glass School, in Washington State, which in its early days required participants to build themselves temporary shelters before using the hot shop. On the top left is an image of the hot shop from 1971 or 1972, and the one below, the permanent structure built in 1973. The following quote is from a 1972 letter from Dale Chihuly and Buster Simpson to registered participants of the second summer Pilchuck workshop that articulates the goal of an integrated lifestyle. They wrote, "Try and develop some of your own ideas for the type of shelter you might want to live in.... It is hoped that the same considerations given your art will also apply to the way you live, the shelter you construct, your food and the way it's prepared."[19]

One of the most interesting illustrations of the craft lifestyle and its intersection with the countercultural desire to live apart from the expectations and constraints of straight society or the mainstream economy appeared in book form. I'm thinking here of Olivia Emery's *Craftsman Lifestyle: The Gentle Revolution*, which was published in 1976 in conjunction with the last of Eudora Moore's "California Design" exhibitions. *Craftsman Lifestyle* brings together the personal profiles of 80 California-based craftspeople working in all media with the goal of capturing their distinctive values, work environments, and ways of life. Moore, who provided the book's introduction, viewed the group as living proof that the craftsman ideal of the 19th century had been achieved.[20]

But this book is much more than a document that connects craft culture of the 1960s and 1970s with the Arts and Crafts movement of the 19th century. It's a very interesting exercise to look at this book as an object that mediated or popularized the crafts lifestyle, specifically its intertwining of work, craft practice, and everyday life for a broad public. By approaching the book from this angle, it can be viewed as part of a much larger phenomenon of countercultural lifestyle publishing in the 1970s that provided expert advice on a wide range of topics that were related to creativity, homebuilding, ecology, communal living, and

19/ Letter from Dale Chihuly and Lewis (Buster) Simpson to participants in Pilchuck summer workshop, 1972, John H. Hauberg Papers, Special Collections, University of Washington Libraries, Acc. No. 2850-7, Seattle, Washington. Reprinted in *Choosing Craft*, 110.
20/ Olivia H. Emery, *Craftsman Lifestyle: The Gentle Revolution* (Pasadena, CA: California Design Publications, 1976).

The reflexive mode of identity to which *Craftsman Lifestyle* spoke is evident not only in the contributors' personal stories about their choice of craft as a practice of self-discovery, independence, and freedom but also in the layout, which was somewhat unorthodox. The photos, shot by Tim Anderson, are captionless arrangements of images of living rooms, gardens, workshops, windowsill arrangements of objects, children's boats, outdoor showers, etc . Within the individual profiles, the photographs provide a record of daily activity, consciously composed to visually dissolve the boundaries between work, craft practice, and everyday life. In addition to the book's layout, the cover of unbleached cardstock complemented the contributors' stories of the rejection of materialism and alienating work for holistic, creative life through craft.

So what became of the craft lifestyle of the 1980s, a decade viewed as a period of backlash against the progressive gains of the 1960s? I'm going to encapsulate all the "evil" of the 1980s with this image of Gordon Gekko, the banker played by Michael Douglas in the Hollywood blockbuster *Wall Street*, alongside some of his well-known lines that became mantras of the 1980s: "Greed is good." "I create nothing. I own." "Lunch is for wimps."

So, given the contempt of the Reagan period for all things countercultural, you'd expect to see the decline of the values that are associated with the crafts lifestyle. However, based on the way the counterculture was appropriated by advertising in the 1980s, it seems that the ideology that promoted life as a product of one's own artistry and the elevation of personal autonomy was actually perfectly well suited to neo-liberal and yuppie visions of self-accountability, individualism, and entrepreneurship. The lifestyle branding of the period, and later, such as Nike's "Just do it" slogan, is a very good example of this appropriation. Its punch derives from a countercultural ideology of self-realization, freedom, and immediacy directed now, of course, toward individual, isolated consumption. Basically, what you have here is an appropriation of identity as a reflexive practice drained of its oppositional character.

the body, among many other topics. The following images illustrate what I mean by countercultural lifestyle publishing. The genre included titles such as Stewart Brand's *Whole Earth Catalog*; Alex Comfort's *The Joy of Sex*; Alicia Bay Laurel's *Living on the Earth*, which is a chronicle of communal living; the feminist resource guide *Our Bodies, Ourselves*; and even Ram Dass's *Be Here Now*.

Each of these books, including the *Craftsman Lifestyle*, promoted a new art of authentic living and functioned as a mediating tool for the reader to understand identity as reflexive—in other words, lifestyle as a product of individual artistry, which emphasized the idea that one had to "work on oneself to enhance one's authenticity through daily lifestyle choices."[21] Craft, along with the practices promoted in these other publications, from homebuilding to spiritual enlightenment, became a locus of lifestyle in this period.

Above:
Garth Johnson, Pottery
Liberation Front logo.

I'd like to return to an example I began with. This is the Brooklyn Industries' slogan, "Live, work, create." It is much more closely connected to the conflation of art and life central to the concept of authenticity in craft but now directed toward a much less radical audience involved in the solitary endeavor of shopping. What is left behind here are the radical implications of a lifestyle marked by the integration of work and creative practice, its resistance to market demands, and control over one's own labor and time.

In this social context, a context in which the discourse of meaningful work, community, or an integrated lifestyle is flattened and made trivial through commodification, can the craft lifestyle or, even more generically, the creative lifestyle, continue to retain an oppositional charge? In other words, is what was valuable about this lifestyle to craftspeople in the 1960s and 1970s still available to craftspeople and others associated with the field today? Is it still capable of inspiring a younger or emerging generation of craftspeople? These are all questions, I think, many of us ask. And, of course, the responses to these questions vary tremendously.

For someone like the architect Will Bruder, the idea of an integrated life and its associated values remain meaningful. This is Bruder's development called Taxi, in Denver, Colorado. I'm only showing you about a third of it (it's quite large and slated for expansion). Taxi is a live/work development designed with the needs of artists, craftspeople, designers, architects, and social activists in mind. The success of this live/work real estate development is a testament to the continued desire for lifestyle shaped by creative endeavor and its association with work and living patterns outside that mandated by the conventional division of work, creative practice, and everyday life. In addition to being designed for people who work out of their homes and live in their studios, this particular complex in Denver also has shared communal spaces for meeting, cooking, eating, and the exhibition of work. Just as an interesting aside, the architect of this space, Bruder, who is based in Phoenix, Arizona, began his career as an apprentice to Paolo Soleri at Cosanti, where he lived and labored communally with other students in the 1960s.

For the contemporary metalsmith Keith Lewis, craft retains its radical anti-establishment edge through the rejection of mainstream production models. Lewis has stated, "In rejecting manufacturing and accepting handwork, in seeking to produce the unique rather than the repeated, craftspeople… are renegades."[22] The "queer" imagery of Lewis's work, connected to his identity as a gay man, also invokes craft as a practice traditionally on the margins vis-à-vis the mainstream market, the art world, and conventional life. His work is a great example of the way craft has been marshaled as a form of self-definition and the critique of culture by practitioners and communities who themselves are socially marginalized.

For the ceramicist Garth Johnson, on the other hand, the answer to the question of whether what was valuable in the crafts lifestyle is still available to craftspeople today is largely no. For Johnson, the path forward requires leaving behind the claims and philosophies of the crafts lifestyle. I'm quoting Johnson here from his manifesto *Pottery Liberation Front* ❶ (you see the home page of the PLF's website on the screen):

In this era of global corporate culture, industry and advertising tirelessly promote the idea that personal identity is constructed… [through] brands and products…. This clever ploy is one that has been used by the cult of pottery since the dawn of the Arts and Crafts movement…. This attitude continues to

22/ Keith A. Lewis, "Renegade Ornament," *Metalsmith* 11, no. 3 (Summer 1991): 10–12. Reprinted in *Choosing Craft*, 288.

dominate the rhetoric used.... [the] hand-made object... somehow [being] an escape from commercialization and industrialization of the modern world.... There is nothing inherently wrong with handmade ceramic objects, but they must be taken for what they are: objects of pleasure and contemplation, rather than a way of life. Any lifestyle defined by objects will ultimately ring hollow.[23]

Johnson's critique of craft as a lifestyle is well taken. He argues that the commercial appropriation of the crafts lifestyle is a changed condition for contemporary practice that craftspeople and artists of all stripes ought to take under consideration. Yet some of the most current and popular manifesta-tions of craft trade heavily on the nostalgia that Johnson finds to be restrictive and a re-tarding force upon the craft world, especially for the survival of studio craft. For instance, there is a large cohort of artists and crafts-

people for whom craft's association to anti-establishment positions—including the opposi-tion to the mainstream economy, consump-tion, or ethical commitment to living life in harmony with nature—remain very viable.

My final examples are selected to show how practitioners associated with Do-It-Yourself (DIY), indie craft, or art activism leverage many of these associations and others I've discussed today. They demonstrate, for better or worse, the way the craft identity and community continue to be informed by resistance to the mainstream economy and the expectations and constraints it imposes. My first example is Radical Cross Stitch . The activity of this group is a good example of how craft's otherness and marginality are used to infuse it with political edge. For in-stance, the ties to anti-establishment and anti-corporate positions so essential to craft's identity in the 1960s and 1970s are marshaled here for a variety of projects. If you take a

Above:
Radical Cross Stitch installation, by Rayna Fahey, from the "Interventionist Guide to Melbourne" exhibition, Melbourne, Australia, 2009.

23/ Garth Johnson, "The Revolution Will Not Be a Tea Party" (August 2, 2000) http://clay.alfred.edu/menu/manifestopage.html. Reprinted in Choosing Craft, 294.

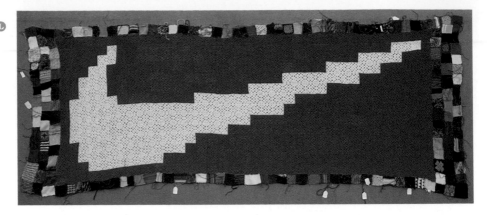

> "Craft is posited as a form of natural work that mends the divide between regular work, craft practice, and everyday life, otherwise ordering one's day in the service of capital."

look at the group's website banner, you see the following slogan: "radical cross stitch will save your soul."[24] The slogan connects this community of artists to the idea of craft restoring wholeness, which goes back even further than the 1960s to the 19th century. There is an aversion to consumerism and a rejection of the art world expressed by the site as well. You see that in the epigraphs on the home page on the top right and bottom right, the latter stating, "Go Shopping. Capitalism Needs Your Addiction."[25] The site also offers examples of urban interventions and a variety of DIY projects that you can print and complete yourself.

MicroRevolt is a project by the artist Cat Mazza that promotes knitting as a form of protest against sweatshop labor. One section of the website allows you to upload corporate logos, mutate them, and print them out as knitting patterns for wearable items. Another section of the site is devoted to Mazza's long-term collaborative project, which is a large knitted blanket to be delivered to Nike's headquarters ⓛ. It consists of a central panel in the shape of the Nike "swish" bordered by hundreds of small knitted squares submitted by people around the world in protest against exploitative labor practices fostered by globalization.

Gestures of Resistance is a creative undertaking of the artists Shannon Stratton and Judith Lehman that takes many forms. I am showing you one example of the group's work here in the form of a website set up in 2008 to promote a College Art Association Conference panel and exhibition in Dallas, Texas. I'm just going to read a small portion of the text so you have an understanding of their position: "Gestures of Resistance... expose[s] the gesture of handicraft as a radical reassertion of agency and restoration of integrity. Already durational, when made public... handicraft becomes politically charged, an active resistance to contemporary spectacle, mass production and uniformity."[26]

If you scratch the surface of any of these sites or writings by these or other artists and people involved in the contemporary revival of craft—and there are many more examples I could have selected—it is easy to find claims to authenticity, wholeness, a restored connection to nature and each other, and meaningful work—the whole range of attributes emphasized by the craft lifestyle of the 1960s and 1970s. In a world where the key oppositional elements that frame the craft lifestyle have been deflated as marketing tools for what is known as lifestyle brands, it should come as no surprise that what opens up are new

46 / 47

24/ Radical Cross Stitch http://radicalcrossstitch. com. Accessed September 10, 2009.
25/ Ibid.
26/ "Gestures of Resistance: Craft, Performance, & the Politics of Slowness," http://www.performing-craft.com/caa-panel-2008. Accessed September 10, 2008.

Ⓜ

spaces of resistance within the same market. This is a form of resistance that has resulted in the renewal of craft's associations with honest labor, anti-materialism, and authentic identity. In some cases, it also results in a picture of personal agency and an obligation to consume responsibly. This could include attention to materials, work conditions, or a utopian form of consumption that privileges the idea of individuals buying directly from other individuals. This is probably where projects like the "handmade pledge" Ⓜ or companies such as Etsy.com come into play—given that they're very much about consumption.

The "handmade pledge," which you can take online at Buyhandmade.org, is a good expression of the consumer phenomenon circling around the revival of craft. As you can see at Buyhandmade.org, there are many craft enterprises connected to the movement listed on the right-hand side of the website, including Etsy.com, billed as "your place to buy and sell all things handmade." As the journalist Rob Walker has pointed out, in this equation, the consumption of craft feels and effectively functions as a creative act and is viewed as a "form of economic independence

within capitalism."[27] If you need more proof, just examine the anti-corporate declarations that are made by people signing on to the "Handmade Pledge."[28]

Against a changed or expanded picture of what counts as craft in culture today—I'm thinking here of many things ranging from studio craft, to the craft of the counterculture, to artists projects like Gestures of Resistance, to what appears on Etsy.com—one thing remains certain: Craft's identity, its communities, and its styles are, and continue to be, shaped through and against the marketplace.

Thank you. ✚

"Is what was valuable about this lifestyle to craftspeople in the 1960s and 1970s still available to craftspeople and others associated with the field today? Is it still capable of inspiring a younger or emerging generation of craftspeople? These are all questions, I think, many of us ask."

27/ Rob Walker, "Handmade 2.0," *New York Times Magazine* (December 16, 2007): 81.
28/ See http://www. buyhandmade.org.

Craft in the 21st Century: Identity, Choice, Meaning

Moderator
/ Sandra Alfoldy

Panelists
/ Claudia Crisan,
/ Tom Patti,
/ Michael Sherrill

Sandra Alfoldy

I'd like to begin by introducing the three panel members, then I'd like to introduce why we are doing this discussion. Our first panel member is Claudia Crisan, who holds a double bachelor's degree in metals and fibers from the University of the Arts in Philadelphia. She went on to get her master's degree in jewelry and metalwork at the Royal College of Art, in London, in 2006. Claudia's work is in both small and large scales and in a range of materials and approaches . In looking at her work and talking to Claudia, I realize that this is a reflection of both her cross-disciplinary background and her willingness to experiment. Currently, she owns and operates, with her husband, a small bakery and edible-art gallery called Crisan, in Albany, New York, and [Alfoldy pulls out a tray of edible art objects by Crisan] she brought show and tell, which will be given out on a first-come, first-served basis at the end of the panel. [Laughter and applause] I've already taken one, just so you know.

The second panel member is Tom Patti. Tom holds an M.A. from Pratt Institute. He trained as an industrial designer and sculptor. In the 1960s, Tom worked with avant-garde multidisciplinary artists and engineers to explore the relationship between art, science, and technology. Starting in the 1970s, Tom was a pioneer in exploring sculptural glass, and today he is well known for both his smaller-scale works and his large-scale architectural installations that highlight his aesthetic subtlety and the pioneering architectural and industrial approaches that he brings to the crafts . His work is collected by the Museum of Modern Art and the Metropolitan Museum, to name just a few.

The third panel member is Michael Sherrill. Primarily a self-taught artist, Michael Sherrill is influenced by the natural beauty that surrounds him in North Carolina. A frequent instructor at the Penland School of Crafts, he teaches at many different craft schools and workshops throughout North America. As a result of his engagement with his students, he developed a line of tools for potters and sculptors in 1995 called Mud-Tools. His realistic and vibrant clay plants are permanent outdoor sculptures at the International Ceramic Museum, in Incheon, South Korea, as well as being in many other collections . So I ask you to join me in welcoming our panel.

We were talking as a group about how to attack these "small" topics—identity, choice, and meaning—in the 45 minutes that we have today. And we decided to do this in a very particular style that we hope will work. So I'd like to do a brief introduction to this panel. As the panel title suggests, craft occupies an exciting moment, one that calls into question many previously held assumptions. There is a great irony, however, in asking a historian to moderate this panel. In my privileged position as a professor of craft history, I have this wonderful job of theorizing and researching this messy, fluid business that we call craft. Students in my classes expect neat packages of information containing a beginning, a middle, and an end. Editors demand this as well

Top to bottom:
Claudia Crisan, *Romance*, wax, 2006.

Tom Patti, *Morton Square Canopy*, New York, NY, glass, 2005.

Michael Sherrill installing *New Growth–Buckeye* at the Gateway Center, Charlotte, NC, steel and porcelain, 2002.

Top to bottom:
Claudia Crisan, *Please Taste Me*, wearable sugar sculpture, 2006.

Tom Patti, design for model housing, 1968.

in the form of nicely completed manuscripts. So it's no wonder that we academics can become a little pompous, and it's no wonder that we like to create hypotheses based on assumptions.

To start this discussion, I'm going to play the role of the pompous professor who's come up with five assumptions, and my panel will deconstruct all of them. We are going to do this David Letterman style—but without any scandal—counting down from Assumption #5. And, panel, just to remind you, you have a whopping eight minutes per assumption.

Assumption #5: You don't need to use traditional craft materials to be a craftsperson. [Shows two images: Claudia Crisan, *Interactive Sugar Sculpture* D; Tom Patti, 1960s model for housing E.] And I'll turn the floor over to my craftspeople.

Tom Patti

I guess I'll start. Although my attention to my work is fundamentally through the glass, I'm interested in bringing to the idea whatever I need to articulate it, execute it, and realize it, and hopefully *it* will lead to other things. I think of the work and the materials as part of a process.

Claudia Crisan

I guess I should go next to support my piece up there [on the screen]. I think that wherever we are trained, we come in contact with craft, teachers, professors, makers. We learn how to make certain things; we learn techniques. We learn how to use certain materials. And then there comes a point when you encounter different materials and you wonder, Oh, can I apply everything I know to this? And then you see what happens. In my case, it happened that we opened a bakery, [laughs], which I think is very feasible from a creative point of view and a monetary point of view.

Michael Sherrill

I think there are traditional materials... I started as a potter, so I found that as time went on, I felt the constriction of living inside of the box that I had to put myself into, the images that I had taken from my other clay people that were my culture. That box became a constraint on me, so I liberated myself from it and started using other materials. I'm still kind of using traditional materials, but, at the same time, I've had the opportunity to work with cast urethanes and things that are really not part of my first-hand experience. But all of it has added to my understanding of material. I'm a material junkie myself. I've heard of this place in New York where you

can go through and look at catalogs of material, just a resource center, and if somebody here can tell me the name of it… I feel like that would be the best place I could go to spend my time, because we're living in a new age where the possibilities of what even ceramics can do are expanding. I'm fascinated with the idea of clay being made into foam-type ceramic or being made flexible, or the possibilities that those can be used artistically and industrially. I have a lot of friends for some reason who are industrial engineers; I don't know, I collect them. I'm not a scientist. I just have scientific questions that they are kind enough to help me understand.

CC

I think it's interesting what [Michael was] saying. We start making sometimes because of whatever is happening around us, and if certain materials happen to be there, you just create. You transform the material into whatever your ideas are. For me, sugar was there since I was born because my mother is a baker. So I grew up around it, and it was just normal to take it and make it wearable, which brings, you know, many other questions, but I don't think it's the time to go into it right now. [Laughter]

TP

Materials are interesting in that in the hands of a creative person you bring a certain sensibility and the potential to discover new ways of working with these materials. I think that's why artists are often interested in industry, because they are poking, pushing it, doing, analyzing it on a scale that you don't see in the natural world, in the physical world that uses microscopes and chemical analysis to break it down and interpret the materials in different ways. But the artists, when they put their hands on these materials, can often tap into something very unique and special. I'm not sure quite how it works, but there's a whole discovery process that takes place, and if you want to break barriers, to open up

new directions, these materials offer opportunities. It's not about old materials and new materials; it's just about getting access to them and spending a lot of time with them. Unfolding them. Spending days and days twisting and turning, poking, pushing the idea often will unravel a new way of looking and using that material that, once you discover it, seems very obvious. But it's hidden; it's often inside the material. But, in fact, often the material is yourself; it's this relationship between yourself and the material, poking and twisting it around.

SA

Boy, my panel's good. That's eight minutes. Thank you. Alright, enough on material. Whatever. No, I'm just joking. [Laughter] **Assumption #4: Craft is an environmental, sustainable set of practices.** [Shows two images of Michael Sherrill's floral ceramic forms Ⓕ.] You can't see, Michael, but the pressure's on you. [Laughter]

MS

Well, I burn a lot of gas, and I use a lot of materials to make what I make. But I try to make something that is not temporal, that has some kind of lasting quality, where the output is hopefully greater than the energy that goes in to make it. I couldn't agree more with Tom's analysis of what happens in discovery with material.

I'd like to jump back just a little bit in that I feel that the role of the artist and the scientist are pretty much the same. But as artists, we are observers of the tactile, visual world. That's just our little gift, and each one of us is going to take it a little differently. I think that's what we have to feed back to the

Top left to right:
Michael Sherrill,
Julesvernium–Seaflower
(detail), 2008, silica,
bronze, Moretti Glass,
porcelain, mokume.

Michael Sherrill,
*The Temple of the Cool
Beauty–Yucca* (detail),
2006, silica, bronze,
Moretti Glass, porcelain.

rest of society—part of our value is that we can open a box that hasn't been opened, just because we see it a little bit differently and bring a different dimension back into our culture. And as far as sustainability, it's an expensive process. What I do is not cheap. I run a shop with employees and pay bills, and I think of the people that keep glass furnaces going all the time. But I think we all are conscious of that, and I'm particularly trying to figure out how to be as responsible as I possibly can.

CC

This really goes hand in hand with the trend that's happening right now in our society. We're really becoming aware of what we are doing to this planet. I think we are looking at craft now because it's a beautiful way of transforming natural materials into something that exists and resists throughout time. Like [Michael] said, I don't know how environmentally friendly we are sometimes because of the techniques that we have to use to get to the final product. For the moment, if I go back to what I do, I kind of stopped any etching or any chemical processes and techniques because I am working with edible materials, which is nice. I did find many other artists

who are so involved in this idea. They are using recyclable, edible materials that they can make into objects that will dissolve in nature after time. Emiliano Godoy, for example, is making these beautiful sugar lamps that will dissolve in water. That takes away from what happens with an object after it's out of fashion, but I think we are going more into the design argument here. Also the German artist Oliver Kessler, he makes these beautiful sugar-cast lamps, again using environmentally friendly materials. I could go on and on.

TP

I have a couple of thoughts. I destroyed half the environment in my neighborhood. I must have killed every frog when I was a kid growing up. I experimented with them, took them apart, ran around with them for days and weeks. It was brutal. [Laughter] But it's interesting how industry has been involved and engaged with this for a very long time. Sustainability is a very fashionable thing now. It's being absorbed in the popular culture, but industry has been actively recycling materials, finding less expensive ways for practical reasons—whether it be profit margin or just the success of a product or so on. But many of

the products you use have been recycled or reprocessed; it's not just the art culture that's doing it.

[References the housing model shown in the first slide.] That home you saw there relates to this idea of sustainability and how the artist or craftsperson relates to it. That white structure is a material I developed that was made out of petrol chemicals, plastics. Inherent in that surface—that skin or shell, which was inflatable and then became rigid as the resin hardened—was a concept that I was developing for global housing issues. That was back in the '60s. That house also

MS

I can just say for myself—and I bet I speak for a lot of people in this room—that when you wake up in the morning, you go to the shelf to find that mug you love, and I hate to use that analogy, but it's so true that there's humanity and warmth in an object that you like to bring into your life. And as a result, it has power. I mean, it has a humble power, but it has power. This morning I've heard scholars way above my pay grade talk about things I can relate to because I know that it's an integration of all of us trying to bring our bodies and our minds and our hands together in one

"There comes a point when you encounter different materials and you wonder, Can I apply everything I know to this? And then you see what happens." / Claudia Crisan

had within those walls a solvent component that when activated would dissolve the entire structure. It could then be reformed into another house or another purpose even other than a house, so you never lost those materials that went into the structure. The interesting thing is that artists can solve and address problems not just in the things they make, but the artist can apply their thought process to larger global issues and affect the world dramatically. [Pauses] That was eight minutes.

SA

I know—thanks, Tom. Whew, I'd better keep in line here, thank you.

Assumption #3: Functional craft is less important than one-of-a-kind work. That's a light topic. I'll just throw it open— eight minutes. [Shows two installation shots from Tom Patti exhibition, Heller Gallery, 2009 Ⓒ.]

CC

I should start because I just get furious when I hear statements like this. I don't even know what there is to say about it in a room full of craft people. I think whether someone makes usable or one-of-a-kind work, it's still the process, the power you are putting into making the object that is the most important part of the object itself. Whenever you make something, you put something of yourself or whatever is around you in it, and I'm not saying this as a funny, romantic idea—this is really how it is. You put your mark on it, and that's why whatever you make is important and beautiful, whether it's mass produced in small productions or one of a kind. How do you react to that, I don't know.

act. I know how giving it is to us as individuals and hopefully how giving it is to the culture that we're in. So the humble work of hand is very important to me, especially when it has an impact on me or others I know. I love pots. I grew up in that culture, but I don't necessarily have to be that. I love other objects as well that really are meaningful. And I hope I don't break them.

TP

A couple things. [References the images of his work on the screen.] The slide that we've been looking at shows design, craft, everything. This is a recent exhibition, and I think of myself as very much a product of all these kinds of things. I sent this slide in because I was reflecting on the questions, and I said, "Geez, I just had a show, and I didn't make those distinctions." And fortunately, my dealer didn't either. You see the one-of-a-kind objects I've been making on the wall, the small, little wall-mounted pedestals. And then you see a wall that I'm working on because I'm doing these large architectural works. It's an exploration of the corner and how you deal with corners in spaces. And then next to that is a table where I'm exploring modularity. It's one table, but it's two parts and they move on the floor plane, so it reconfigures itself both sculpturally and functionally according to whatever space it's in. So I'm a contemporary craftsperson working today, and I don't make those distinctions. The purpose of my work is to explore new areas with those basic ideas that I have. And I try to stay true to that. Fortunately, I have a dealer who has a similar approach and allows me to create an

"Someone said to me about a week or so ago that we are watching things change really fast, but some things don't change—our nature, our preferences, and the way we go about our daily life. We lean into what we need to survive, and my feeling is that I'm lucky enough to have figured out a way to make for a living and to be productive and survive." / Michael Sherrill

environment like this in a gallery in the city. An interesting thing: Two years earlier I had another exhibition. There were mostly artists and collectors there. At this exhibition, it was mostly designers—I knew many of them—and architects who were there. While I was setting it up, there was a tremendous amount of photographic activity, just getting information on what was there.

SA

You guys are good. It's 11:30. Good. All right, **Assumption #2: Making it by hand makes it craft.**

[Shows images: Claudia Crisan, *Whisper* ⊕, 3-D wax printed; Michael Sherrill, ceramic floral form ❶.]

CC

You had to choose like the strangest pieces to put up there.

SA

I know, I couldn't help myself.

CC

When I was at the University of the Arts in Philadelphia (actually two of my teachers are here, and I'm so happy to see them), I was obsessed with hammering, chasing, and repoussé, and everybody around me knew that because they couldn't stand me; I was so loud. The same thing followed me in London. It's about pushing and pulling a material until it becomes volume, shape. It takes life. From a flat sheet of metal, something that was in my head and comes out and is formed, somehow—I still don't know how. I think Professor Richard Sennett was explaining that very nicely. You can't even call it intuition—it just happens because of what you are taught to do. So I took those tools, that craft that I learned by working with my hands, and I brought them into a three-dimensional, virtual environment in the computer. I used this 3-D program that revolves an object, where you push and pull a mass—exactly the same way that you hammer a piece of metal. It's

fantastic because this program is usually used for animators, and I used it as a maker. What's interesting is that even though the hand is not literally touching the material, you are still forming and shaping this piece the same way because you have this connection between your mind and your hand, which goes through the mouse. Now the shock is what happens when this three-dimensional piece in the virtual space comes out as a 3-D object printed by a 3-D printer in starch or whatever material you use. You are shocked, because it's there, but it's different, and you feel that you made it, but you didn't.

[Refers to the image of her piece *Whisper*.] That little piece that's in my ear, we like to call it "a little whisper of my subconsciousness," was printed in different sizes, so one was in starch about hand-size, then exactly the same piece was printed at about an inch—I use centimeters, so that's a little confusing when I start to translate—in wax, which was cast through lost-wax casting in rose gold. So I made a piece that I could not make with my hands in the traditional way I used to do, which still shows what I wanted to show, so it is still craft, even though the hand is not there. You are using these new tools on the computer, but the important thing is that you do have the basic knowledge and training that you are transposing into this other environment. That's what makes the computer your tool; otherwise, like we were talking about in the CAD/CAM [discussion with Dr. Sennett], you don't really understand what you are doing; the computer knows what you are doing. Or it becomes just a 3-D animating thing…

MS

Sort of in response to that, I work as a designer of tools for potters as sort of an offshoot of my making. I've always made tools, and I've always liked carrying them around and sort of digesting whether they are working or not and sticking them in my pocket.

Well, I do the reverse of exactly what [Claudia] said. I don't think that we have to always make things by hand, I'm not saying that at all, but in my practice the fact is that I have to be tactile with materials. So I'll make a physical model. And I'll carry that thing around in my pocket and knock it around, and when I go home I think about it and live with that thing for a while. And then I do the reverse of exactly what she's talking about. I go to someone else to computer model it because *industry* deals in computer modeling. They build molds, and they do the processes and production through a different way. Because I don't have the time at this point to become really skilled at computer modeling, I'm best working through people who do have the skills. I have to go to their place usually, wherever they are, and I have to forge *them* into position, because they don't always get what I'm seeing or what I know, what I feel about an object. As a result of that kind of collaboration, I feel like my objects have the longevity and multipurpose qualities that I think need to be there for them to function. But my practice is tactile. At the same time—and I'll close with this—a piece is already finished in my head before I start it. Before the hand is ever worked, it's there. The comment earlier today about the whole idea of how things unfold as you work is such a true thing for me. The whole idea of something unfolding and maturing in front of me is a part of my process, and I don't have to have every little nut and bolt in position; I just have to have the spirit of the object to move forward. Once that's there, then that's my plan of action and I get going.

TP

My work looks very machine/industrial made, but it's all made with my hands. Whether I draw it, sculpt it, build it three-dimensionally, whatever, there is something very special that happens through the hands. And it's not whether it's craft or fine art, whatever you want to call it. You know, you put the brush to the paint to the canvas—a computer's not going to put it down that way; there are too many serendipitous things that happen in the process that you can't explain, that are just accidental, that you're inherently responding to as the process moves forward. Another thing is that when you engage your hands, you're not just using your hands; they are part of your body, connected, and your brain is in there somewhere, but your whole self is engaged in the making of something. And your body starts sweating and your heart starts pounding—all these things start

happening. I don't work with a computer, the way [Claudia] describes, but I doubt if that kind of experience happens to one…

CC

Ah, it does.

TP

It does? OK, OK. It does. I know that when I'm carrying something and lifting it, and it weighs 150 pounds, and I'm dragging it across the floor because I need to do something, I say, "How does the computer do this?" You know, "How would I imagine it?" But I get it over there, I lean it, I say, "Geez, it looks better leaned this way than it would have another way." Because now the difficulty of handling it becomes a component of what it even is. So when I finish a piece, I have all these experiences that I relate to, and when I look at it, in some way, they all come together, consolidate. That work, you know, *is* me. It's just a hand, and I can't separate it. I have a very difficult time doing it any other way.

CC

This is an important topic to me. I'm not a computer savvy, is that what you say? But I am amazed by this tool. I think it's something similar to what happened when photography came to be. What happened to drawing? We are still drawing. It just depends on how you choose to make certain things. And it's a beautiful thing to know how to take advantage of what's happening in today's crazy explosion of technology and whatever is happening around us…

TP

It doesn't matter that I make it by my hand or she makes it with the computer; in the end, it's the purpose of what it is and the result of that purpose…

CC

Right.

TP

And it needs to be looked at in the broader culture.

Top let to right:
Claudia Crisan,
Whisper, 3-D digital
print in wax, 2006.

Michael Sherrill,
Dream of Wildflower,
mixed media.

CC

Probably most of you are teachers, and whenever I interact with students, it's amazing to see this. They know they are learning the traditional way of making, but they are so aware of what's happening right now. And they're the generation that's going to combine everything and just make a different way of making, which is, I think, fantastic, because you know we are on the verge of a revolution here and I don't think many people really acknowledge it…

TP

I think they do. I think they do.

CC

Probably. That's why we are having this discussion, I guess.

TP

Yeah, it's a big, it's a major part of it. It's interesting—where craft was a reaction to industrialization at the turn of the century and then again in the '60s, the computer is now the machine. It's digital versus analog, and gears and grease and oil versus electronics, but we're dealing with that thing again. But it's interesting that this culture embraces it, whereas if we looked at the information from the previous speaker [Elissa Auther], it was a reaction against it. You are seeing now this subtle acceptance, embrace of the tool. For me, the tool is unimportant. I always say to anybody who works with me, "Break the hammer if you need to do the job." You know, if we need to get to where we're going. Never make the tool more important than the work, whatever it is. But that probably costs a lot with a computer. [Laughter]

SA

That's right, that's right. Wreak havoc on computers. Stay away, Tom, stay away! [Laughter] Well, and I'm so glad I got to save our lightest topic for the last.

Assumption #1: The craft field is dying and DIY will save it. [Shows image of *Martha Stewart's Encyclopedia of Crafts*.]

CC

Oh gosh.

SA

Any thoughts?

MS

I can just say that as long as there are people like me, it's not going to die. I mean, we're fighting a fight of trying to be makers. Someone said to me about a week or so ago that we are watching things change really fast, but some things don't change—our nature, our preferences, and the way we go about our daily life. We lean into what we need to survive, and my feeling is that I'm lucky enough to have figured out a way to make for a living and to be productive and survive. And I hope that I can be, with all of you guys, models for the next generation to come along and say, "You know these guys did it, so maybe I can." In fact, one of the reasons I moved to the part of the world I live in, in Asheville, was because there was a history, there was a craft culture already there. It was this simple: I was a hippie kid in the '70s who moved to the mountains because of the Southern Highland Craft Guild; if you were a member, they would buy pottery in the wintertime. That's why I moved there, because I thought I could live through the winter as a potter if I became a member of that guild. That's how simple my thinking was. But somehow that thinking was the step that led me into this culture that I live in, enjoy, and really care about. I have young people in my studio, and they're looking at the fact that they have a bill for their education, wondering how they're going to get their insurance coverage, how they're going to get equipment together, how they're going to get the time to do or to be practicing artists or artists/teachers, either/or. I can't say that I am a perfect model at all, but I am a model, and there are other models in this room. If we open up our experience to those who are coming along, I think that's maybe the best way to say that we're not dying. Any healthy

"Artists when they put their hands on these materials can often tap into something very unique and special…. It's not about old materials and new materials; it's just about getting access to them and spending a lot of time with them. It's this relationship between yourself and the material, poking and twisting it around." / Tom Patti

group of people is inclusive of the greater. It's a biological principle, but I think it's so true to us today.

CC

I like Martha Stewart! [Laughter] I like her because she's a very smart woman who made an empire on, well, you know on what. [Laughter] But the thing is—of course craft is not dying! How can it die when you look at all the schools and kids that are so involved in it? They've never been so excited about it, and you know what's nice about Martha Stewart and people like her? She makes it fashionable. It's fun, it's funky. It's cool, so young people get interested, become interested in crafts through them. Of course it's kitschy. Of course it's, you know, Jo-Ann's and Michaels, but this is how *kids* get involved in it. They start with simple beading projects, and they're, like, "Wow, I really like to do this. Can I study this for real?" And, yes, you can. You get a beautiful class in high school, and so on—I think you know what I mean. So, [Michael], I do agree with you, and I respect the traditional way of living as a craftsman. I think it's very hard to be true to it in today's society, and I guess that's why I opened an edible art gallery. I'm very proud of it, even though sometimes it's hard to show people that you can still make art while you are making a living, without teaching. I can't be a teacher, so I had to find something else to do, and my husband was so good to do this with me. He's a musician, so it's not that far from being a craftsperson. But, you know, we see this as a craft. He rolls croissants every morning; they are the most beautiful croissants I've ever seen. We have our little things, and then I make sugar brooches for special events. Sometimes they explode in the oven, but that's the way it goes, I guess. But we are still making, and that's important. And the nice thing about it is that people want to come and work with us. People want to come and see what we do there because we're not just baking; we're making. We're making. It's a way of living, and it's going back to what the beautiful book *The Craftsman* said. We live upstairs. It's our little world. We live by doing this, and I think that's how it is with you [gestures to Michael].

SA

It's so tragic, eight minutes just fly by. We have to wrap up the whole panel, but I can't end without giving Tom a couple of minutes.

TP

It's interesting what's going on. It's fascinating. You know since the '60s, it's finally democratized, and here we are trying to, like, change it again. Now everybody's doing it—it's what we wanted. But now we're going to have to organize it and build criteria. [Laughter] But crafts made by people working today are going to be as strong as they are. It's not going to go away if we keep pushing boundaries, keep being innovative, keep making meaningful work with purpose. It can't be threatened. If it goes away, it's not going to stop the people from working. It's not going to stop me. I went for years where I'd work for six months to make money, then go into my studio to make my own work for another six months. I did that for ten years. And I thought that was my life. Then somebody said, "Maybe you can sell all those things lying around the room," and I said, "You think so?" [Laughter] And then Sienna was born and off I went to New York. I cleaned my pieces up and said, "Yeah, maybe I can do something with them." That was my career, but I thought it was just going to be searching and researching for my whole life. But if more people approach it like we are here, I don't think it can be threatened. You know, it's just more stuff to look at.

SA

Now I feel happy. Thank you. ✦

Mixed Taste: Tag-Team Lectures
/ Adam Lerner

With

/ Jennifer Komar Olivarez,
/ Kristin Tombers

My name is Adam Lerner, and I am the director and chief animator at the Museum of Contemporary Art Denver. This is a program we call Mixed Taste, and maybe we can call it the traveling edition of Mixed Taste. To just give you a little context, Mixed Taste is a program that I have been running since 2004 at an institution that I founded called the Lab at Belmar. The Lab was basically in a shopping district in the suburbs of Denver. As you can see [shows images on screen], we were right across the street from Dick's Sporting Goods, and we actually had a sign in our window saying, "Welcome to The Lab. We're not Dick's," which we got in trouble for. I won't go into that story.

So I founded this whole institution with this program called Mixed Taste. The concept of Mixed Taste is simple: You have one speaker speak on one subject, then a second speaker speaks on a completely unrelated subject, paired at random. And then you have question-and-answer for both at the same time. During the first two talks, the speakers are strictly forbidden from making any connections between their subjects, but during the question-and-answer, anything can happen. So we started Mixed Taste in 2004 with this program: Andy Warhol and Artificial Lighting. We had an art historian talk about Andy Warhol and then a leading expert on artificial lighting come and talk about that. This is what one season looked like: You'd have Carnivorous Plants and Color Field Painting, Earth Art and Goat Cheese, Capoeira and Le Corbusier.

Now I say we paired these things at random, but we really don't; we just pair things that sound good together. This just sounded perfect: Capoeira and Le Corbusier, Chinese Opera and Alfred Hitchcock, Walt Whitman and Whole Hog Cooking, Tequila and Dark Energy in the Universe (which is basically the same thing), Soul Food and Existentialism, Prairie Dogs and Gertrude Stein. And then the summer blockbuster was Marxism and Kittens, Kittens, Kittens. Now I'm not going to go into the philosophy too much, but I just wanted to say that when we started this program, on the first day when we did the Andy Warhol and Artificial Lighting program, we had 12 people there. This is the suburbs of Denver—Lakewood, Colorado. Kind of like the Flushing, Queens, of Denver. It's not the Upper West Side, and it wasn't known for being a cultural center, so getting 12 people there seemed pretty good. And half of them were my friends, and that was okay, they

came out to support me. But the numbers grew exponentially. We had 20 people the next week and then 30 or 40 people the next week. Then by the end of the season, we had about 100 to 150 people coming.

We did these once a week. Here's this teeny little program, basically the only good idea I've ever had. I say that because really everything else I've done after that I learned from doing this one thing. And what makes it special is that we managed to figure out a way to enable a conversation on sophisticated subjects while disabling the pretensions around those subjects. I don't consider this to be education in any way because I think it's too interesting to be called that, and I actually don't like that term. For me, what education aims to do this does better; essentially, it makes people comfortable and not afraid of things that are unfamiliar to them.

The context for this created this extremely robust audience. Eventually, we were regularly getting 180 people. When we did this season, we would actually sell out weekly at 330 people.

[Shows an image of a typical Mixed Taste audience.] And you can see here what happens is you have these sort of hipsters with bed-head and tight-fitting retro T-shirts sitting behind NPR-listening retirees who come in half an hour early to get the front-row seats. That combination is very rare for a museum audience, and what we've done is we've managed, on some level, to combine curatorial education and marketing that taps into public imagination, that's got a creative dimension to it, but you also learn at the same time.

All this took place within a contemporary art context, so this was an international contemporary art center where we would have exhibitions of art and also other things that interested me. Of course, much to the dislike of any grant givers, none of our educational programs had anything to do with any of the art. Nothing we did was actually about interpreting the art for people or connecting people to the objects; they would just sort of run alongside.

I should just tell you now the end of the story is that all of these programs now happen at the Museum of Contemporary Art Denver. While I was director of the Lab at Belmar, there was a vacancy at the directorship of the museum, and I applied for that position. Then the two organizations merged, and all the programming of the scrappy little Lab at Belmar then became a part of this very respectable organization called the Museum of Contem-

Top to botton:
The Museum of
Contemporary
Art Denver.

Postcard for the
Mixed Taste tag-team
lecture series at
the Lab at Belmar.

porary Art Denver, where now I am the director and chief animator.

So then basically the class clown becomes the class president, and the programming that we run continues in this broad context. We ran "Art Fitness Training" ("Tone up your contemporary art muscles. Don't be bullied by art critics anymore. Feel more confident at art museums."); "Taste Test: Random Encounters in the History and Science of Food"; "Feminism and Co.: Art, Sex, Politics." That program is actually co-directed by Elissa Auther, who you heard this morning, and there we would again have a "mixed taste" concept around the same idea or around a similar theme. For example, you'd have a theme like "Girls, Girls, Girls," where you would have a music historian talk about riot grrrls (this sort of post-punk girl-band phenomenon that emerged in the 1990s), then you would have a psychologist talk about girl bullying, then you would have a panel of mothers and daughters talk about dolls. So if you want to know what a nine-year-old thinks about a doll, you have a nine-year-old there talking about the doll. And it all sort of comes together and weaves into one circus of ideas.

So that's the context for what we're going to do today, and we decided to provide you with a version of that even though I'm not coming from the craft field. I've invited today two speakers who probably stretch as far as what might be possible within the universe of making to discuss Meat Fabrication and Prairie School Architecture. "Meat fabrication" is another term for butchery, and I think it is a great pleasure to be able to introduce this sort of Mixed Taste traveling edition where we have two great speakers tonight. We will have Kristin Tombers, who is the owner of Clancey's Meats and Fish. She was recommended to me by a writer for *Food Arts* magazine, who said that if you want one of the most sophisticated people in the food industry in Minneapolis you need to go to Kristin for that. We're thrilled to have her here. And to talk about Prairie School architecture, we have Jennifer Komar Olivarez, who is associate curator of architecture, design, decorative arts, crafts, and sculpture at the Minneapolis Institute of Arts [MIA]. She has curated many exhibitions on art and design. So we're actually going to start with Jennifer and Prairie School architecture.

Prairie School Architecture

Thank you, Adam. Some of you may know me from this context (I'm a card-carrying member of the American Craft Council), but I have my Prairie School hat on now because I do a lot of programming with that collection. So without further ado: I was asked to do a bit of a potted history of Prairie School. Those of you who were on my tour yesterday know that we now incorporate textiles into our department, so to shorten the impossibly long title that we had, we are now the Department of Decorative Arts, Textiles, and Sculpture, but that still incorporates all the things we do with architecture, craft, design, etc.

When I start telling the story of the Prairie School, really, we think of Louis Sullivan as the father of the Prairie School, being the forefront of what we think of as the Chicago School of architecture. Chicago became the center of American architecture in the late 19th century because of the opportunities for rebuilding after the 1871 Chicago fire. New technologies were developed at that time to give form to what we now call the skyscraper. Those included the development of the steel frame, allowing for non-load-bearing walls with larger-size windows (which we all appreciate today) and the development of the elevator, which is very important in climbing ever higher and higher.

Aesthetically, the work of H. H. Richardson—the rustication, the Romanesque revival architecture—played a large part in the development of the aesthetic of the Chicago School. So let's look at a couple examples. Here's H. H. Richardson's Marshall Field Wholesale Store Ⓐ, in Chicago, looking kind of like an Italian palazzo. So you see that rustication of the stone, definition in the upper levels, the use of the arch, of course, which is something that Sullivan brings into play. An example of the load-bearing wall is seen here in Burnham and Root's Monadnock Building Ⓑ. The north half of the building does have the load-bearing walls, which are six feet thick, so you can see what they've done to modernize it with the abstraction of the walls, very unornamented. So you're getting that early abstraction, but the building itself has the traditional masonry walls, so that means these walls are incredibly thick.

The Home Insurance Building, in Chicago, is considered one of the first in the development of the modern skyscraper because of the steel frame that was employed for the non-load-bearing walls, which, again, allowed for many more and larger windows. This is the development of what we now call the Chicago window, which is a fixed pane in the middle and movable smaller glass panes on either side.

Now Louis Sullivan, within the Chicago School, developed what he called an organic approach to architecture, and you can think of this in several different ways. One of the things that was very much a concern to him, and to those in the Prairie School who inherited his beliefs, was the development of an indigenous American architecture. Sullivan felt that the Beaux-Arts canon that he actually studied in France—looking to ancient Greece and Rome and applying that style to buildings in the United States, as they did for civic buildings and universities—you don't really know what you're looking at since the forms are applied to many different building types. So Sullivan wanted to develop aesthetic forms that were indigenous to the United States and also really think about what a building should look like and have the forms spring from that, grow from a seed, as it were. This is where you get form following function, as opposed to a standard façade, which we have at the Minneapolis Institute of Art, with our Mc-Kim, Mead, and White building, so it is kind of interesting to talk about that in terms of our own Prairie School collection. [Sullivan developed] an organic system of ornament by looking at the flora of the American Midwestern prairie, adapting and abstracting those forms in the late 19th century as well as thinking about the use of color, which is really quite a departure from the Beaux Arts.

Here's Louis Sullivan in what I like to call the milkman pose . We'll look at a couple of different examples of his work, so you can see the similarities between the Marshall Field warehouse and his Auditorium Building . In the interior—and you can go into this building today, it's part of Roosevelt University—you see the use of the arches, how he's kind of elongated the building and accentuated the verticality by creating these arched areas that incorporate several different floors. This is what [Frank Lloyd] Wright ended up doing with horizontality. There was a system of ornament in the interior of this building that included, first of all, the use of the electric lightbulb, whereby the bare bulbs were celebrated and not hidden behind shades. That embrace of newly developed technology can

Top left to right: Henry Hobson Richardson, Marshall Field Wholesale Store, Chicago, IL, 1885–87.

Burnham and Root, Monadnock Building, Chicago, IL, 1892.

Middle to bottom: Louis Sullivan, Auditorium Building, Chicago, IL, 1886–90.

Louis Sullivan, interior of auditorium from balcony, Chicago, IL, 1886–90.

Louis Sullivan, photographed by Frank Lloyd Wright in front of cottage, Ocean Springs, MS, 1890.

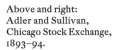

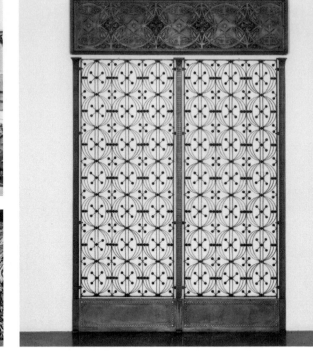

Above and right:
Adler and Sullivan,
Chicago Stock Exchange,
1893–94.

Louis Sullivan, detail of
ornamentation on capital
from the Chicago Stock
Exchange, 1893–94.

Far right:
Louis Sullivan, pair of
elevator grilles from the
Chicago Stock Exchange
Building, c. 1893–94.

Below:
Louis Sullivan, interior
view of main lobby,
National Farmers' Bank,
Owatonna, MN, 1907–09.

Louis Sullivan, detail of
lamp, National Farmers'
Bank, Owatonna, MN,
1907–09.

62 / 63

be seen again in the use of the arches and the integrated ornament, which was both painted onto the plasterwork and used in the color scheme and the murals that were incorporated into this building.

In Sullivan's design for the Chicago Stock Exchange ⓔ, you can see the Chicago window employed and, again, the use of the arch above more than one story. This building was sadly demolished, and pieces of it are distributed throughout the country. We have in the MIA's collection—as I'm emphasizing our collection with this talk—one of the elevator grilles ⓕ, and you can see within the metal the different interpretations of natural motifs. On the frieze, you see an abstraction of plant forms, which was something that was very prevalent in Sullivan's work. I like to think in looking at the main part of the elevator grilles that he's looking at a seed, incorporating the whole philosophy of organic architecture. He's looking at the smallest component or unit that was known at that time, which was what he called the "seed germ." And, of course, things would grow from that. But to me, in the 20th and 21st centuries, it looks almost atomic, which, for us, is the smallest component. So Sullivan was thinking of the growth of a building from the smallest component.

Locally—and if you haven't seen this, I encourage you to do so—a very good exploration of this new organic architecture is at the National Farmers' Bank, in Owatonna ⓖ, Minnesota, where Sullivan really helped redefine the bank form. He really designed this building thinking about form following function, with the building really looking like a strong box or a safety deposit box. It's large, it's square, it has a very strong mass to it. This looks like a very safe place for farmers to put their money. So the form of the building is important, but the ornamentation is also very important. It was very carefully conceived by Sullivan, along with Louis Millet in Chicago and George Grant Elmslie, who would later come to Minnesota after he left Chicago to work for William Gray Purcell. You can see again in this building the incorporation of the arch into great window walls of art glass. The color scheme is very much being taken from the earth.

George Elmslie was responsible for a lot of the drawings for these extremely elaborate terra-cotta lunettes and other elements that decorate the building, the mosaics you can see encircling that as well. Talk about technique and taking advantage of the craftsmanship of the time. This is really kind of the

heyday or the full flowering, I guess you could say, of organicism in ornament, and it was all conceived to be part of the interpretation of the building as a whole. On the inside, you have these massive electroliers, again with the exposed bulbs. There's also plasterwork on the inside, with this wonderful autumnal color scheme that's extremely beautiful, and you can see some of the detail work with the plaster as well as the terra-cotta bands below. You can see how he explored those things.

Now when we think of the inheritance of the Prairie School, we kind of go in two different directions. I always look at Purcell and Elmslie because they were local practitioners and they were very prolific next to Frank Lloyd Wright. Frank Lloyd Wright worked for Sullivan in the late 1880s until 1893, when

One of Frank Lloyd Wright's most influential designs was published in the *Ladies Home Journal* in April 1907–"A Fireproof House for $5000." It was meant to be kind of a prototype or a model home. One of the things he did that a lot of the Prairie School architects took to heart and interpreted in their own work was pulling out the stair hall from the main block. If you think of this as a Foursquare, Wright was sort of pulling it out and using a terrace, these different elements that increase the horizontality of the house and allow for greater flow within the space. The development of the open plan was really important, so once you move that stair hall out of the plan, it allows for the rest of the space to be much more open and free within.

These elements come into play in the Francis W. Little House , in Peoria, Illinois,

> "With these two movements, one of the things you see in common is that you're drawing from the particular landscape and traditions of this area." / Jennifer Komar Olivarez

he went off and started his own practice. Elmslie worked for Sullivan for 20 years, so he really learned from the master. So this sort of goes off in two different directions. Wright and Elmslie were contemporaries, and they really emphasized the application of these organic ideas to other forms, including residential architecture, which was not a strong suit of Sullivan's. [Shows floor plans for two houses.] Thinking about what Frank Lloyd Wright was doing around the turn of the century, you can see in the Wright floor plan on the left what he's doing to play with the elimination of walls, for example. You can see how he's created window walls on the left part of this slide, and on the right is a more conventional house from Tuxedo Park, New York, from 1885. The Frank Lloyd Wright house is from 1902, so he's taking a similar plan, and he's rearranging the walls, fireplace, and stairwells to really open up the interior spaces and incorporate more windows into the plan.

from 1902, where you can see the terraces and the horizontality and the extension of this main block in both directions to emphasize that horizontal. Interestingly, there is a little archway above the entrance door. You can see also the window walls in this slide, where even upstairs, where there are probably two rooms, he's linked those windows so it looks like one interior space.

[Shows two images of furniture designed by Wright for the Little House .] You can see Frank Lloyd Wright's furniture here, which is, of course, well known for being uncomfortable. In these examples, he's taking a very geometric or planar approach, so this is really kind of an early modern abstracted form here in these two chairs from that house. The one on the right is the Morris chair, but it's really kind of an arrangement of planes in space. You think of Gerrit Rietveld and those who came in years to come. So Wright's looking at abstraction and form.

Really, where this comes into play is in

Right and below:
Frank Lloyd Wright,
detail of interior window,
Frederick C. Robie
House, Chicago, IL,
1908–10.

Frank Lloyd Wright,
the Frederick C. Robie
House, Chicago, IL,
1908–10.

Clockwise from above:
Purcell and Elmslie, side
chair from the Edward
W. Decker House,
Wayzata, MN, c. 1914.

Right and above:
Purcell and Elmslie,
dining room, Decker
House, Wayzata, MN,
1911–12.

Purcell and Elmslie, the
Decker House, Wayzata,
MN, 1911–12.

the Robie House in Chicago J. I just took this slide a couple of weeks ago; the house is undergoing a major restoration. It really is an abstract arrangement of walls, of rooflines, of terraces—it is an abstract sculpture. He's taking this to a different level. So it's not a logical house—you don't really know where you're supposed to enter, you don't know where there's more than one room. This is, for me, a high point in terms of sculptural design with Prairie School architecture and horizontality. And you can see the interior with the custom furnishings, kind of creating a room within a room with the dining space, and the very graphic treatment of the dining-room interior.

I'm going to speed up to talk about Purcell and Elmslie, who worked here in Minneapolis. Purcell worked here from 1907 to around the time of the First World War, and the firm broke up in 1921. They had a bit of a different approach, a little more thinking about the client's needs perhaps than Frank Lloyd Wright. [Laughter] They were really thinking about social responsibility in architecture; it wasn't necessarily just about conceiving and executing an aesthetic ideal. They had that in mind, and the integrity of the architecture was really, really important.

They conceived of houses with these wonderful horizontal modern forms. The Decker House K, in Wayzata, which is sadly no longer there, was in the shape of an airplane, often called one of the "airplane houses." Again, you see that integrated furnishings were very important and the stenciling as well. We have the dining-room furniture from this house [at the MIA]. It was a part of that whole conception of the interior.

The Prairie School house that's part of [the MIA's] collection was Purcell's own house from 1913. It's called the Purcell-Cutts House L. Again, you're seeing some of the same elements: the window walls, this has stenciling on the exterior, a wonderful prairie color scheme, buff-colored stucco with a graphic treatment in between the windows, abstracted ornament by Elmslie. Here, a motto on one of the beams reads "Gray Days & Gold." So these different decorative elements were personal, but they were also part of the unified design of the building. Things like these very wonderful, whimsical window designs by George Elmslie that are part of this whole scheme—integrated artwork with mural above the fireplace, custom-designed furniture, and stenciling in the interior. Different zones for activity—this was really a modern house, so Purcell was literally thinking about breaking out of the box in terms of living in the spaces. He wanted multipurpose spaces instead of spaces that forced you to do specific things. The house allowed you to explore what you wanted to do at particular times of day, and light is a very important part of that, too.

Purcell and Elmslie carried on the bank tradition after Elmslie left Sullivan and came to Minneapolis. Another extant bank that's wonderful to go see is the Merchants Bank, in Winona Ⓜ. It has had additions over the years, but it's a more abstracted form. It doesn't have that heavy cornice and solid base, it has a lot more severity of design, but it shares a lot of the amazing details: George Elmslie's designs for terra-cotta that were executed by American Terra Cotta from all these little sketches that he did. He often would do just a corner of the sketch, and then they would send them off. The fabricators were incredibly skilled to be able to mold this terra-cotta and have it shipped, of course, by train and installed on the building—the whole thing was a leap of faith, as far as I'm concerned.

And then the interior, with these amazing light standards emphasizing the verticality, the window walls, the skylight, agrarian murals with scenes from around Winona. So there's the whole appropriateness of the decoration for this rural bank. The furniture, which we have some of in our collection, is also sort of cubelike, dare I say, like the bank itself.

Now I'll just end with kind of an extreme example by George Washington Maher, who's a Chicago architect. He designed a building in Winona, too; it was kind of a little laboratory for progressive architecture at that time. He did several buildings for the Watkins family in Winona. Perhaps the best known is the one that's no longer with us, which is called Rockledge. This is what they call in Prairie School a "blank check house"; I guess you can still build one of those today.

Left:
Purcell and Elmslie, Purcell-Cutts House, Minneapolis, MN, 1913.

Middle:
Purcell and Elmslie, writing nook, Purcell-Cutts House, Minneapolis, MN, 1913.

Bottom left and right:
Purcell, Feick, and Elmslie, Merchants National Bank, Winona, MN, c. 1911–12.

Grace Watkins King and her husband commissioned this house. George Maher's whole philosophy was what he called the "motif rhythm theory," where you would take a motif and repeat it through the house. The more you used it, all over for all the decoration—the furnishings, fixtures, you surrounded yourself with these repeated motifs—it would provide more harmony for you as you're moving about and using the house. (I think in a way that may be even more constricting.)

You can see some of the interiors here that reflect the flattened arch; there was also a lily design. These elements were repeated throughout the furniture, in all the built-ins, all the fixtures—everything was designed by George Maher. Here's one of the armchairs that we have [in our collection] with that flattened arch motif. This silver service 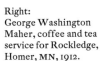 was commissioned from the Gorham Manufacturing Company and done to the highest standards of Martelé silver. When Mrs. King was presented with the design, she said, "Okay, we might as well do it, otherwise the house just is not going to be the way [Maher] wants it." [Laughter] I think she really felt that it was a little too much, but said, "Okay, well let's go ahead and complete the design." They did end up remodeling in the 1930s, but

everything was kept, and when the house was torn down, all that material came onto the market. When the architects could design down to this level—the silver that was on your dining table—what they were trying to achieve was not so much about control but really thinking about that whole unified design philosophy.

Those are just a few different examples [of Prairie School architecture]. I hope in the little time that I've had I've introduced you to some of the concepts behind unified design and the different philosophies that they were looking at, in an early modern way—thinking about developing architecture that resonated with Americans instead of a transplantation or an acceptance of something that was the status quo. They were really thinking about a reexamination and how you redefine that for modern Americans.

Right:
George Washington
Maher, coffee and tea
service for Rockledge,
Homer, MN, 1912.

Meat Fabrication

I'm Kristin, and I'm the owner of Clancey's Meats and Fish. I'm going to explain a little about our business because it's probably not very familiar to see someone like me standing up here talking about meat fabrication. [Laughter] I bought a butcher shop, an existing shop, about six years ago. We're going to have our six-year anniversary on Halloween this year. I thought, How in the heck am I going to fill 20 minutes talking about meat fabrication? And I realized that what was so crucial and important to what we do, and we wouldn't really be in business without this, is the farmers that we work with. I've got photos here of three of the main farmers that we work with so as [the images] run through I might refer to them.

We are a little unique in the way that we buy our meats. The farms that we work with are all local Minnesota family farms. We are very lucky to have a duck farmer who raises mallard-Muscovy cross ducks for foie gras. That was one of the reasons [the food writer] Juliet Glass was really interested in our business. Juliet had written an article for *The New York Times* about foie gras. So these are a lot of pictures here of Christian's ducks.

I was thinking about kind of the art of what we do. It was such an accident that I ended up purchasing this business. I was relatively angst-filled and very frustrated with our government a few years back, and the loss of farmland, and how we eat, and where the food comes from. As I happened to be selling seafood at the time, the gentleman that owned the existing butcher shop kept telling me to find a chef around town that might be interested in buying this business. After a while I thought, Maybe this is something I can consider doing. It took a lot of nerve, and it took my mom basically telling me that if I didn't figure out something to do with some of the angst and anger that I had and maybe talked about something other than politics, I might not have any friends left after a while. [Laughter]

So I wish I could say there was some long germinating period where my frustration with confined-area feeding operations and overall disgust with our food system would have led up to this. It's been in the past six years that it's all kind of come together in a way that makes more sense than it ever could about our food. It's kind of a critical issue right now—how we eat and where our food comes from. *The New York Times*, speaking of, has done a very good job lately of covering some of these food issues where they're getting national attention, and so we in turn are getting a lot of attention.

These are photos from Hidden Stream Farm; they're our hog farmers. We do bring in steer, hogs, lamb—everything comes in whole animals, and this is where the meat fabrication comes in. There will be slides showing you some of the whole pieces that we get, which are called primals. All of these animals that we get are raised on pasture, they're cared for. I mean, you'll see, especially from Eric and Lisa (they're kind of my heroes), they have taken this old vision of farming and made it very real again today. They raise hogs, chickens. Andy, Lisa's seven-year-old son, is now raising goats. We're going to get a goat from Andy next week. They're really just doing an exceptional job caring for their animals. [Refers to photo on screen.] Those are kittens in there with the chicken, which I guess animals do that once in a while just to keep warm.

[Refers to two photos of pigs at Hidden Stream Farm.] These are my two favorite slides. These are animals that are raised on this farm. From this stage, the hogs come to

Counterclockwise from left:
Piglets run home for dinner at Hidden Stream Farm.

Au Bon Canard ducks and farmhouse, Caledonia, MN.

Hog families in Hidden Stream Farm hoop houses, Elgin, MN.

Clockwise from top left:
Pork loins and sirloin,
filleting Alaskan sockeye,
short loin, short ribs.

Right and below:
Trimming fat from Hill
& Vale Farm rack of lamb.

Cutting down rack
of lamb.

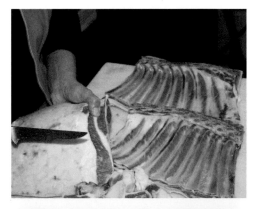

us in six to eight pieces, the steer in six to eight pieces. Obviously, there is a big size difference. The round and the chuck from the steer are going to be about 150 pounds, that whole carcass is 700 to 800 pounds. The whole hogs weigh anywhere from 80 to 90 pounds.

We've been with these same farmers for the six years that we've been in business, and it's really been kind of a neat progression in terms of the relationships maturing and the friendships that have developed. I've been down to visit all the farms. My favorite is the duck farm. I just like going and doing chores, so I'll go down there and work with them. Lisa, I don't know how she does it, has all of this going on with the farm and five children. But I think it's really a belief in a need to change our food system and the way that people have access and the way that people think about our food that is driving these people to work as hard as they are, and getting more of what they can do so well on their farm to the city. I feel lucky every day. I had a hard time writing notes because I just kept looking through these slides and thinking how I'd like to be closer to this type of life and yet living in the city. Our shop is in southwest Minneapolis, so every week we get these animals coming up from the farms. We've all grown together. Eric and Lisa have now gotten a new truck—a new, big refrigerated truck—so everyone is really working very hard together to keep this system going.

When we get these meats, or primals—subprimals, primals, they're all a little different, the way they're cut—they'll arrive at our door, and we get them into the backroom onto the cutting table. I didn't really have a lot of photos of our shop, so next you're going to see a picture of Clancey, who is my yellow lab. I named the shop after my dog, which fortunately for the neighborhood that we're in, makes a lot a sense. There are dogs everywhere, so it's a very dog-friendly business, as are the neighboring businesses around us; there's a lot of dogs everywhere. Clancey's actually 13, so he's moving on in years. The only shot I had of the front [of the shop] are these [refers to photo with 13 dogs tied up outside of Clancey's]. There's a guy that walks dogs in the neighborhood and, literally, he's been written up in the local press for walking 13 at a time. This is Halloween decorations one year, so it seemed fitting. This is pretty much all I have of our storefront, and now we're going to go into the slides of the meat production and the meat cutting.

It's really to me a thing of beauty when

I can see this [refers to photo of primals]. When we get that bright-red beef, it hangs at the processor for about two weeks before we get it, and we continue to age it. It makes me very proud when I can see every week that we can still afford to do this. We hang the meat and age it for anywhere from two days, depending on what we need to cut immediately to put out in our meat case, to an additional two weeks. I've learned a lot in the six years that we've been doing this. In the middle are the fancy cuts, the rib eyes and the short loin. You don't really see them there, but that's what we have to fabricate, that's what we have to take and turn into cuts that we can sell to our customers. It's been kind of a long process in educating people about the difference between purchasing meat this way versus the stuff you see wrapped in packages at the grocery store.

That's a picture of the inside of the meat case, what it looks like when we put it out. So I consider it to be very artistic, although I never thought I would talk about meat as being so beautiful or pretty or even cute sometimes. We'll see a little lamb skirt steak that's *this big* and it's, like, oh so cute. Those were crosscut beef shanks. It's really

which is used for just about anything with a bone in it. To me, it's just so beautiful. I don't know, I didn't see these things growing up—I didn't grow up on a farm, I didn't go hunting. Somewhere along the line, I guess I just decided that I was either going to be a vegetarian or I was going to learn more about meat. So it was sort of a natural accident, or stumbling upon that shop being for sale and having the nerve to take this on and make it happen. It's been a pretty great experience, learning about this and knowing that we can offer these things to people that you can't get many other places (I think that

Top left to right: Clancey's storefront in Minneapolis with a pack of dog admirers.

Post-dinner-party staff photo in Clancey's kitchen.

"Somewhere along the line, I guess I just decided that I was either going to be a vegetarian or I was going to learn more about meat." / Kristin Tombers

been such a work in progress getting to this point. When we first opened, we really didn't know a lot about what we were doing; we knew what we wanted to do, but we were pretty much self-taught and managing the meat cutting. The guy that I originally started the business with had taken some butchery classes—I think Bob the Butcher was his professor's name at the California Culinary Academy. So we had some basis for getting started. There's a book called *The Meat Buyer's Guide*, and it was a lot of looking through that and making phone calls and working through the muscles and the seams. Not a lot of cuts; I don't tend to cut myself, but you're using pressure. I poke myself when I'm cutting a lot. It's a puncture thing, but it doesn't happen very often.

We have a big cutting table in the back of the shop, and that's where all of the action happens, whether it's the beef, the lamb, the pork. We keep things separate, and we have our cutting days. That is our band saw,

there are a handful of co-ops around town).

That's a full pork loin. It's about probably this big end to end. And that's a little pork roast cut off that loin. So those cuts, anywhere from the beef to the lamb to the pork—the pork generally requires most of the fabrication or the cutting because we make so many different things out of the pork. There's the bacon, and we do pancetta out of the bellies. I put the salmon in there just to show again sort of the craft of cutting and what it requires in terms of attention to detail. We have had quite a few people, young people that work in restaurants, who want to come to Clancey's and learn about cutting. Oftentimes just to put a knife in someone's hand thinking maybe they've had some proper training working in restaurants and having gone to school, it's amazing what can happen to a piece of meat or fish if someone doesn't know what they're doing. Things can literally just be shredded, so it definitely takes time. I think there's an art to it.

Adam had asked me to talk about the art of the fabrication, but, again, I'm just thinking about all of this as one big picture, not being able to pull this off without the farmers, and, again, just the beauty of that raw material that we get from the farms every week. Now we're going into a series of photos—we also do dinners in the back of our shop, and this is where we get a little bit of a reward for all of the hard work. It's not an easy job cutting meat and selling meat retail. It's obviously a very perishable product, and we work pretty hard. Behind that counter it's a lot of education, so it's always a lot of work, but what we get as payoff is these dinners that we do. I really think of it as payoff. I have a hard time sometimes when it comes to settling a bill feeling right even charging for them because we all have so much fun doing this.

This is seared foie gras wrapped in nori leaf and panko bread crumbs. This is smoked duck breast. I put these pictures in there because I just love them, and it's all about the beauty of the food that we have at our fingertips and disposal, really, because we have these relationships with the farms. The meat producers that we work with have set us up with CSA boxes. I don't know if anyone's familiar with Community Supported Agriculture, but this year, Clancey's took in CSA boxes from four different farms. So we're just a drop site: The customers that pay for the CSA boxes come to Clancey's to pick them up. It's a pretty good relationship because we are able to talk to them about what's in their CSA share. I get to see little kids rifling through the box excited about vegetables, and then maybe they'll pick an animal protein to go with their vegetables.

[Refers to photos of prepared food dishes on screen.] Again, these are just sort of the end result of what we get to do in an artistic, creative way. The dinners kind of came about because we were asked to cater in the very first year, and I was reluctant to do any catering because it always seemed to me to be an even harder job than retail meat. And then we sort of came to a decision that we would do this if we were able to do it with our own license, to make things the way we want to make them without anyone telling us what to do. I guess now after six years of doing this I feel much more comfortable.

That's just beautiful. That's seafood sausage we've made in the past, not enough because it's really good. These are baby amaranth from a grower that we work with. So I guess for me to be able to relate to all of you what we can do from farmers with food is pretty amazing, what we've accomplished in six years. And again if it wasn't for the hard work of the farmers... I'm so grateful everyday that we have the relationships that we do.

These are ramp sausages. Ramps are wild leeks. We also work with foragers. This is a full loaf of foie gras—rather fancy. We've had a lot of questions over the six years about foie gras and whether or not it makes sense that we would be doing it. I guess, for me, it's the issue of small versus big, huge, industrial, and corporate, which is what's happened with our food system, which has just gone wild and out of control. If you're interested enough, the articles that have been written recently in *The New York Times* are pretty amazing, and it's just that we're getting national attention for what is really a big issue. Our food system is completely unsafe, unstable. I guess, for me, I don't even know what I would have been eating if we didn't start Clancey's, because I have a hard time remembering sometimes to feed myself because I work really hard and I'm running around. I'd gotten to the point where driving around, maybe I'd go for coffee, but I would never quite know where to go for food. Now, I'm surrounded by it and it's just really a beautiful thing.

So I think this was my way of showing that all of the food that's in these photos is from local farms. That art of fabricating meat... if you have the opportunity to work with a butcher wherever any of you live, to find someone that's sourcing meats from local farms, or even if you have to drive out of your way, it's a pretty neat way to eat and think about living, and almost, really, kind of critical. This is the group of us, and I finished with this photo of a piece of chocolate-covered bacon, which we actually did before the Minnesota State Fair put theirs out, and ours would have been much better, I'm sure.

Bottom and right: Clancey's housemade halibut sausage with greens from Dragsmith Farms, Barron, WI.

Bayley Hazen blue cheese from Jasper Hill, Greensboro, Vermont, served with Dragsmith Farms micro greens and housemade lingonberry sauce.

Q&A Segment

Adam Lerner

Now we have question-and-answer. Just so you know, this is the time where you *can* make connections between the talks but you're not *required* to do so. We can just let the connections emerge or merge afterward, or merge in your own minds or in your conversations afterward. Again, anything can happen.

QUESTION

My name's Amy Shaw. I'm from Brooklyn, New York. My question is kind of for both of you. I'm really interested in sustainability and keeping things local and that sort of thing. Maybe it's obvious how it relates to the food situation, but I was wondering if you both have something to say about why it's important to source materials locally for craftspeople. Maybe not everyone can get their clay from a regional source or something like that, but maybe there could be more effort toward that. I'm just wondering why people care about locally produced materials, in terms of food and maybe even in terms of the architecture. I don't know where some of the materials were sourced for these beautiful buildings, but I'd imagine some of them were local, and I'm wondering how that is valuable to the people who use them and to the people who build them.

AL

That's what we call a crossover question.

JKO

It's a very good question, and I think part of it is, as Kristin was saying, identifying the people with the talents and the same mindset as you. I think that with Purcell and Elmslie, the incubator was Chicago, and they were an extension of that, but it was still part of the Midwest. They were using a lot of the talent that they knew about both in Chicago and Illinois—also locally. Almost all of Purcell and Elmslie's leaded glass, their stained glass, was done by a man named E. L. Sharretts right here in Minneapolis. The idea was to develop these working relationships with people who could help you fulfill your needs, your ideals, your philosophies in a satisfying way to both of you. I was looking at [Kristin's] slides, and that question really brings to light that there was this great relationship between [Purcell and Elmslie] and the talent pool that they knew about.

I mean, this was an avant-garde movement, sort of like what's going on now with the whole back-to-the-way-things-used-to-be farming movement. And so I do think that it was important for them at least to find the connections between like-minded people who could help them fulfill the craftsmanship at the level they were looking for, who had the skills, and even helped them bring in the culmination of all these parts, execute their vision at that level. It almost becomes greater than the sum of the parts when you look at some of these buildings. It becomes the synthesis of all these great talents that, in large part, were local. Using local brick and stone, things like that, was incredibly important if you read Purcell's writings.

KT

I think, too, if you can't find something that you want locally… I've struggled with this a little bit. We carry a lot of product in our shop that's imported from Europe, and we've got pastas and olive oils and vinegars, and we've got one bottle of Sicilian olive oil. Over six years, many customers have come in and said, "Well, I've been there, I've met the old man that presses those olives." So it is researching enough and educating yourself enough that you're comfortable with your source, whatever it is.

QUESTION

I'm Mary Kay Baumann from Minneapolis, and actually I shop every Saturday at Kristin's shop, and it's fantastic. She really brings a lot of craft to our food, so I applaud her. But I wanted to ask a question: A lot of people think of innovation happening either in New York or Los Angeles or San Francisco, and it occurred to me in listening to both of you that so much innovation happens here in the Midwest. And it often doesn't get recognized, I think, because the news media is on the East Coast. But if you could address that in any way, shape, or form.

KT

It's funny, because I was going to start today by asking how many people had read Michael Pollan's *Omnivore's Dilemma*. I was explaining to Jennifer before I even started that I don't get out much; I get to do this today and I get to go to the orchestra tonight, so this is kind of a big night for me. I'm trying to change my life a little bit from the small-business owner to feeling like I can manage this and let go a little bit and get out and experience some of what Minneapolis has to offer. I was thinking about how to talk about the things that are important to me today, and I was speaking with a girlfriend last night who said that there's some perception about Midwesterners—or Minnesota, Minneapolis, in particular—that we're kind of quiet and humble, don't necessarily talk big about what we know. And I thought that was kind of interesting because there is so much going on, and I don't even know the half of it. Jennifer asked if I knew about the meat dress at the Walker, and I don't. [Laughter] I really should. I guess it's just a perception, and I asked her, too, I said, "I think most of these people would be coming in from both coasts.

QUESTION

[Keelin Burrows] I was just interested in hearing each of your perspectives on this idea of local and regional. In both cases, I'm wondering if you see this local or regional aspect of culture being accessible to only a particular class.

AL

Hmm, interesting…

JKO

I can probably do a little bit shorter. Now when you look at a house like the Purcell-Cutts House, that house was $14,000 when it was built. It's a pretty small house, so that

"A lot of people think of innovation happening either in New York or Los Angeles or San Francisco, and it occurred to me in listening to both of you that so much innovation happens here in the Midwest." / Mary Kay Baumann

Do you think it's safe to assume that everyone reads *The New York Times*?" And she said, "No." So I thought it was interesting that that was her perception, that there is a difference. And however it is that we've arrived at the point where there is that thinking that somehow we're a little behind or slower in the Midwest is really… I don't know that there's any truth to it.

JKO

I guess my response to that would be that I really like that observation because I was born in Missouri in a rural area, and I think that you often do get glossed over here. But I think, in particular with these two movements, one of the things you see in common is that you're drawing from the particular landscape and traditions of this area. I was sitting there thinking it was so strongly reflected in what's going on. To me, it's so evident in the Prairie School architecture, drawing from the palette of this area and really thinking of this as the place where you can kind of have this clean slate to go back to. I was looking at the palette of the salad with the carrot that [Kristin] showed with the baby amaranth—it looks like all the ornamentation. The palette that she's bringing in from the farmers is similar to the palette that Sullivan was envisioning in his mind when he was looking out in the landscape and thinking what was appropriate for Midwesterners to live amongst. I guess I was also thinking maybe we have more time for contemplation, how we can improve our lives by drawing on what's around us.

was at a level of craftsmanship that was very expensive. But one thing that Purcell was interested in, and Frank Lloyd Wright to a certain extent by creating these plans that hopefully other architects or developers would adapt, they were interested in social responsibility in architecture. They did want to have a trickle-down effect. But it was one of those ideological barriers that they came up against that was similar with the Arts and Crafts movement, in that if you're designing a home that is so personal for somebody and reflects how you're talking to them and trying to create a home based on how they live and what they want, well, that's not really something that's easy to replicate. You can't really get a Sears home that's going to fulfill that for you, so people would obviously go and buy a Sears home. Purcell really struggled with that, but that was something that he did want to do. His piano tuner came to him and said, "I only have a fraction of what you spent on your house, but I would like a house that's similar," and Purcell spent a lot of energy designing a house that had some of the similar flow of space and, frankly, a better bathroom. That house still stands, by the way, down on 36th Street in Minneapolis. It has a similar look, and the piano tuner was very, very pleased. That house cost like $2,600. So there was this interest in creating a model using that philosophy, but it wasn't necessarily executed by the Prairie School architects. It sort of got taken over in a more mass-produced form by, for example, the Sears houses. And, of course, with his Usonian houses, Frank Lloyd Wright was able to fulfill that to a certain extent, but that was later, so it's kind of beyond this particular period. But there was definitely a philosophical imbalance between something at the level of our house, Purcell-Cutts, or even something for [a client like] Robie and what most middle-class families could afford. But that's a really good point.

KT

I guess as far as I can say, if anybody has time to find this, or maybe some of you have seen it, there's a new documentary out called *Fresh*. I believe the woman that made the film is from Holland, and she started out with the idea that she was going to make this movie about how she was going to raise her kid, and across the board, she ended up narrowing everything down to food. In this film—it's probably one of the best documentaries I've seen on food, there's a ton of them out there right now—she interviews Will Allen. He's been awarded a genius grant. He is working in Milwaukee, Wisconsin, in an urban area, and he has an indoor tilapia farm and hoop houses for chickens and all of his greens, and it's an enclosed system. He's educating urban people in Milwaukee about what they can do to feed themselves. So I think that if there can just be more open discussion, whether it's about food or any material, about the importance of the quality and the integrity behind the quality that you can get on any level, in any form, talking about that is maybe what will take it out of this class distinction where maybe only certain people have access to it. If I can (I've got the form), I want to take EBT cards at our butcher shop, and that would force me to figure out ways to put packages together. And I get phone calls, so those questions come in. So I think that there are a lot of people who want this to be accessible, all of it, whether it's the food or the fabric or whatever it is that someone might use to create something. I think the communication and the relationships matter and talking about all of it all the time.

AL

Can I ask a question? One of the great things about being the moderator is that you get to just ask questions. This is for Jennifer. We got a really broad range of culture here, and in many ways I really feel that this is a great illustration of the French and German distinction between culture and civilization—those aspects of society that are kind of reified into what we call art and the lofty pursuits but then also the things that make up our daily

lives—this architecture and this fine ornament, and yet the culture that is our daily lives. And I guess what I want to know is, from these architects, whether or not their organicism went so far as to actually include food. The design was totally united, totally integral—everything from the furniture to the fixtures was all kind of one. But did they have any sense of what people would actually be doing in that house and that lifestyle and how they would be getting their food?

JKO

I don't know of any specific writings that address that per se. I know that Frank Lloyd Wright even did design dresses for his clients and their wives, or if the clients were women, he did design some reform dress for them to wear.

AL

Not a meat dress, though.

JKO

Not a meat dress, no. So it was about introducing modernity in all these different ways. I think this sort of enlightenment came in stages, even though Purcell and Elmslie were very progressive. They had a woman architect working in their firm as early as 1908, and she worked there for almost ten years and was treated as an equal in the firm and was given credit for what she did. So there was this recognition of equal rules within the office and also in their house. The house was named after Purcell's wife, Edna Purcell, and she helped design the house, gave input into what she wanted, and kind of had equal say. But she still came from an upper-middle-class family in Chicago, and you still see her with the high collars, and they also still had a domestic servant, as most people of middle-class backgrounds did until World War I, when everybody's fortunes changed. She probably also employed somebody to come in and cook if it wasn't the maid. So, as far as what they actually served, I don't know, because I don't think Purcell really talked about that too much, and I don't know that from the other architect studies. Now when you look, for example, at what George Maher did for the King family, that's a really formal house in the end. So when you have the coffee and tea service designed in a very formal way, it's not necessarily about a relaxed way of living.

However, Purcell does talk about moving the dining table to where it made sense. One thing he does say about food is that it really makes no sense that when you have such beautiful surroundings, and all the windows placed to maximize them, that you dine staring down at the food. So for him, I guess the food wasn't necessarily central, or the experience of eating was enhanced when it was moved to a place in the house during the time of day or time of year where it could be enhanced by a relationship with nature. So I guess that's maybe as close as I can get for you. For Purcell, it wasn't about staring at each other and staring at the food and eating the same way you always did. He loved the idea of sidewalk cafés in Europe and bringing that kind of sensibility into your own home, to enjoy your house in a new way instead of getting stuck in a rut

again, I understand that we have to make money, and if we weren't in business after these six years, a lot of people would be very disappointed, and I feel very lucky for that. I guess I think that the relationships have become so important, and if I didn't have the commitment that I have… I just said to Adam over lunch, I think I'm coming off six years of adrenaline, and I really have been in that shop nonstop for six years, and I'm only just this year learning how to take time away. I guess in the community that we're in and the neighborhood that we're in, that has probably shown—people come in and see me and see

74/75

> "I think what your two presentations help this conference do is understand how craft is really a social practice." / Keelin Burrows

the way the box-type houses forced you into.

QUESTION

[Jennifer Hinshaw] First of all, I think this is for Kristin, hearing your talk is such a great case example about what Richard Sennett was talking about this morning. I think if there are any questions about whether a craftsman or crafts can extend beyond the materials we typically think of, your talk was a perfect example. My question for you has to do with the marketplace. You mentioned how much you've learned in the last six years and how proud you are of what you've learned. That came through mainly for me in how you talked about learning to work with meat, but what can you say about learning to work with the marketplace? Because, after all, you wouldn't be here after six years if you hadn't also built a customer base and figured out the ways to connect in such a way that you are still in business. And I think that's a question for the crafts in general, because to stay in business and stay viable and to sell is about figuring out how to make a marketplace for it. So I'm curious what you can say about what you've learned in that regard.

KT

A woman that I know who sells dog food wholesale to retailers—it's an all-natural dog food, and she's very hard-lined—said to me, "If you're not in the business to make money, you might as well sell to someone else and go get a job." It's been hard for me because my initial feeling was just that I had to develop these relationships, and I like people so much that it was very easy for me, and yet anytime we needed to make a price increase, these things always make me cringe. But,

my level of commitment. In the neighborhood we're in, people are just hungry for the handcrafted, whatever it is, and so for where we are in south Minneapolis, again, we're very lucky. I don't know that we would have had the same fortune in any other location. There was a gentleman who wants to move into a space adjacent to us, and he wanted to know what I thought about him coming in, and he said, "I'm trying to figure out what to put in there as a business. I think a dog boutique might work." It occurred to me that he was just sort of grabbing something out of thin air to open up a business, and I realized when he said that that the people in that neighborhood, with their loyalty, probably wouldn't accept this guy because they would probably pretty quickly identify that there wasn't passion behind it. So I think that passion and that trust and that level of commitment really matters a lot to people right now—no matter what it is.

JKO

Can I just carry on that idea just a little bit further to talk about the idea of patronage with the arts in general? Thinking about this with the Prairie School, like I said, it was avant-garde. There were these forward-thinking people that oftentimes worked in industry, like Frederick Robie manufactured bicycle parts. They were looking at technology and were the early supporters and early adapters of this modern movement at that time. So I think that wherever we are in thinking about supporting the arts at a very high level—like the honorees at [the awards luncheon]—those people have helped support craft or craftsmanship at a very high level. That is something that can't be ignored and is essential.

I think this is something that is definitely in common with both of these topics—that you have people who are willing to support artistic vision. In fact, one of the Prairie School architects talked about how Midwesterners... you know, you think of innovation on the East and West Coasts, but at this time, it was thought that Midwesterners were really problem-solvers, and they were looking at something that was practical. And if it happened to be more modern, then that's fine; they had trust in the architect. So I think there was a lot of belief in these new forms because they were helping to be logical and solve problems in a new way, which is a characteristic of Midwesterners that I think is quite often recognized—our sensibleness.

QUESTION

[Bennett Bean] Hi, I have a confession to make, and that is that I am deeply involved in a romance with pork. It started out with a Duroc. It has moved to a Gloucester Old Spot. Now I've settled on a Hampshire, and I'm considering a Mangalitsa. These are antique varieties of pigs. These are pigs that are not the "new white meat." These are lard hogs. They are spectacular. These are hogs that have pretty much gone out of style. So I see a very close parallel between antique houses and antique pigs, and I'd really like you to comment on the interplay between those two.

AL

I don't know, do we need a comment on that? I think we could pretty much end it at that. But, OK, we have one more "must ask" question.

QUESTION

[Keelin Burows] I just wanted to quickly say what I think is interesting about each of your presentations—and perhaps you could briefly comment on this further—is that I think what your two presentations help this conference do is understand how craft is really a social practice. Your presentations, I feel like, really draw out how we have shifted our perspective and how we look at craft as not only a static object or craft as a creative process but also as a social activity that provides critical reflections and, hopefully, logical solutions to contemporary needs in our society.

AL

That's a pretty good way of ending, too. That's beautiful, let's keep that. Please join me in thanking our two fantastic speakers. They were amazing. Thank you. ✢

The Marketplace and the Personal: A Story of Thread / Natalie Chanin

It's hard for a Southern storyteller to pack it all into 20 minutes, so I'm going to do my very best to run through it. The slideshow runs relatively quickly, and what I'm going to talk about is not necessarily tied to the slides, but the slides have everything to do with what I'm talking about. I'm going to give you a little bit of background first, so you'll know where I come from, who I work with, what we do, and about our company.

So, first, since this is about the personal, I'm going to tell you a little bit about who I am. First and foremost, I'm a designer. We make what would be called "couture garments" with fabric that is not really known for couture, which is cotton jersey. That's pretty much the only material that we use as far as garments and textiles go. I'm the owner of a lifestyle company called Alabama Chanin. There has been some talk today about lifestyle companies and commerce and if that's an evil word or not, so maybe we can address that in the Q&A time.

I'm a craftswoman. I produce all the garments that we design. There's a word in architecture called "design/build," so I own a design/build company, but instead of working with wood and concrete, I work with fabric and thread.

I'm an agent. I represent 30 to 40 artisans who live and work in and around the community of Florence, Alabama. Florence is about eight miles from Tennessee, so some of our artisans live in Tennessee and some down in Mississippi.

I'm a writer. I wrote a book about sewing that touches a little bit on cultural preserva-

tion in the form of sustaining textile traditions. We have another book coming out in February called *Alabama Studio Style*, which is a follow-up to our first, *Alabama Stitch Book*. I'm also a mother, a cook, and a gardener. So I loved the stories about meat [in the Mixed Taste session with the butcher Kristin Tombers]; they were right down my alley. I think there's also a big correlation between meat and sewing, and we can talk about that as well.

I just want to give you a little bit of a background about how I got started because what happened to me is so incredibly personal that my business is so tied to my history of growing up in Alabama and the stories that I lived from that point out. In the year 2000, I took a sabbatical from my life, and I wound up in New York City. I was going to a very fancy fashion party, and I didn't have anything to wear because I'd been on sabbatical for four months. I didn't really have money to buy anything, so I took an old T-shirt, and I cut it up, and I sewed it back together again by

Clockwise from top left:
Natalie Chanin.

Repurposed blue baseball T-shirt.

Quilted American flag.

Bottom left to right:
Ceremony whites.

Ceremony quilt.

Top left to right:
Stick bowl.

Stacked farm chairs.

hand, sitting on my bed at the Hotel Chelsea, in New York. And it was a very strange thing, because I wore that T-shirt to the party that night—what I deemed to be a very fancy "fashion party"—and everybody at that party touched me.

Now it's a very strange thing in New York City if people walk across the room and touch you. I woke up the next morning, and, of course, I was overjoyed that all these fancy fashion people loved what I had on. But what really struck me was that I was just so taken with the joy of actually making something with my own hands. I'm trained as a designer, and I worked as a stylist for ten years—I had been designing for over 20 years—but it had been a very long time since I physically made something. So I got up the next morning and I made another T-shirt, and the next morning and the next, and that whole thing evolved into me permanently sitting on my bed at the Hotel Chelsea and sewing and, consequently, trying to find a manufacturer in New York who could help me produce a line of 200 one-of-a-kind T-shirts that I wanted to present with a documentary film about old-time quilting circles.

Well, I've gotten a little ahead of myself. Let me just talk about the manufacturer. I tried to find a manufacturer in New York, and so many people thought I was crazy. I was going into these garment factories with a bag of cut-up T-shirts—I think they literally thought I was a bag lady. I bring these cut-up T-shirts, and I want to do this extremely beautiful embroidery and handwork on these recycled shirts. You could just see their minds going, "Eeeeeeh."

So I was standing on a street corner in New York and looking at the clothes one day, and I was like, I'm so dumb. This is a quilting stitch. Both of my grandmothers were quilters. I grew up with quilters in my community. I slept under quilts. It took me a real long time

to figure out that all I was doing, as a writer from *The New York Times* called it, was "channeling my grandmother." And in that moment, I remembered that there were still craftswomen in my community in Florence, Alabama, some of whom had sewn with my grandmothers, and I realized that I had to go home to get these T-shirts made.

So I went home. I raised the money to produce these 200 one-of-a-kind T-shirts. I raised the money to make a very short documentary film called *Stitch* about old-time quilting circles. I manufactured the T-shirts and took them to New York City during Fashion Week in 2001. Now, I'm a bit of a hybrid, because I am very attached to the craft world and I live in craft every day, but I also work, as the [conference] brochure says, in a global marketplace. As you can see, we sell to stores like Barneys, in New York, and Bergdorf Goodman and have sold to stores around the world.

I took these T-shirts to this Fashion Week, which is really like the global marketplace, or the first of several global marketplaces, for clothing. I kind of had this idea that we would sell these 200 one-of-a-kind shirts, and we'd take that money and go back to the artisans to make a few more. But what happened was Julie Gilhart from Barneys came in the door and sent in her buyers, and they looked at the shirts and said, "We'll have 12 like this, and 12 like this, and 12 like this,

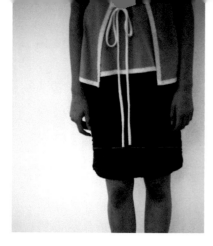

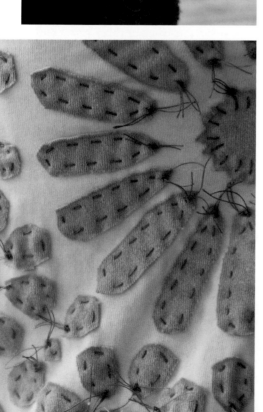

Top row, left to right:
Maggie's top.

Red bolero and long
beaded skirt, from the
spring 2010 collection.

Middle:
Red negative reverse
coat, from the spring
2010 collection.

Bottom:
Negative reverse
ceremony mannequin.

and 12 like this." And I said, "Wait a minute, these are one-of-a-kind pieces," and they said, "Well, you just do something kind of like it."

One of my very first design problems when I was in design school was a project where we had to design a toy, and we had to make that one toy. Then after the toy was made, we found out that we actually had to make 12 more of them for everybody in our studio. Any of you who have ever done a problem like that, or ever gone into production, know that it's very easy to make just one thing but that it's a lot harder to make two. It's harder to make 12. It's a lot more difficult when you start making a hundred or a thousand of them. The problems just grow exponentially.

I called our ladies in Alabama who had sewn—I just ran an ad in our local paper that said "part-time hand-sewing and quilting" to make those first 200 shirts—and said, "Are you guys up to this? Do you want to make more?" And they were like, "Yeah!"

So I went home and I became a manufacturer. That was in March of 2001, right after we had presented the shirts, and I never left. I've been at my home at Florence, Alabama, since then. It will be ten years next year that I've been doing what I do.

So it was all a little bit of an accident. I would love to say I'm very clever and I had it all planned out, but it's really not the case. I'm not that clever. I just kind of followed my heart and the heart of my community, and we're still there and we're still sewing.

We wanted to talk a little bit about thread, and I think this is a really important story. Some of you may have already heard this story before because I know some of the faces in the audience. I think it's really important because it's kind of at the core of what we do. I like to liken sewing to physics, and people always laugh when I say that, but, really, it's no different than building a building

Top to bottom:
Revolution black and
white spiral dress, rose
dress, and mini coat.

Beaded-facets pillow
close.

or a beautiful piece of furniture. You have materials that you use. If you're using metal, you use screws and welding to tie those materials together. If you're using fabric, you use a thread to tie those materials together. It's the same thing. You know, my dad is a builder and wanted me to become an architect, but I told him, "I am an architect and a builder. I just work with thread and fabric."

Those of you who sew know that thread starts with a fiber. I work with cotton fibers, so I'm going to talk about cotton. When they make thread, they take all those little squiggly cotton fibers and comb them into two rows. You have two rows of these little squiggly fibers, and they twist one way, called an "s" twist, and they twist the other way,

which is called a "z" twist. Then they cross them over one another, and they twist them again, so only through properties of torque and tension—again, back to physics—is that thread held together. So if you've ever tried to sew a button or hem a pair of pants and that thread knots, it's only because of excess torque and tension.

So when I first started hand sewing, I realized this is a real problem when your thread knots all the time. I started doing this thing called "loving your thread." It's not something I invented—I think it's more something like a memory that I had—but it's my story now anyway, and people call this my "Oprah moment." So I'm going to share with you my Oprah moment.

When you're getting to start one of our garments—some of the garments can take one woman three, six, eight weeks to make—you take that thread, you thread your needle, you hold the thread in your fingers, and you run your fingers along the thread, and you say, "This thread is going to sew the most beautiful garment that's ever been made. The person who wears it, it will bring them joy or peace or love or warmth or happiness or healing or any of the wonderful things that you might want to wish for a person." You tie your knot off, and you start to sew and your thread will never knot again, right?

It's a property of physics. All you've really done is released that excess torque of tension. But it's also a way of embracing the thread and preparing the thread to make the most beautiful garment that's ever been made.

This is really at the core of what we do. We make one-of-a-kind garments, but we make them in limited editions; no two garments are ever alike. You may have seen some of the labels in the pictures. Each piece is numbered. It's initialed by the artisan who's sewn it. It's this personal connection. I am the representative of those artisans. I mean, I've written a book about sewing, but I don't really sew that much anymore. I'd love to say that I sit on my bed every night and sew, but I worry every night about cash flow and dye lots, things like that these days. But this personal connection has been an amazing, fantastic, and an incredible journey. This little thing like a quilting stitch drove me to my home, a very personal journey back to where I grew up, and my family. It's about this personal connection between me and my artisans. It's about their connection to farmers who grow our cotton. It's about the connection of the artisans signing their name, their initials in

"This thread is going to sew the most beautiful garment that's ever been made. The person who wears it, it will bring them joy or peace or love or warmth or happiness or healing or any of the wonderful things that you might want to wish for a person."

that garment, and then that garment going out in the world.

Now our pieces are extremely expensive. As any of you who are craftsmen know, you know what it takes to make something that will last a lifetime. On some of the little threads you'll see that we leave a long thread tail, which is kind of unusual, because as you wash and wear a garment, the thread will get shorter and shorter. So we like to leave these long thread tails so that the knot will not come untied, because we like to say that we're sewing for this generation, for the next, for the next, and the next. I imagine this room is filled with people who want to make beautiful things that last through the generations.

So not only is it a personal connection between a woman who lives in rural Red Bay, Alabama, to a garment that's selling at a store

in Paris and the person buying that, wearing it on the streets of Paris; it's also, hopefully, the connection between our artisan and the woman-walking-the-streets-of-Paris's daughter and, hopefully, *her* daughter. In all the stories, and in all the ways that we've built our market, there's always this thought of the connection to what it is that we do, to the quality.

I'll tell you just a little bit about our business model. When you talk about marketplace and a personal connection, this is something I'm really proud of. I think it's something that all of us can do.

We make couture garments. This has to do a little bit with sustainability as well. But I also think it has to do with craftsmanship, because, as we heard today, craftsmanship has... You know, I never thought that

This page:
Alabama Chanin in Paris.

I'd use my design skills and my craftsmanship to solve labor law. All of our women work in their own homes. We work in the cottage-industry style. It's not really favored by the IRS or the Department of Labor. There are all kinds of ways to craft a business, and I would say my business is equally or more carefully crafted than the beautiful dress that you saw in the windows at Barneys.

I'm just going to tell you a little about that, and the slides will run out after that.

We work with a fiber that's grown in Texas by farmers who I consider equal artisans to our sewers. The fiber is spun in Ten-

wrote a book about how we sew, teaching people to use the methods. I mean, I hear all the time, "It is so wonderful that you are able to invent reverse appliqué." I have to tell them I think the Aztecs were doing it. I'd love to take credit for it, but it wasn't mine. What I hope is that we just use these very ancient techniques in a contemporary way and perhaps bring light to them. Because when you can teach someone young, as you will learn from Faythe [Levine] next, there is a whole generation coming behind us that is hungry and starving for more, for knowledge, for wanting.

"I just kind of followed my heart and the heart of my community, and we're still there and we're still sewing."

nessee, it's knit in South Carolina, and we dye it in North Carolina and Mississippi. We cut, paint, and sew in my office or my studio in Florence, Alabama. Then the garments are sewn in Alabama, Tennessee, and Mississippi, and from there, come back to us and are shipped all over the world.

Now the process of making a garment is extremely wasteful. There's a lot of fabric left over, so we use those fabric scraps for a home-furnishings line. What's not used for the home-furnishings line, we up-cycle into pieces of up-cycled furniture, so we find farm chairs and incorporate fabric with farm chairs. Then what's left over we've started baling just like with a straw baler. And then we either sell these bales or we use them to build with, like we have a couch in our office. Some are being used for architectural installations and things like that.

The only complaint I've ever had about the work that we do is that it's very expensive and not affordable for a lot of people. So I

So while the complaint about our clothes is that they are very expensive, I said, "You know what, I'll give you our two best-selling patterns. Here are all the instructions and you can make it yourself." In the process, many people in my industry, in my market-place, told me that I was crazy. Once again, I've been called crazy a lot in my life.

What I found was that a whole new part of our business opened up. We sell books now. I'm paid as a writer. We have a whole crafting community, a DIY community—there's been a lot of talk about that today. We sell our materials directly. It's been very difficult for people to find organic materials—cotton and fabrics. So we just decided, we'll give you the pattern, you can buy the same thread that we use, and we can sell you the scissors that we use. Everything we use to create our garments we now sell from our online store so that anybody who wants to make that dress right there has the opportunity to do it.

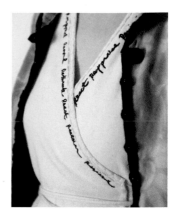

Everybody said, "People will stop buying the clothes." Well, you know what happened? People found out that it's really hard to make our clothes. And it takes really a long time and a lot of patience. Actually, I lost nothing; I only gained. Unfortunately, I'm not going to be able to be here tomorrow, but you'll hear something about the Long Tail [theory], which was really a strong influence in crafting my business model.

So we sell our fabrics now. We have a crafting business. I've been collecting oral histories from textile workers because when I came home I saw sort of the end of NAFTA in my community. My community was a vertical community. They grew cotton, they did everything. We cut it, we sewed it. So, about the time that I came home, about 5,000 people in a community of 40,000 had lost their jobs, and that doesn't include the service industries built around that industry. I realized pretty quickly that my three-year-old daughter is not really going to know about that because a lot of the people who worked in this industry are older and will have passed away by the time she's my age. So I think it's really important to document that craft.

I want you to know that while many of us don't go to high school or college and think, "I want to work in a factory," the people in my community and the people that I work with were very proud of the work that they did. There's a woman that you saw a picture of earlier—her name is Faye Davis—she worked for 35 years in the textile industry. That's all she knew, and she's a very proud woman and very proud of the work she does. And to be honest with you, she sees herself as a craftsman. And if you saw her and she talked to you today, you would also see her as a craftsman.

So if I can do anything with my voice, I hope that I can break down the borders between the marketplace and the craftsperson,

and, hopefully, I can help children and adults—all of us—to realize that there is a very fine line. There is craft in everything that we do. We really have to preserve these cultural traditions because they're such a part of our lives and, if ever we were to lose them, we would be missing a great hole in our society. ✚

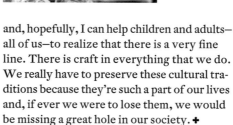

Top, left to right:
Nude corset and tiered
skirt, from the spring
2010 collection.

Abbie's flower appliqué
coat, from the spring
2010 collection.

Revolution words
wrap top.

Bottom:
White all-over spiral
coat, from the spring
2010 collection.

A Handmade Nation
/ Faythe Levine

I have a lot to say about a lot of different things, and this is such a varied group of people. So for those of you who are familiar with a lot of these things, I apologize if I am reiterating things that you know or people that you are familiar with. And for those of you who are not, hopefully, you will get excited about some of the people I'm going to be talking about.

I just actually, about an hour ago, added this quote to the front page of my talk. This is a quote from a punk band from the early '90s called Huggy Bear [referring to quote on the screen, "This is happening without your permission/The arrival of a new renegade"]. They were a riot-grrrl band, which was a movement of women who played music and were kind of taking back music for themselves. I grew up in Seattle in the early '90s, and punk music and DIY for me was about music and about the underground music community that I was exposed to there, and that was sort of my gateway to DIY.

Like a lot of the people I've interviewed in my work, I've always made things. I work in a variety of mediums and music. The creative community that surrounds the DIY music scene that I grew up in opened up and was a permission-giver to me as far as doing DIY and doing things for myself.

Zines, hand-published magazines, were a life-changing point for me when I was 14. I was at a show watching bands at an all-ages venue, which was a really amazing resource for me as a teenager, and I came across these little photocopied magazines. You could do a zine about anything. There were no rules. And that was what was appealing to me about DIY.

Skip ten years ahead: I was still making things. I came across online other people who were my age who had a similar aesthetic also doing things, and through that online community, I became exposed to the work that I have continued to document and explore.

This is the "craftifesto" Ⓐ, which was written by two women in Chicago who do a show called the DIY Trunk Show. They have this on their website for their craft fair that they do in Chicago. They are indie. For those of you who aren't familiar with the word "indie," it's independent. Indie is the word that we throw around. You've probably heard it a lot this weekend.

They had this "craftifesto" on their website, and when I started working on my book, I really wanted to adapt it for the book because I feel like it really sums up the DIY movement. Something that I kind of want to put out there before I go into all of the people

Top to bottom:
Handmade Nation logo, designed by Faythe Levine.

Craftifesto, written by Cinnamon Cooper and Amy Carlton and illustrated by Kate Bingaman-Burt.

Ⓐ

that I am about to show you and talk to you about is that DIY is this huge, huge term, and it kind of encompasses and blankets a lot of different types of people. So, as I realize that opening quote was a little aggressive, I sort of feel like I'm slightly defensive when I hear certain people talking down on DIY because I feel like it would be like saying, "I don't like dogs" when there might be the sweetest little dog. There's just so many things that fall under this one term, so many different types of work, so many different quality levels of work. I know quality is a big topic of discussion here this weekend, and so I just want to remind everyone that just because someone might identify with the DIY movement, it doesn't mean that their work is of a lesser quality. And even if it is, it doesn't mean that it's not important and valid, because those people are making things and it empowers them. I think that's what's really exciting about what's going on right now. [Applause] Thanks.

I had a company that I started of things that I made. I became familiar with the online community I participated in through a craft fair in Chicago called Renegade Craft Fair. It's one of the largest indie shows that goes on. It started in 2003. Renegade is now all

be willing to travel around the country with me and shoot what was going on, so that's what we did.

I funded the film myself, and I had the support of a lot of community members. I did a lot of fund-raising. I'm still paying for it. We started shooting in 2006 and spent a year and a half shooting. Over the course of that time, I started a blog. (This is all relevant to the people I'm going to be speaking about.) I started a blog at the very beginning of the production because I felt like I was documenting a community. It's a very online community. It's a very tech-savvy community. I wanted people

"One of the things that will come up as I continue to talk about people involved in the community is the collaborative aspect of the DIY community and how it's such a big part of who we are and how we support one another."

over the country. They have shows in a lot of larger urban areas. I had such a fantastic experience at Renegade Craft Fair that I wanted to have a show like that in my hometown where I live in Milwaukee, Wisconsin. And so I started a show in Milwaukee called Art vs. Craft, and we're now in our fifth year of that show, and it's going really well.

I also felt like Milwaukee lacked a space where you could find all this work online through all these websites, and you could go to these craft fairs in your local city if you were lucky enough to have a show that people produced there. I felt like Milwaukee needed a space where you could come and physically handle the work. So I opened up a brick-and-mortar space called Paper Boat Boutique & Gallery with my friend Kim Kisiolek. We recently closed in May due to the economy and the fact that I'm never home, so it was kind of hard.

All these things were happening, and I was traveling to all these shows as a designer, and I was producing my show and curating shows in my gallery and doing freelance curatorial work. I was just meeting… I mean, I already knew amazing makers and artists and musicians and performers, and it was just going on and on. I mean, the Internet was basically blowing my mind. I felt like it really needed to be captured and documented. So in June of 2006, I started working on *Handmade Nation*, the documentary. My best friend, Micaela O'Herlihy, is a very amazing artist and filmmaker, and I asked her if she would

to know where I was going, and so people started following the blog and following my progression around the country. What I ended up doing, without really realizing it, was building an audience for my film as I was going through pre-production. This is not the normal way people go about making a film. I now do lectures to directors who are trying to think outside the box, which I was doing without really knowing it, because it angers some people that I've had such success with my first film without having any film background.

I was making a film, a DIY film, about a DIY community. It was a one-camera production. I had a local editor who is also a friend of mine who edited on her single laptop in her studio. And what I'm about to show you is the trailer that a lot of you may have seen circulated on YouTube. It's gotten something like 100,000 hits. It's a little outdated at this point because the film is out. However, I felt like it—just in case people hadn't seen it—puts everything into context and gives a lot of the makers a voice. Because I am just one person talking about such a large community, oftentimes people direct very specific things at me because I represent a lot of the people that I talk about.

I'll go ahead and play it. And then as a side note, the trailer that you're about to watch was also the reason I got my book deal through Princeton Architectural Press. Someone from the publisher saw the trailer on YouTube, and they approached me about doing a book based on the research I had done for the documentary. We'll go ahead and watch that, and then I'll continue on.

[Trailer plays.]

I haven't watched that in like a year. It's almost painful for me. I'll come back to that film a little bit later.

Out of that trailer I was approached, as I said, by Princeton Architectural Press, which put out the book *Handmade Nation*, which features 24 of the people that I interviewed for the film. Not everyone who's in the book is in the film, and vice versa. I did a lot of different interviews with a lot of different people, so it was a nice opportunity to have some of the people who didn't make the cut in the film get represented in the book.

Another nice thing about the book is that I had the opportunity to work with Kate Bingaman-Burt, who is an artist that I had worked with at my gallery. Kate did all the typography for each of the individual featured makers as well as illustrating the timeline that's at the beginning. One of the things that will come up as I continue to talk about people involved in the community is the collaborative aspect of the DIY community and how it's such a big part of who we are and how we support one another.

I pulled some stills of some of the screenings that I've done so far. The film came out in February, and I've been touring since February around the world but mostly within the United States, and it's been really interesting for me.

I do all my own programming, so people contact me and bring me to events, and it's anything from a college bringing me in to lecture and doing a screening that's also open to the public. We had the premier at the Independent Theater, in Milwaukee, and I had 800 people come out to see my film. It was really exciting. It was a very local production, and it was supported very well locally, which was very flattering for me because there aren't really 800 people in Milwaukee who consider themselves DIY hardcore makers.

I got to go to this really great performance space in Germany, in Hamburg. I recently visited the Renwick Gallery, and I was also out at the American Craft Council Show, in San Francisco, recently, and it has been a really amazing opportunity for me to see how wide and international my audience is for this film, which has become a lot more of an educational tool than I was originally expecting.

Along the lines of talking about collaboration, I wanted to discuss a little bit about the ways that the DIY community taps into one

another's abilities and skills. The next few slides are posters for indie craft fairs that happen around the country. Art vs. Craft is my show. This is the postcard for an upcoming event in November . I work with the design team called the Little Friends of Printmaking, and they're featured in the film and in the book.

Something that I think that the DIY community is very good about is design. People respond to design, and it's something that we were talking about within our marketing convenings group yesterday. I feel that the importance of design and getting your message across to the general public is so important, and it's interesting to see the different shows that happen in the different cities and who they work with and how they tap into the design pool that we have at our fingertips.

Feltclub is an event that happens in Los Angeles put on by Jenny Ryan, who just opened up a space called Home Ec., in Silver Lake, that is sort of a DIY lounge where she is offering all types of classes. I don't think she's doing it this year because she just opened her store. Jordan Crane is an illustrator/comic book artist who did their posters in the past.

Craftland is in Providence, Rhode Island. Craftland just opened up as a year-round gallery and brick-and-mortar. They were a monthlong craft show. It was an interesting concept: They would work with the city of Providence, which would give them an office space downtown; they would work with the mayor. Providence has an incredible arts community. They would open up and have this store for three weeks to a month. They would work with Jen Corace, who is an illustrator and artist who also does craft fairs as well.

And then the Renegade Craft Fair. This is a poster for their last show in Chicago. Mat Daly is a poster artist who does a lot of posters for bands and works with the Renegade Craft Fair ladies.

I'm going to move into events and people that I have worked with in the community

Top and right:
International Fiber
Collaborative, World
Reclamation Art Project
(W.R.A.P.), otherwise
known as the Gas Station
Project, Dewitt, NY, 2008.

and blaze through a bunch of stuff here. This is a show that I curated at the University of Wisconsin, Green Bay. "Craftivism" is a word that has sort of popped up over the last five years or so. Betsy Greer is a writer and a theorist who has a website called Craftivism.com. I'm pretty sure she coined the term. That might be debatable. I don't know if it's really important. I don't think she cares. Betsy Greer is a fantastic resource for those of you who might be interested in reading more about craftivism. She just wrote a book called *Knitting for Good*. It's on Shambhala Press. [The "Craftivism" exhibition] featured a bunch of

people that I work with on and off.

One of the artists that I featured in the "Craftivism" show is Jennifer Marsh. I really like sharing this work. This has been published pretty widely, so some of you may be really familiar with it. This is her gas station project ○ [in which a collective of artists created fiber panels to cover the exterior of an abandoned gas station]. Besides the visual appeal to me of this project, which I think has a lot of impact, apparently a lot of people hated this locally in this town. They thought it was just the biggest eyesore. They'd much rather look at an abandoned gas station than the awesome gas station covered with all the panels, which I don't understand at all.

Jennifer works with a really wide range of people. She works with schools, and basically she has these projects, and this was, I think, her first one. She did an open call for people to make a panel to be a part of this giant cover for this gas station. I really like it because it involves all different levels of skill, all different types of people. It was an outreach project. It was raising awareness about our dependency on oil and consumption. It has the whole awareness angle as well. And it was cool when in the "Craftivism" show we had these prints hung up, and then we also had panels that were rather moldy because they had been out in the weather for quite some time. But it was a really interesting way to show a lot of the students in Green Bay just how you could do these outreach projects and really work with the different types of communities.

These are some photos of an artist in San Francisco. She actually lives in Oakland, excuse me, Monica Canilao. And Monica's quite young. I think she is under 25. This is a studio visit I did with her. Monica does a lot of different work, and she had just started doing these headdresses recently for a show. She works with a lot of craft-based materials. She also works with a lot of salvaged materials. This is an installation that she did at my gallery in Milwaukee as well. The quilt piece was a piece of quilt that her grandmother had made and had been passed down to her. Her work is incredible. If you're attracted to this, I highly recommend looking her up and looking at her extensive body of work. It's absolutely amazing.

[Shows postcard image for "Devotion to Thread" exhibition.] This is a show that I curated in Milwaukee at a book center that has a really fantastic gallery, Woodland Pattern. They've been around, I think, for 25 years. This piece was for the show and is by the artist Orly Cogan , an embroidery artist—another amazing woman who does amazing things. I don't know if you can tell, but it's these ladies snorting lines of cocaine and shoving cupcakes in their mouths. It's called *Sweet Obsessions*. This piece is rather large. This is four feet by five feet. Her work is very large scale. Most of it's amazing. I had a chance to do a studio visit with her, and it was pretty incredible.

The "Devotion to Thread" show, I think there were 12 people that I got to work with for it. I really have a bad habit of cramming a lot into a small space, so it was kind of a tight squeeze for all the people that I worked with. It was a great opportunity, though, to bring a lot of work to Milwaukee that people hadn't had exposure to before in person. I also got to bring Garth Johnson of Extreme Craft to do his amazing Extreme Craft lecture, which—if you ever get an opportunity to hear him, do—is fantastic. I also decided to handmake 300 show catalogs by myself. It was a terrible idea.

But I think, also, this is going to lead into the theme of makers having that obsessive "I'm going to do all these little details down to

every last stitch, and hand bind this thing, and then wrap it with this hand printed…" Just this really intense, detail-oriented sort of mindset that I think is a common kind of thread through a lot of the people that I have worked with. I wanted to have these little spools that would represent the show. They were in these sewing baskets, so everyone who came to the show got to take a little spool of thread away with them.

And along the lines of obsessiveness, I'm going to go back to talking about Kate [Bingaman-Burt], who did the typography for *Handmade Nation*, and she also did the packaging design for the movie DVD that's coming out next month. If you're not familiar with Kate's work, it's fantastic. I'm a huge advocate. She's here today as well, so if you get a chance to meet her, she's great. She's a design professor at Portland State University.

Kate's work surrounds consumption, documenting her consumption, and making things. She works with a variety of mediums, and it's really amazing what she does with her work. She does daily drawings that are cataloged into monthly zines that you can subscribe to . She also works with textiles and embroidery.

The dresses [shown on the slide show] were hand-sewn by her and then embroidered with her credit-card APR rates. She also draws her credit-card statements. On her website, you can find all of her stuff cataloged on Flickr.com. But if you search "obsessive consumption," you'll find Kate's work. She also has a book coming out from Princeton Architectural Press of her daily drawings, so keep an eye out for that next year.

Steve MacDonald is an artist who does machine embroidery. I've had the opportunity to work with him in a few shows. He's great. Again, I have so many people that I like and who fall under the work that I talk about that

Top to bottom:
Orly Cogan, *Sweet Obsessions*, 2007, hand-stitched embroidery and paint on stretched cotton.

Daily drawings from Kate Bingaman-Burt's Obsessive Consumption blog.

Right:
Xander Marro,
Bed of Knives, 2008.

Bottom:
Stephanie Syjuko,
The Counterfeit Crochet
Project, 2006.

I figured I would throw a lot of these things in here.

I've never met this guy, Cory Thompson, before with these photos of these dolls. They are these plush little sculptures of if someone fell backward and smashed their head on cement. They lay flat, and I found these at Craftland the last time I was in Providence, and I was really excited about them. They are really beautifully made. The faces are all hand embroidered. Each of them is one of a kind.

I'm also a huge fan of Ashley Brown's work. She goes under the company name Fern, and she makes these little hand-sewn animals. They are very tiny, three inches big, and hand-sewn, and she embroiders all their faces. They're really beautiful.

This is a company called Something's Hiding in Here, and it's a husband-and-wife design team. They produce all their work together. I just pulled these off of Flickr yesterday, and this is their booth from Crafty Bastards, which is a craft fair in Washington, D.C. But they do a really amazing job of executing design with their displays and also with their product design, and so I like to share their work.

Xander Marro is a printmaker who also

quick clip in the trailer. Xander mostly works on paper, but then every time she does a print on paper, she also does it on fabric, and then she does these incredibly crazy quilts Ⓕ. Her mom is a master quilter, and she learned her quilting skills from her mother. These quilts are used in their house. When she shows them, they are on loan from their household, so they are not art pieces. They are exceptionally well made and so beautiful in person. This is just a small detail shot of a larger blanket.

Stephanie Syjuko is an artist, a conceptual artist, and a crafter. She's based out of San Francisco. She does a number of things.

'I believe that the simple act of making something, anything, with your hands is a quiet, political ripple in a world dominated by mass production, and people choosing to make something themselves will turn those small ripples into giant waves.'

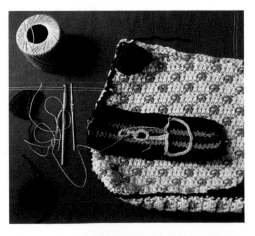

works with fabric and textiles. She's a poster artist and she's a part of the feminist art collective called the Dirt Palace, of which there's a

One of them is a company called Anti-Factory, which has the tagline "Because sweatshops suck." She works with all-recycled materials and reworks them into one-of-a-kind wearable items. Stephanie also has a project called the Counterfeit Crochet Project Ⓖ, which is super awesome. She works with home-based crocheters and asks them to reproduce their favorite designer handbag with crochet or knitting. Then the bags are put into a larger show and put on display. It has traveled around the world. I was lucky enough to get about five of the bags for the show in Green Bay. It was really exciting to see people there react. People really react to the designer labels with knit and crochet represented that way. She also has a downloadable PDF of the Chanel bag if you're interested in making your own. You can follow her pattern.

Left:
Lisa Congdon installation
at Paper Boat Gallery, 2008.

Bottom:
Michelle Ott's Postcard
Machine at the 2007
Renegade Craft Fair
in Chicago.

This is Jamie Vasta. I've never worked with her. She's actually studio mates with the next artist I'm going to talk about, but I'm a huge fan of her work. She's a painter, she's a glitter painter. She works exclusively with glitter, and she does photo realistic paintings with glitter, and you can see in the background, at the top, that's glitter. And here's a little more of a detail shot. She masks out certain areas and has her favorite brands of glitter and whatnot that she uses.

Her work is absolutely stunning in person and, as those of you who work with shiny materials know, it's very difficult to photograph because it's reflective. If this interests you at all, I suggest looking at her website because her work is absolutely stunning. Her subject matter is very strange. She does a lot of teenage-girl-hunter images, which is pretty interesting.

Jamie is studio mates with Lisa Congdon. Lisa was here yesterday, but she had to go back because she lives in San Francisco. She owns a really fantastic store called Rare Device. Lisa is a really good example of a working artist who does lots of different types of things. She's the shop owner, so she works with a lot of independent artists through Rare Device, which also has a gallery space.

She also has a very successful illustration and fine-art career. Lisa is a self-taught artist. She started painting in her thirties and is very widely known. She has a line of products through Chronicle Books, and she does a lot of different things. She's a friend, and I'm a huge fan of her work. This is part of an installation that she did at my gallery .

This is the Postcard Machine , and I wish I had a video clip of this because it's really funny if you can actually hear the woman, Michelle, who's inside. Michelle has a really interesting story. She's a performance artist who also made things by hand, and she wanted to figure out a way to mesh her performance art with her craft. What she came up with was the Postcard Machine. What she does is she sits inside, and she has a little megaphone, and she talks in a robot voice, and she can see through that little middle window. She sits in there all day at craft shows. It's pretty intense, and it's really hot out. She talks at people as they go by and interacts with them, and she's really good at it, and it's really funny. People gather around, and it's very engaging. You can put your money into the slot, and you turn this dial (which you can kind of see on the right-hand side on the right photo up there). Her whole booth is handmade, and it has all of these different options. This was in Chicago, and I think there was a "Chicago option" or "pick your favorite color." You spin it and then pick your subject, and then out of one of the slots comes this handmade postcard that she's made. It's really awesome and really amazing the way that she's been able to incorporate her two passions of creating and performing. There are clips on YouTube of this as well if you're interested in seeing it in action.

Because of *Handmade Nation*, like I said, I've had a lot of opportunities to travel. I got to go to Australia this year, and I did some programming with Craft Victoria. They are a fantastic organization and resource. The show that was going on there was this group Chicks on Speed, who are a band and performance-artist group of women. There are four of them, and they are international from all over the place. They had this installation here called *Viva la Craft*. I was doing some programming with Chicks on Speed through Craft Victoria because I just happened to be in Melbourne at the time doing some other work with *Handmade Nation*.

[Refers to photo on screen of Craft Victoria workshop.] What I like about this

Right:
Knitta "tag" on a statue near the Eiffel Tower in Paris.

Far right:
Lacey Jane Roberts, *We couldn't get in. We couldn't get out.*, 2006–07. Hand-woven wire, crank-knit yarn, steel poles, assorted hardware.

Bottom:
Mallory, a.k.a. Miss Malaprop, recycled FEMA blue tarp bustier and skirt with flower choker, 2007.

92/93

specific photo is that I feel that it really encompasses, again, the idea of collaboration. I'm doing an embroidery workshop with embroidery patterns that Jenny Hart of Sublime Stitching put out—a limited-edition embroidery pattern of *Handmade Nation* designs that Kate drew. And I'm in Australia with these designs and with my "Craftivism" catalog from Green Bay and in the gallery showing Chicks on Speed, which is a collaborative performance-craft group, and on the wall is this fabric that was printed for them through this amazing company called Third Drawer Down, which is an Australian company that puts out limited-edition artist textiles. You can see it's a knit pattern. That's the pattern on the fabric that's draped in the background. On the monitor I was showing a film by Sabrina Gschwandtner, who does *KnitKnit* magazine. It's just amazing—all these overlapping people and ways to share all of this information that I feel is all very relevant and is very exciting to me. I feel like this photo embodies a lot of the community.

I was invited to the Kohler Art Center, which is in Sheboygan, Wisconsin, to do a weeklong residency there. I got to do some embroidery classes with kids and community people who came in for programming. I did a screening of a short clip of my film (it wasn't complete yet) with people who came in one night. I got to hang out there for a while, and it was really cool.

This is Knitta, which you saw in the clip. They do the knitted graffiti. There are a number of people who do work similar to Knitta; they are just one of many groups.

There's actually a book that just came out called *Yarn Bombing*, so if you're interested in that phenomenon or anything surrounding that, I suggest picking it up. I think it just came out last month.

These are some of the images I pulled off of Knitta's website. They've had a lot of success within the last few years within the gallery world, and they get to travel and do site-specific installations in different countries. They bring their work with them on the streets when they do that.

This is work by Lacey Jane Roberts, who is actually here as well. I had never met her before, so this was an exciting weekend for me. I use her work in my presentations all the time. I usually use her work in my "Craftivism" talks that I give, and I feel like these pieces sort of speak for themselves. This is a knitted, hand-woven fence installed in an alley in San Francisco. I just love this piece in general. Another piece I pulled from Lacey Jane's site.

This is a woman named Mallory, who lives in New Orleans. Etsy had an up-cycling fashion contest, and she entered. She has lived in New Orleans, and she's based there and was there for Katrina. She decided to work with what was around her at the time, which happened to be these FEMA tarps that were everywhere, and she created this incredible bustier and skirt from the FEMA tarps. Again, I feel like it speaks for itself, but it's just kind of an amazing presentation of working with what you have around you.

This is a website called Cast Off. I like to use this slide because, again, it goes back to the whole community idea. Weddings are this very personal thing that people have that are very family-oriented. You invite your best friends, you keep the list small, it's expensive. One of the women from Cast Off was getting married, from my understanding, and she basically made her wedding open to the public. She wanted to have a knit wedding entirely. Everything in her wedding she wanted to be knit. It was an open call to the public; if you submitted something to her wedding, then you were also invited to her wedding. They encouraged everyone to knit during the wedding. [Refers to photos from the wedding.] These are all online, and I just pulled them off. I don't know these people, but I talk about them all the time. Her bouquet, her dress, as you can see, the camera, disco ball, there's a lot of photos. And I also just put this one in here. You can see the [knitted] champagne [bottle] at the bottom of the photo. This woman is one of the ladies in this group called the Shellac Sisters. This doesn't really have anything to do with craft, but I feel like, again, it crosses over within these fringe communities. The Shellac Sisters are a group of women in the U.K. who deejay from 78 records, so they use windup gramophones. They do all sorts of events, and they were the deejays at this wedding, which I thought was really awesome.

Going back to Whitney Lee 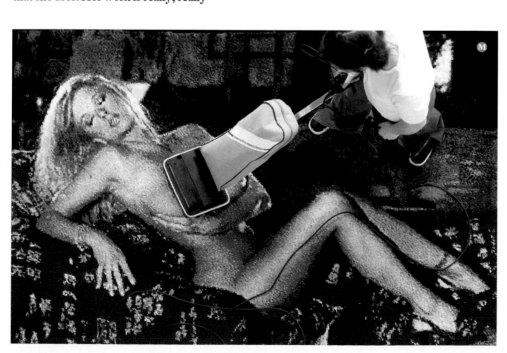, whom you saw in the trailer. Whitney does a number of things. Latch hook is one of the mediums that she uses. Her work is really, really impressive. Her philosophy behind what she's doing and why she's doing it is also very interesting. I could explain to you a little bit more about her work, but I feel it would be better for you to just read it on her website. She takes most of her images from pornographic sites, old and new. You can also buy her latch-hook kits. She makes large-scale, huge pieces. She has gallery representation, but then she also has these kits that you can purchase if you want to buy one and do it yourself. Again, the idea of making work available on different levels—expensive gallery work and then more affordable ways to bring it into your home and do it yourself.

I guess I'm coming near the end. This is just a quote that was in *American Craft* magazine [September 2008], and it kind of sums up my motivation for what I'm doing and why I'm documenting the people that I'm documenting and the importance I feel of what's going on and the future of what's happening and how we're reshaping what's to come. I'll just read my own quote:

"I believe that the simple act of making something, anything, with your hands is a quiet, political ripple in a world dominated by mass production, and people choosing to make something themselves will turn those small ripples into giant waves."

I'm just going to leave this up during the Q&A because I love it and I think everyone should read it.

Thanks. ✦

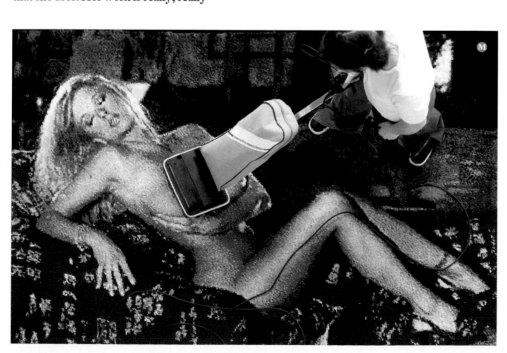

"The whole broad idea of craft seems to be sort of up for grabs in a way that might not have been the case four or five years ago. And it seems to me this is not such a bad thing." / Rob Walker

Day 2
Saturday, October 17, 2009
9:45—10:45 am
Marketing Craft on the Internet

See page 110

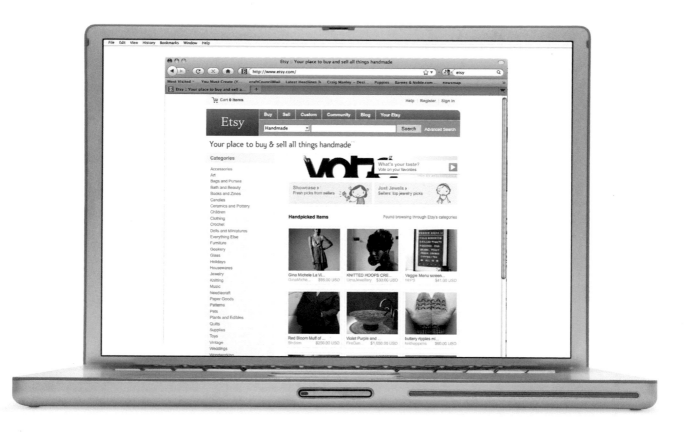

A screenshot from the
online store Etsy.

Day 2
Saturday, October 17, 2009
11 am—12 pm
Men in White
See page 120

The design team at
Unimark Milan, ca. 1965.

Day 2
Saturday, October 17, 2009
12—12:30 pm
Good Craft + Good Design = Good Sense
See page 130

Vintage Heath Ceramics
casseroles from the 1950s.

Radical Jewelry Makeover
creation by Melisande
Inness-Brown.

Day 2
Saturday, October 17, 2009
2—3 pm
New Models of Marketplace
See page 140

The Pioneers of
Change "LAND!" sign
on Governors Island.

"I believe in a Craft Nation, something vast, unquestionably real and yet deeply mystical… some of it professional, some of it hobbyist, some of it pure catharsis."

/ Garth Clark

"Question: Should craft become the example of critical making, parallel to critical thinking, in our culture? The majority of you answered yes to that, at 84 percent." / Sonya Clark

Handmade 2.0
/ Rob Walker

So our theme is "creating a new craft culture." I suppose I should start by saying that my focus, as a journalist, is not craft. My focus is on consumer behavior and, more broadly, consumer culture. And I guess that with that in mind, my perspective is that there is no "craft culture."

Craft *cultures*, maybe so.

In the 21st century, "craft" means many things to many people. Different definitions are being affected by generational approaches, by varied motivations, by technology, and, of course, by the marketplace. Traditional craft, or fine craft, has a long and well-documented history. Then there's a modern iteration that's associated with mainstream hobbyists–stores like Michaels, practices like the huge contemporary scrapbook scene. Then you throw in a phrase like "do it yourself," and maybe you're talking about Martha Stewart or how-to-ish TV shows, and so on, oriented toward decorative projects.

Finally, there's the so-called new wave of craft, which I'll get to but which itself encompasses a pretty wide range of ideas about craft.

To top it off, it seems to me that each of these craft cultures is in flux right now. The upshot is that the whole broad idea of craft seems to be sort of up for grabs in a way that might not have been the case four or five years ago. And it seems to me this is not such a bad thing.

Given that my subjects are consumer culture and consumer behavior, I'm very much an outsider, but maybe that's a useful perspective for you to hear. I certainly hope so, because I'm not really going to talk much about, say, specific examples of craft creators that I've written about or whose work I like or find interesting. Instead, much of what I'm going to do is explain my interest in craft cultures as they relate to that bigger picture, because, as you know, consumer culture and consumer behavior *in general* are quite in flux right now. So it's an interesting time–a good time–to consider what these versions of craft mean to the consumer market, and vice versa.

So let me set this up a little bit. One of my recurring themes as a writer is that what I'm interested in is contradictions–or tensions, as I prefer to think of them. Consumer culture, consumer behavior, the marketplace, the world of commerce–these are full of tensions. So, for example, consumers tend to be attracted to novelty *except* on those occasions when what they really want is the very familiar. Or consumers really want to feel unique and express their individuality *except* when they want to connect with the like-minded and feel like part of something bigger than themselves. They demand the best *except* when they demand the cheapest or the most convenient.

It sounds like I'm suggesting consumers are crazy or a bunch of hypocrites. But I prefer to frame it as a matter of resolving tensions between hardwired but contradictory impulses that exist in all of us. There are, for instance, evolutionary reasons for being attracted to novelty and to the familiar.

So let's get to craft. I became very interested in the new wave of craft, or indie craft, alternative craft, the DIY scene, whatever you want to call it, a few years ago. I wrote an article that more or less used Etsy.com as a kind of organizing device for talking about the stuff I was interested in. And later, I explored those themes in a different way in one chapter of my book *Buying In*, trying to put what I was seeing into the broader context of consumer culture in the 21st century.

Along the way, I've become familiar with the fact that there are *other* kinds of tension hovering around the idea of "craft culture" in the last few years. Some people told me Etsy was a catastrophe for the idea of craft. Among other things, they said, it pitted spare-time, hobbyist crafters who didn't need the money against pros who did, and in the process, privileged low price over high quality, which drove down prices and drove down quality. I also know that a lot of alternative, or indie, crafters have complained of feeling marginalized or dismissed by traditional crafters and by the mainstream craft industry as well. I'm aware of all that—but I have nothing in particular to say about it. This is where being an outside observer just really gives me a different perspective. I understand why the various parties involved feel the way they do, but I don't really have a horse in that race. All along, I was interested in what the audience for this stuff—the consumers,

"The whole broad idea of craft seems to be sort of up for grabs in a way that might not have been the case four or five years ago. And it seems to me this is not such a bad thing."

basically—were responding to.

I'll tell you why. My interest in tensions puts me very much at odds with what I'll call the "trend industry," which is all about sweeping pronouncements. They're constantly framing things around a "new consumer," who has always just arrived on the scene and marks a radical break from all prior iterations of material culture. And the analysis is always flattering to the now, in a way that insults consumers of the past.

The trend industry, for reasons that mystify, is often the dominant voice on what is supposedly going on in consumer culture. I'm a very small voice trying to point out that consumer culture is too important to treat in broad, simple strokes. In this case, I think the trend industry had three related pronouncements, each of which I think is approximately half true.

The big one is: The new consumer *craves authenticity*! And that's what this trend is about (they said). People reconnecting with lost hand skills! They want the quality of crafted goods, not cheap, throwaway crap! It's a backlash against a century of industrial production! Handmade is in and mass made is out! Wal-Mart is toast! This was sort of the level of analysis just a few years ago.

Needless to say, craft skills never *actually* disappeared. And craft as a superior response to mass production—craft as the exercise of self-expressive skill—that idea wasn't invented by the new-wave crafters either. The Arts and Crafts movement, John Ruskin's writing on the idea of the individual craftsperson—these responded to the second big wave of the industrial revolution, not a hundred years after the fact but pretty much in real time, before the turn of the 20th century.

Now I do think it's true that many consumers are kind of anxious about how things are made and that in the mass marketplace it remains maddeningly difficult to figure out the full backstory of a box of dog treats, or a sneaker, or a T-shirt, or a bookshelf bought at some big-box store for an unbelievably low price. I also think it's true that many people are on some level anxious about feeling "de-skilled." Many people have the sense that they just don't know how to do anything anymore. We depend on these big, abstract conglomerates for our food, our clothes, our soap, for everything. All we know how to do is shop.

But I think it's important to be honest about how we got to that point. It seems counterintuitive to say that mass production has anything to do with novelty, but it actually allowed access to maybe the most attractive form of novelty—progress. People *wanted* to be able to make a tasty dinner more quickly, with access to a greater variety of food choices. They *wanted* to be able to buy soap and clothes, instead of having to make things themselves. They *wanted* cars instead of horse-drawn carriages. They *wanted* air conditioning and airplanes. They *wanted* machines to do the laundry with synthetic detergent, instead of washing things by hand. And later, they wanted iPhones.

In every case, for the same reasons, mass production resulted in things that made people more efficient, made previously impossible things possible, made difficult things easier, saved time, made life feel better in some way. Progress.

If there's a rejection of mass production, it's a very, very selective one. So the way that I would think about it is that this new version of craft, of the handmade, that was getting so much attention, it wasn't that it represented a backlash. It was that it represented a way of resolving tension: tension between wanting progress and wanting a connection to some version of the past.

The second trend-industry pronouncement: It's all about new-consumer *ethics*. Again the old consumer was a thick-headed indifferent ingrate, but today's new consumer cares about labor conditions and the environment and so on. And there's all this empowering technology that's creating a consumer revolution. In reality, there have been many consumer revolutions in the past, often with ripple effects that change society in general and the very contours of American life.

The notion of "ethical consumption"—a very trendy phrase today—dates back at least to the turn-of-the-20th-century Progressive era, when reform groups like the National Consumers League sought to leverage collective buying power in order to influence both the quality of products and the conditions under which they were made. Progressive reforms included the Pure Food and Drug Act and the Federal Trade Commission Act. They managed to pull that off without even starting a Facebook group, if you can believe it.

In his book *The Marketplace of Revolution*, the historian T. H. Breen even makes a case that collective consumer action was crucial to nothing less than the founding of the United States itself. "The colonists' shared experience as consumers," he wrote, inspired them to unify in a (grassroots-led) refusal to purchase certain English goods, opting, in what is obviously the most famous example, to fling unfairly taxed tea into Boston Harbor. This consumer unity became a means by which they "made goods speak to power," as Breen put it. Again, just to clarify, this is before Twitter.

I actually think in the great sweep of American history the consumer movement is in pretty sorry shape these days. It's been in decline since the late 1970s at least, since the defeat of the Consumer Protection Agency and the decline in popularity of figures like Ralph Nader. It's not gone, but it's not robust.

In large part, the ethos that replaced it had less to do with changes that benefited society in general and, as the historian Lizabeth Cohen has put it, turns more on individuals in the marketplace demanding to know, Am I getting my money's worth?

Interestingly—and with apologies for possibly inadvertently invoking hippies—the connections between craft and consumer ethics is kind of a 1960s/1970s idea. That said, there's no question that the new iteration of craft culture interested me very specifically because of the almost ideological overtones of some of its participants on the creator side. I was struck in particular by how many people used the word "movement," for example. Some people took it in an overtly political direction, arguing: "In the age of hyper-materialism, Paris Hilton, and thousand-dollar 'It' bags, perhaps making stuff is the ultimate form of rebellion."

Now maybe that's a bit much, especially if you start thinking not just about the people who hand*make* stuff themselves but about people who buy stuff that somebody else handmade. But that sort of "movement" attitude seems to me to offer two possibilities I found a lot more interesting than blogging about lousy cable service or a bum laptop.

First, it offers another way of resolving one of the tensions I mentioned at the top—the tension between wanting to feel like an individual and wanting to be something larger than yourself. An independent crafter who is part of a movement perhaps resolves that tension. For that matter, a shopper supporting a given crafter might be doing the exact same thing.

Second, and more important, it's an attitude that is in effect positioning craft as a way of making goods speak to power in the marketplace itself.

The third trend-industry pronouncement is that the new consumer is all about quality. This is kind of a spin-off of the rejection of mass-industrial products that I've already addressed, but I want very briefly to break off one small piece of this idea here because it brings us into the new tensions of the present.

The idea for the first six or seven years of the 21st century was that the new consumer was willing to spend more for quality and that this was evidence of new savvy and virtue.

Now, of course, that's changed. The trend industry has pivoted and said the new consumer is all about being thrifty and frugal and saving, not spending. And this is evidence of... new savvy and virtue.

This matters to the craft culture idea, or ideas, because a lot of traditional craft has been seen as better quality, yes, but in a way that, for a lot of people, connoted luxury. In being the opposite of mass, it was also the opposite of accessible. "Handcrafted" carried with it the idea of special, but special in a way that was ultimately exclusive.

The new-craft phenomenon, in my view, did not and does not carry that connotation. The stuff may be more expensive than mass goods, and it may feel singular in some sense, but it's pretty accessible. Partly this is about raw price point, and partly it's about the Web.

This is one of the reasons I actually think it's a good thing to avoid really hard-and-fast definitions of "craft culture" that tend toward excluding rather than including. It's a good time to think about being as inclusive and accessible as possible.

Now that remark maybe threatens to bring us back to the whole debate over what it means when a hobbyist selling not very original or well-made stuffed owls for fun sort of hijacks the halo of handcrafted and literally cheapens it by selling at a losing price, hurting everybody. You know: That's not craft. I get that. But I want to try to sort of flip that debate over.

I've just given you the reasons why I as a journalist got interested in the new wave of craft and how I think it relates to some of the tensions that animate consumer culture. So now let's look forward. I have a few conclusions to offer, as an outsider, having to do with the creator side and with the consumer side.

In both cases, I want to suggest the deeper, and to me more important, reasons why it is that I said at the beginning that I think it's good that there's really no such thing as a single craft culture.

On the creator side, I would say this. First, when I was reporting on the new wave, handmade 2.0 version of craft, I was repeatedly struck by

> "Maybe, in some sense, one idea about craft is a kind of gateway drug to others, and then to a whole different way of thinking about material culture."

how incredibly supportive the participants were of each other. I've avoided talking about specific crafters here, but in *Buying In*, I write a bit about the Austin Craft Mafia as an example. It was founded by nine women who each had their own businesses and were essentially helping each other in a quasi-formalized way, and they've continued to expand on that in their relationships with the other Craft Mafias they've inspired around the country. And it isn't just that example, and, yes, of course, there are conflicts and problems along the way. But I write a lot about indie entrepreneurs in many consumer-goods categories, and I've really never seen anything like the general sense of "let us help each other" that characterizes this handmade 2.0 business world.

And not only let us help each other but let us help others who we don't even know—right down to publishing genuinely useful how-tos, which is pretty routine in this DIY, handmade new wave and is, if you think about it, pretty remarkable.

There's another tension here that interests me—the tension between the urge to compete and the urge to cooperate. Again, there are reasons tied to evolution for both of those urges to exist in us all the time. The way that this particular group of entrepreneurs was resolving that tension is something worthy of attention. And to me as an outsider, the more that spirit can be extended across or even be sort of poached by all versions of the craft idea to find common ground, the better.

Second, a real unsung element of pretty much every version of the craft idea that you can come up with is the idea of story.

When we talk about authenticity or quality or the ethics of an object, what we're really talking about is story. You buy a mass-produced object, and it doesn't come with a story. In fact, it comes with the opposite of a story. You'll *never* know who made your iPhone, where exactly it was made, what, if any, connection there might have been between the maker and the thing.

Almost anything that we describe as crafted—and this applies to the most elegant handcrafted piece of jewelry, the sorriest hand-sewn owl, even to scrapbooks—is the opposite of that. The most interesting thing about such objects is their resistance to anonymity. There's always a story. I think this might be a true binding element of all versions of craft—not just people making things but the story of that making.

But there's another story that's even more important—or at least it's more important to those of you who are engaged in the marketplace in some way—and that's the story of the person you're selling to.

It's my firm belief that what animates consumer behavior, at bottom, is the story we tell ourselves about ourselves. I believe a very common mistake that creators make is to think that the important story is their own story. It isn't.

Let me give you a weird example. I wrote recently about a healthy-pizza business. They started out calling themselves World's Healthiest Pizza, and all their communication with the world was about them and why what they did was so important and noble and good. Then they wised up. They realized that they were expecting everybody else to come to them on their terms, to love their story. But if you weren't immediately attracted to their story, there was really no reason to pay any attention. They were, without meaning to, being exclusive.

They changed their name to Naked Pizza. They lightened up their attitude. They didn't change their product, and they still made their story available if you cared to learn all about how their views on the gastrointestinal system inspired them to undertake this study of ingredients and blah, blah, blah. They still had something to say, but their starting point became: Hey, it's good pizza. Which is a better conversation starter, as it were. If you want to dig deeper, great, we have answers. If you don't, totally cool. It's not about us.

I'm certainly not saying that your own personal standards about craft don't matter. They should matter—to you. You shouldn't expect them to matter to everyone else the same way. The new version of handcrafted that came along in recent years fit into the stories of a lot of consumers, in a lot of different ways. Sure, some of those ways had to do with authenticity and ethics and quality. But some didn't. Some people just saw a cute owl on a shopping blog, and they didn't know anything about the Renegade Craft Fair or the politics of DIY, let alone John Ruskin.

And thus here we are today, with these multiple versions of craft culture out there right now. One response to that would be the formation of different camps looking at what the others are doing and saying, "That's not *really* craft."

But what I wonder about as an outside observer to *your* world isn't, well, which definition of craft will prevail. It's more, can these various definitions of craft draw strength from one another and become a bigger and bigger voice in the marketplace? I really hope so, because there's never been a more important moment for that to happen.

Right now, as I mentioned, there's a lot of discussion about a new frugality, a new thrift, and maybe a sort of change in American values. We'll see how that all works out. Unfortunately, a lot of what the "new frugality" seems to boil down to is, in fact, attaching virtue to cheapness. I've read too many stories where the examples involve, you know, a half-priced flat-screen TV or incredibly low-priced shirts from Costco, that sort of thing. Things that revolve around, Am I getting my money's worth?

Another element that maybe all the versions of craft culture have in common is that at the very least they are concerned with asking a more so-phisticated version of that question—a version of the question that isn't just about cheapness, in other words. As you know, getting what's cheap isn't always getting your money's worth. And it is pretty much the opposite of making goods speak to power.

I want to be careful here. I've mentioned a bunch of caveats to the sort of trend-industry version of what's happening in the consumer marketplace. My view is that it's a lot more dynamic and tension-filled than they suggest.

But having been blunt with my caveats, let me close by reiterating what I like about *all* the versions of craft culture and why I think maybe hav-ing multiple versions of what craft means is just fine. The good news is that most of the various players who inhabit the world(s) of craft by and large seem to have a common interest in, at the very least, understanding each oth-er. I mentioned various discontent and squabbling earlier, but in each case, there has been good evidence in the aftermath of a lot of the players looking to find common ground. I hope that spirit persists.

Because maybe the fact that there's more than one version of craft culture means there is more than one way for more people—the broader con-sumer marketplace—to be drawn into the discussion. Not by expecting them to listen to and accept the proper Story of Craft, but by making it as easy as possible for ideas about craft to fit into their personal stories.

That way, maybe the fact that some crafters' handmade objects ap-peal to many consumers for reasons that have nothing to do with the history of traditional craft or consumer ethics or whatever is, indirectly, a strength.

"Can these various definitions of craft draw strength from one another and become a bigger and bigger voice in the marketplace? I really hope so, because there's never been a more important moment for that to happen."

Maybe, in some sense, one idea about craft is a kind of gateway drug to others, and then to a whole different way of thinking about material cul-ture. Maybe that's a way to draw broader groups of consumers into the be-ginning of a more wide-ranging conversation about the goods they buy—about what "your money's worth" means.

As an outside observer, it does seem to me that the most important idea all the different versions of craft seem to have in common is opening those kinds of conversations, not ending them.

On the broadest level, it's the opening of conversations that will help us all recognize and face the tensions of American consumer culture and the tensions in each of us as participants in that culture. And, who knows, maybe it helps in finding new ways, for each of us, to resolve them. +

Riding the "Long Tail": Marketing Craft on the Internet

Moderator

/ Namita Wiggers

Panelists

/ Lisa Bayne,
/ Amy Shaw,
/ Maria Thomas

Namita Wiggers

We realized that it might be a good idea, even though I have a feeling most of you have visited these sites at some point, to have just a couple of slides up while I do the introduction, and then I'm going to take those away so that the conversation isn't about what you see on the screen but more about what you guys do as businesswomen. I'd like to thank Monica Hampton and the conference committee for the tremendous work they've done with this conference. I'm really honored to moderate this panel with three businesswomen, each of whom is connected with an Internet site through which craft, like many, many, many things, is available very readily and very easily.

First, I'm going to introduce you to each of the panel participants and then very briefly describe the site with which they are connected. Following these introductions, I'm going to explain very briefly a kernel of the Long Tail theory that serves as a pivot for this conversation about marketing craft on the Internet. And I say that because I want to clarify that I'm an art historian and a curator. I am not a businessperson, nor do I really know a whole lot about marketing and marketing theory except as a consumer. In trying to find some sort of theory or frame or idea to pull all of these three kinds of sites together, the Long Tail theory was something that my husband, who develops websites and has for the past 15 years or so, pulled together and introduced me to. It seemed like a great way to start off this conversation.

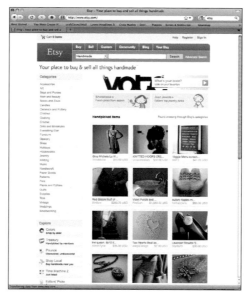

So, our panelists today are Lisa Bayne, CEO of the Artful Home Ⓐ, Maria Thomas, CEO of Etsy Ⓑ, and Amy Shaw Ⓒ, blogger and former owner of the craft gallery and blog Greenjeans. Lisa combines extensive retail experience with such companies as J. Jill, Gymboree, Smith & Hawken, and Eddie Bauer with a fiber-arts background in her position as the CEO of the Artful Home and the Guild. Bayne holds a bachelor's degree in textiles and fine arts from California College of the Arts and an associate's degree in fashion design from the Fashion Institute of Design and Merchandising. Her role as CEO at the Artful Home is to drive the company's vision, strategy, and marketing. I'm reciting her C.V. to emphasize that Lisa brings a number of things to this conversation. She brings experience in brick-and-mortar stores, experience with catalogs and print marketing tools, as well as with the Internet, in addition to having a strong textile and fiber background.

Just to give a brief background about the Guild: Founded as an art publishing company in 1985, the Guild rebranded itself in the past few years as the Artful Home. Through its annual sourcebooks for designers and architects, catalogs, and website, first launched in 1999, the Artful Home directly connects customers with works of art from the studios of hundreds of artists. It's a connection that I have personal knowledge of, having been an Artful Home artist for about a year or two before I took this job. You can't really be a curator and make art; it's not easy.

Maria Thomas is the CEO of Etsy and is League of New Hampshire Craftsmen, which, as many of you know, is one of the oldest leagues of its kind in the country. From 2005 to 2008, Shaw and husband, Jay, co-owned and ran Greenjeans, a shop and gallery for new craft in Park Slope, Brooklyn, as a craft shed—a place to bring world craft to the urban setting. In the process, they discovered a new wave of urban crafters as well.

In 2005, Shaw started the Greenjeans blog as an alternative to a website for their brick-and-mortar location. The blog provided a link to communities and to what Shaw describes as a "hands-on, real-world MBA."

"There's a lot of tension in the craft world with the Internet and technology, but the Long Tail theory seems to be a model to put forward for how the Internet can actually serve a community that's based on individual objects, one-of-a-kind, or small-production pieces in a different sort of way." / Namita Wiggers

responsible for helping the company scale its operations and expand its global presence. Prior to joining Etsy in 2008, Thomas served as the senior vice president and general manager of digital media for NPR, where she built and managed NPR's online, podcasting, and mobile operations. She began managing Internet-based businesses at Amazon.com, where she played a key role in the launch and management of Amazon's camera and photo store. With an MBA degree from Northwestern University and a BS in accounting from Boston University, Thomas brings her expertise and experience with Internet businesses to the rapidly growing Etsy. Founded in 2005, Brooklyn-based Etsy was described by Rob Walker in a 2007 *New York Times* article, "Handmade 2.0," as a "very much for-profit entity that bills itself as 'your place to buy & sell all things handmade.'" While eBay rose to prominence decades ago as an endless garage sale for the auctioning of collectibles and bric-a-brac, Etsy is more of an online craft fair or art show where the idea is that individuals can sell things they have made.

Brooklyn-based writer, blogger, and curator Amy Shaw is committed to craft sustainability and conscientious living and learned a great deal of craft from her mother, who organized craft fairs. She said to me earlier today that she got her education with the

After working as a Web-only enterprise from 2008 to 2009, as well as maintaining a space at the Brooklyn Flea, Shaw decided to close the virtual doors on Greenjeans earlier this year. She recently began a new blog, Found Curve, which she describes as about "art, craft, design, and sustainability, kept by a New Hampshire girl born and bred on good, traditional craftsmanship, who now, having lived in New York City for eleven years, is as at home in the fringy art galleries of Bushwick as I am in the woodwork shops of Canterbury and, in fact, appreciate their similarities as much as their differences." Shaw holds a degree in international affairs and an MA in humanities and social thought and is currently employed with an international sustainable development NGO.

To go back to the Long Tail, Chris Anderson, editor-in-chief of *Wired* magazine, first wrote about the idea of the Long Tail in an article in October 2004 and then later expanded this idea in his book *The Long Tail: Why the Future of Business Is Selling Less of More.* You can get the article off of the Internet. It's fairly accessible.

I bounced this off of everybody when we had our conversations prior to the panel, and the kernel of the Long Tail theory that seems particularly appropriate to the way the Internet functions today in terms of craft is this idea that it is sort of undoing traditional retail. In traditional retail, there is this 80/20 rule, where you've got this curve, the bell curve. The idea is that 20 percent of the products account for 80 percent of the revenue, so that's what's up at the top of the curve selling the most. It means that if you're a store like Wal-Mart or Barnes & Noble, you're making most of your money off of selling these most popular, best-selling items.

But Anderson noticed that something different is happening down on the tail end of the curve. Here is where the mainstream is splintering off into a countless number of niche markets. If you add up all of these items down at the tail end, the items that are low in demand or sales volume, the amount of sales and the revenues on the Internet exceed what's happening up here with the more popular items.

What does that mean, then, in terms of craft? It basically means that things are flattening out. It means that things that are one-of-a-kind or individual items are actually selling quite well on the Internet when you add them all up together. It makes for a very different and interesting way of thinking about the Internet. There's a lot of tension in the craft world with the Internet and technology, but it seemed to be a model to put forward as a way of thinking about how the Internet can actually serve the craft community that's based on individual objects, one-of-a-kind, or small-production pieces in a different sort of way.

So, with that, we are going to start by having everybody introduce what they do and tell a little bit about the business model for their companies. Lisa, do you want to start because your company is the oldest?

Lisa Bayne

Sure, I'm happy to start. You've gotten my background, so I'm not going to talk about me. Namita just mentioned that the Guild, which is the company, or the Artful Home, which is the consumer-facing brand, is the oldest of our three companies here. I'm not actually the founder. Many of you know Toni Sikes, who founded the business Guild.com in 1999 as a remarkably forward-thinking business to sell art online. It was so forward-thinking that it nearly went belly up rapidly because consumers weren't ready yet to buy art online. The original site and the original catalogs that were produced were brilliant. I look at them almost every day for inspiration. But the public wasn't yet ready.

Since 1999, when the company was founded, and now, the company has evolved and is now–knock on wood and the recession not withstanding–successful. It's successfully connecting artists from across North America with consumers, generally from across North America but sometimes internationally. The base of the artist network and consumer network was founded in the world of craft, and this still serves as the majority of the work that is sold through the Artful Home. We are also a purveyor now of work by traditional fine artists as well: 2-D, printmakers, painters, and sculptors.

I was thinking about the panelists who are here today, and we are in many ways the new world/old world, the new guard/old guard. The Artful Home is considered by brick-and-mortar galleries and by consumers who are used to either the art-show or brick-and-mortar experience to be new-fangled. Speaking about [Rob Walker's writings about tensions in the craft world], there is definitely a tension between brick-and-mortar and online retail, but we are also a catalog company. Actually, I'm not supposed to say those words, because we are so far from being a normal, predictable catalog company where you put up a picture of a polar fleece turtleneck and sell 50,000 of them. We are a "long tail" business using a "short tail" marketing vehicle of a catalog as a way to draw consumers to our site. That's probably far too much introduction, but I want to talk lots more because the picture that was up there portraying our business was in an email, and it was a very particular email that very succinctly described our business.

Maria Thomas

Good morning, everyone. It's a real pleasure for me to be here. I've learned so much over the past couple of days. My name is Maria Thomas, and, as Namita mentioned, I'm heading up Etsy, which has been invoked here more than I expected over the last couple of days. I've been at the company for 18 months. Like Lisa, I'm not the founder of the company. The story of Etsy is that it was formed about four years ago by five young guys in Brooklyn. Really, I think it was a story common to many Internet start-ups. Young people, because they're not bound by convention and are generally not afraid of risk, see opportunities and try them. In a nutshell, that's what happened with Etsy. I'm happy to talk a little more about that. The site was put up in June 2005, and relatively quickly it gained a lot of audience.

So I came to Etsy in the spring of 2008 to try to help with the growth of the company, to focus on our values and our mission and, at the same time, try to build a successful and lasting business. The business of Etsy, very similar to Artful Home, is a marketplace environment. We connect makers and buyers. The general principle is that makers are able to set up a shop on Etsy.com and connect directly with buyers, as you've heard from Marty [an audience member who sells on Etsy] and a little bit from others in the room. Etsy actually makes money in three ways right now. One is to take a commission on the transaction, another is a listing fee for each item on the site, the third is a kind of proprietary promotional model inside the site whereby makers can purchase slots on the site to promote items. So that's basically how Etsy is making money.

In terms of the larger purpose and values of Etsy, Rob Walker's comments were really resonating with me. Of course, I have seen his article and read his book but have never met him or heard him speak. Today was the first time. There were so many things he said that really resonated with me and things that we speak about at Etsy. The one thing in particular was the story. The story from both sides—the maker's story (and we have a lot of work to do on Etsy to tell those stories more forcefully and more powerfully) but also the buyer's story. I think that's very important. What I have tried to bring into the company over the last 18 months is not just the operational focus, and all the things that we have to do to build the foundation of our business, but also that idea that connecting people and their stories is really something that Etsy should be focusing on and should do well.

Amy Shaw

My name is Amy Shaw, and I owned Greenjeans, in Brooklyn, New York, with my husband. We started two months before Etsy launched, actually. We're talking about business models. Our business model was a little bit more naive than others. We decided to open our doors—we had four artisans that we'd signed on at that point. Our idea was to open a space and offer work by independent artisans from around the country, from traditional craftspeople to the craft new wave, and try to build a bridge between these two realms of craft-making that didn't seem to be communicating very well, or at all, at that time. That was sort of our concept. Our business model was based more on a concept than a business model.

The Web portion of it came after we opened the doors, because, in terms of storytelling, I wanted to be able to tell the story of starting a business. I didn't realize it at the time, but we were craftspeople making a space, making a gallery, making exhibitions, making connections between buyers and makers, and trying to close the gap between the producer and the consumer. We didn't have a website, so we started a blog. (I started a blog; Jay really didn't do anything with the website part of it. It was me.) [Laughter] I started a blog, so I could tell the story and also tell the stories of some of the artisans and craftspeople that we were working with, and show pictures. As I got into it and really got into the craft world, I started covering events that were happening in the craft world and doing virtual studio visits with the artisans that we were representing. All of that is still on the Greenjeans blog. I have about 700 posts that are all there. And I started a new blog after closing Greenjeans due to the economy. It's called Found Curve, as Namita said. That's where I'm now blogging about the craft community. I'm still involved online as a writer and not so much as a business at this point. Maybe in the future.

NW TO MT

I thought we'd start out with one thing that struck me in our conversations, which is how you have worked with the Internet in a number of different capacities. I wonder if we can start our conversation now with you sharing a little bit about how the Internet has changed in the last decade or so.

MT

That's a big question, Namita. I was so happy that you started with the Long Tail because I finally get to use a word that ever since I graduated from business school, which was many years ago now, I've never been able to use in conversation, which is the Pareto principle. So I think I just got back the value of my education. That's the 80-20 principle, the Pareto principle.

Let me just give a little context to the question before I directly attempt to answer it. I always say I got my Internet degree at Amazon.com. I was telling this story in the convening session that we had the other day about how I ended up there. Because, as you heard about my background as a businessperson, like Rob Walker, I don't come from the crafting culture, other than being a buyer who appreciates the qualities of craft and qualities of the heart. I ended up at Amazon because I was teaching a class back in 1996, 1997 on finance. I was teaching about how companies access capital. I was using an example of what the initial public offering process is. What is that, how do companies go through it? I chose to use Amazon because it was such a remarkable example in 1996 of a company that raised an extraordinary amount of money on a business model that was not understood, in an industry that was really new and highly disruptive. I was using that as a model. In order to teach that class I had to do quite a bit of research on Amazon. I became so enthralled and interested in the model that I wrote cold to the company and found myself working there about a year later. I joined Amazon in 1999, and my comments, there-

location ready to receive the story—I was sort of the disrupter in that model. Part of the premise of NPR.org was to capitalize on the archival notion of the Web, applying the Long Tail principle that stories could be archived over time and people could access them. So it was also about accessibility. Just quickly trying to tie that to Etsy: I think that while some changes have happened over time, the Long Tail principle is still in play and not just in the companies that I've mentioned (think Netflix, many other examples). There are a couple of big changes in the Internet. One is mobile, one is social, and another

"We are a 'long tail' business using a 'short tail' marketing vehicle of a catalog as a way to draw consumers to our site."

/ Lisa Bayne

fore, are going to look over a period of about ten years, or more than that now. Three years at Amazon and about six and a half years at NPR. At NPR, I was also building a digital media business in the context of a nonprofit institution.

Maybe I'll start with the Long Tail and just make a couple of quick remarks. I think that the Long Tail principle and the Internet are exemplified nicely by Amazon. It really had to do with the idea that on the Internet real estate—by that, I mean space—is inexpensive. The cost is not zero, although the cost has declined sharply in recent years, but you have a lot of space. Space is almost infinite on the Internet. Of course, you have to pay to deliver goods, so to speak, into the space. But the idea is that you can service a lot of different tastes and choice for a variety of kinds of consumers because you're not limited in your shelf space or your store space or whatever kind of physical space. So Amazon really exemplified early on the power of this principle, because in books you have millions of titles, but in a physical retail store you can only show so many.

So that was a very strong principle that I learned early on at Amazon and, interestingly, applied at NPR. You know, radio is an ephemeral medium, but the Web is an archival medium. One of the key principles that I brought from Amazon to NPR is that notion that people are interested in a lot of different things. Some stories resonate with many, some stories resonate with few. The notion of this one monolithic radio audience that's there at a particular time of day at a particular

is real-time. These are the trends right now that are upon us when I think digital.

NW TO LB

This makes me think about the difference between Etsy and Guild. I really don't want to get into the questions about what the products are quite yet. But if we could then talk about what the model is. How has that changed? I'll be honest, I remember when Guild.com first introduced their website. You would go on the page, and it was just strings of images. It was very, very difficult to navigate and find anything. It's a very different kind of a model now. I think that has a bit to do with newer ways of thinking about how to navigate the Web. But it also has to do with other companies coming out and giving us different structuring systems. I wonder if you might talk a little about that.

LB

There's an interesting fundamental difference, which I'll follow the trail of in a minute, between Etsy and the Artful Home. (I'm going to keep trying to say Artful Home because the company is the Guild, but really our brand is the Artful Home. That's the problem when you're a small company with two names.) The core fundamental difference of these two businesses that sell handmade work online is jurying and editing. I'm not going to spend a lot of time talking about Etsy—that's a democracy, anything goes. Artful Home is a business that's built on representing the work of many artists, but all the artists must be juried onto the site by a panel of experts that is headed by Michael Monroe, who was actually honored yesterday at the awards luncheon. That's a really important difference. It's important to the artists who we represent, and it's important to the consumers because it's a first filter. Yet that is a difference that has been challenged and continues to be challenged in the world of the wide-open Wild West of the Internet. It sometimes seems like a difference that is archaic, and we talk about it all the time. While Guild.com started juried, and today we still are, we understand now that there is a balance —a tension, if you will—between representing a "long tail" of art and helping consumers focus and find what they're interested in.

I'm going to refer to the email that was pictured at the very beginning [in the slide show], which was all white ceramics. It was an email that went out within the past month at the same time that the big Beatles release happened. I saw an opportunity to capitalize on "The White Album," and the buzz that was happening then, but also to focus on a wonderful resurgence that seems to be happening in ceramics right now. We're noticing consumers are interested in ceramics. We're noticing a lot of really interesting explorations going on. We have the ability because we are an edited site to say, "Notice this, notice that," or to notice something and to spread the word.

So what's different between then and now is that while we're still edited, we now have a dialogue with consumers. We now can react to what's going on. And by blogging about it, by emailing about it, by Twittering about it, get a real dialogue with consumers. And that "White Album" email—I've had more interactions with artists, with consumers, with people who have never considered ceramics, but because of the "White Album" connection, have said, "Oh, that's interesting, and it's not mass made." So it's a very different place that we're at now than when the company was started. Is that what you asked me? [Laughter]

NW

It leads to a very interesting thing that you brought up with me before. We had a conversation about how certain websites link you in a more personal way. We were talking about Anthropologie, for example. If I click on *X* sweater, and it happens to be this yellow sweater, Anthropologie will suddenly pop up with other clothes that they think I would like. We were talking about how that is not something that works with craft. This ties in with some of what we've talked about, too, Amy, about the way craft functions. I wonder

if we could move into talking about that a little bit. What is it? Where is it? We know that we can navigate a little bit. We can pull out from the products. We didn't talk about how Etsy is structured, but Etsy has different ways to navigate as well. What are the other kinds of filters that are going on that are helping people navigate on the Web, that are functioning differently in what you all do than what you would expect from some of these other retailers like J. Jill and Anthropologie and so forth?

AS

I think the blogs are a major element to that. Websites can do so much to make suggestions—the way that you were saying, for instance, Anthropologie does. That's a whole programming issue, too. You have to have a whole team of people. I was the only person managing our website, so I would never have been able to make that leap technologically, I don't think. As far as editing goes and filtering, I think blogs are really a big player in that now. As most people know, craft blogs are in great number. There are lots of people who are blogging not only about the stuff that they are making but that other people are making. I think the people who are following these blogs are getting to know work that is being made in greater variety than if they perhaps were just looking at blogs where you can shop.

In terms of the way that the Internet has changed over the last few years, clearly things have gotten more and bigger. But I think the big change is that more people are adapting to the Internet and more people are getting involved and going online and being less afraid of the technological barriers between the concrete real world and the virtual world. I did a presentation a year and a half ago at the American Craft Council Show, in Baltimore, kind of introducing the idea of craft and the Internet and blogging. I felt like it was an opportunity for me to introduce this technology, perhaps to a generation that isn't as involved with the Internet, to see that this is a tool. It's not this monolithic crazy thing that you can't understand. It's a tool like any other craft tool that you have to take your time and learn to use and slowly adapt to using in your own life. I think that's the big change—it's that more people are getting comfortable and familiar with the Internet. As that happens, it becomes a more fertile place for communication and exchanging ideas and showing work. It's more fertile as a thing to leverage in a business respect as well, because you can rely more that people are checking your site. They are following your blog, they are reading your emails, and they are involved in that way. So I think that's a big change, that people are involved.

LB

What we all have to recognize in marketing online is that the consumer owns their experience. Those of us who are responsible about it set up ways for the consumer to navigate their way through the way they want, because that's really what marketing on the Internet is all about. In some businesses, like the old world I was in of J. Jill, it was fairly

comment specifically about what you were talking about. I think the notion of "if you like… you might also like… ," which was promulgated by Amazon—I can speak for Etsy—is not going to work for Etsy at all, certainly not based on purchase behavior. Amazon's technology—I'm so happy that I get to use my terms! [Laughter]—is called collaborative filtering. Notice the word "filter." It's totally based on purchase data. So if Lisa purchased things from Amazon, and I happen to be browsing or buy the same item, it's going to look in this vast database of information and return recommendations based on purchase

"I started [the Greenjeans] blog, so I could tell the story of starting a business… and also the stories of some of the artisans and craftspeople that we were working with, and show pictures." / Amy Shaw

predictable; that if you like this sweater, you'd very likely like these pants. For that kind of business, it's a lot easier to set up the algorithms. It's easier to use the research that says, "Okay, the women who like this also like this. Great, show it to them and refer." In the world of art and craft, it is so personal that the idea of, "Well, if you like this ceramic bowl, you may also like this fiber piece because one other person bought a ceramic bowl and a fiber piece," does not work at all in my experience. I was challenged by one of our customers who is a very active customer and active collector, who said, "Don't send me all those emails. Just send me other things I might like based on my purchases." I know what her purchases are, and I happen to know her personally and know that she is an extremely progressive, left-wing collector. I also know that there is another extremely affluent collector of a lot of the same work that she buys who is extremely right-wing, could be no more different politically and lead no more different a life. They do like some of the same things, and then they diverge completely. So in the world of art and craft, we can't follow the same norms. So this "long tail," making it possible for the consumers to find what they are interested in, is what we have to be able to do the best. Whether it's various filters and search navigation, that's the key to it really working.

MT

I agree to what both of you guys said, and you both used the word "filter." Just to

behavior. For all the reasons Lisa mentioned, that's not going to work at Etsy.

The thing that I think is interesting when it comes to thinking about recommendations is social filters. The notion of questioning: What is a filter? I'm not going to profess to be one of those experts, because I'm not. I feel a little bit intimidated by all the experts in the room. But I think that a principle that's been shown over and over again on the Web and may apply here, and certainly does apply at Etsy, is the idea that the community itself can be a filter. For example, we on the site today have a notion of "favoriting." I would argue that many people who come to Etsy have no idea what they want and may not be there to buy something. It's the idea of shopping as, dare I say, entertainment. They trust that they are going to see beautiful items and browse around and so forth. But if you are browsing through Etsy and adding items to your favorites list, right now that sort of becomes a place where you keep your favorites. We don't make it that easy to share that.

We do make it possible to share, but there are many more things we could do, such as: If I know—actually, I do know for sure because I know Lisa and she has finer and better taste than I. [Laughter] So I might want to "follow" Lisa. It's an age-old principle. You've done it all your life. It's the idea that you know who in your group of friends, who in your social circle, who in your family has the best taste in clothes or in wine or whatever it is. You ask those people. When I go shopping in a physical store, I usually don't go by myself because I'm not that good at it. But if I knew that Lisa had good taste, I might want to follow her on Etsy. I really think that's part of the power of opening that process and letting the community curate. We have a place on the site today called Treasury. For those of you who are familiar with the site, that is a way for anybody that comes to Etsy to sort of curate a small collection of items on Etsy on any theme they want. Then we use those curations throughout the site, principally on the home page but in other ways as well. There is a whole book, *The Wisdom of the Crowd*, and the notion that within any large group of people there is wisdom. I think that's one of the differences in terms of how to curate these giant collections of items. At least for Etsy. I think the wisdom and the curation, ultimately, if we do our job well, will be to enable that.

NW

But then this starts me thinking about a couple of things. One: I watched you, Amy, in your store when a customer came in. She was someone you knew personally. You had talked with her. You cultivated this relationship with her so you could physically guide her. It then makes me think of the story that you shared, Lisa, about your experience walking around at the American Craft Council Show, in San Francisco, and the interactions with people about what you were wearing. If you could talk a little bit about that personal interaction. This has come up a couple of times already in this conference. What people are worried about is that the interpersonal relationship, that conversation, the story, the connection is gone on the Internet. Share some of your experiences like that that we've talked about.

AS

When we decided not to re-open the brick-and-mortar and then kept the Web shop alive for the following eight or nine months, I then decided to close the site, not because we weren't selling things but because I missed the space. I missed guiding the customer around and interacting personally, making exhibitions physically. I really missed the physicality of it and the tactility of it. To me, it was not my milieu to be only online. So I closed it for that reason. Different from the Artful Home and Etsy, our website was—and I think this could be true for many brick-and-mortar stores and galleries—about information. Often what would happen is that I would get a phone call from somebody who

would say, "I saw something on your website. I wanted to ask you a question about it." And then the actual transaction would take place over the phone. We *would* sell things just online, and I never knew who bought them. I'm not sure if it was more often than not, but it was quite frequent that it was more about the information, about the artist, the price, the dimensions, the materials, the story, the picture, the different angles of the picture, and then the phone call. So that was my experience, and I think that may be common for other physical spaces that have Web elements: It's more about the information than the business exactly.

NW TO LB

For the story, you told me—I think you blogged about it on the conference website—it ties into the emotional reaction to what people were wearing.

LB

What Namita is referring to is an experience I had at the American Craft Council Show, in San Francisco, and actually I was wearing a sweater that I was wearing yesterday, that ties in an interesting way. I spent most of my day at the show tying and untying and tying and untying my sweater because all of these women came up to me and said, "Wow, what is that? How does that work?" And I was struck by the community of women at the ACC show who were obviously interested in art to wear and who dialogued with each other and were very comfortable stopping and talking to a complete stranger. I was comfortable undressing and re-dressing in front of these women, the same way that I am in dialoguing via Facebook and putting something out there and having women—frequently women I don't know—ask me a question, and we'd get into a dialogue. I think I was really responding strongly to something I had heard about how the new craft community was all online; it was all younger, and it was all sort of different and passing me by. I realized that was not true at all. That community that happens face to face also happens online, and I'm engaged in it every day online. Our company has always said that our single greatest asset is our relationships with our artists. We now are saying that our single greatest asset is our relationships with artists and consumers, because those dialogues are critical. People who love beautiful things often want to talk about them. They want to explore them and touch them. That can happen online, but it obviously happens in person. It's happening here at this conference.

NW

This relationship-with-artists thing is interesting because one of the things that I know Maria does when she travels around is that she has a meeting with Etsy sellers whenever she goes to another city. [To MT] I know that you had one while you were here in Minneapolis to talk to the Minneapolis Etsy contingency. The conversations that you were having were with the artists very directly. It started me thinking about these conversations about the relationship between the Internet and the consumer or collector and the Internet and the artists. I wonder if you could talk a little more about that. When you say "community," the community that you're working with, are you working more directly and having those personal relationships more often with the artists than the customers who are buying the work? I'm just curious.

MT

When we talk about community at Etsy, I think we're talking about a lot of different types of constituents or people who are interested in what we're doing, either because they have a direct interest in what we're doing or an indirect interest in what we're doing. So when we think community, we think very broadly. Like Lisa, we think both about makers and buyers, of course, because those are the direct participants in the marketplace. But we also think about people who are coming to the site, maybe browsing, maybe not even coming particularly for an item but maybe coming for some of the content and information like Amy mentioned. Maybe they come to look at a video we're showcasing or a how-to type of process. So there's a larger community that aren't buyers or sellers that are interested in what we're doing for one reason or another.

The community also, for us, includes all kinds of different parties: perhaps the media; certainly the investors; our employees, which I would put at the top of my list. It is true that whenever a number of us in the company travel for different reasons, we always organize wherever we are going what we call a little "meet-up." It's very informal. I post on our blog that I'm going to be in Minneapolis. I ask our Etsy "team"—a self-formed group of sellers in a region or around a type of technique or a type of work that come together for the purposes of sharing—to help me set it up. We put it up on the blog. We did it over at Nye's, which is a really cool place in town. We just gather for however long they want to gather for. I talk about what's going on in the company, what we're prioritizing, give an opportunity for Q&A. Mostly I would say for them it's an opportunity to get their questions answered directly. Frankly, I watch this in many cities, not just in the United States, but also in Europe I see this happening. They come together, and they say, "Oh, you're so-and-so!" and they call them by their Etsy shop name. They've dialogued, and they've talked, and they've shared their stories and their interests, and the hugging starts. It's remarkable. It's a very satisfying part for me.

NW TO LB

It's very different than at the Artful Home.

LB

It is different, though I would say that we have more one on one, and we don't have the same community networking among the artist community. But another difference is that we send out a personalized email to every single customer who shops with us, and we engage in a dialogue with them, so we really can develop a relationship. I would say it's more one on one. I haven't figured out whether a real community relationship is viable. However, when we introduce reviews next month, I think a community will develop that's outside of our control, and that's fabulous.

AS

I really like the idea of what Rob [Walker] was saying earlier during his talk about how the idea of *a* craft culture is not as functional as the idea of multiple craft cultures and, similarly, multiple craft communities. I'm starting to envision these overlapping spheres of communities: all these different sets of makers and buyers and businesspeople and writers and bloggers and all of these intersecting spheres. For me, that was what Greenjeans, and I'm sure any other institution, is about. It's about the intersecting of all these different communities who are interested in craft from different angles. ✦

Men in White / Julie Lasky

Welcome back from your break. I'm Julie Lasky, and I'd like to begin my presentation with a clip from a film many of you know, Alfred Hitchcock's 1959 masterpiece, *North by Northwest* .

    This clip is taken from one of the great seduction scenes in all of cinema. Cary Grant, a New York ad executive who's been mistaken for a secret agent and is being pursued for a murder he didn't commit, has leaped aboard the 20th Century Limited train heading for Chicago. There, he encounters Eva Marie Saint in the dining car. Here's a bit of their exchange.

CARY GRANT
Don't you think it's time we were introduced?

EVA MARIE SAINT
I'm Eve Kendall. I'm 26 and unmarried. Now you know everything.

CARY GRANT
Tell me, what do you do besides luring men to their doom on the 20th Century Limited?

EVA MARIE SAINT
I'm an industrial designer.

    Now it's time for a show of hands. How many of you never saw or don't remember this movie?

    Among those who just raised their hands, how many of you believe that Eva Marie Saint is an industrial designer?

    Of course she isn't. She's a double spy hanging out with evil people with foreign accents who are clearly no friends of democracy while she reports back to American intelligence. And Cary Grant, in true Hitchcock fashion, doesn't have a clue about any of this.

    When Eva Marie Saint claims she's an industrial designer, the screenwriter Ernest Lehman is having his little joke, asking us to picture her stomping around a factory floor inspecting the apparatus for injection molding. Can you imagine a less appropriate job for this woman? Plus, her character's name is Eve, for Pete's sake, the world's most notorious manipulative female.

Above:
In *North by Northwest*, Eva Marie Saint's character introduces herself as an industrial designer to Gary Grant's character.

Above:
Designers in their own
chairs, which accompa-
nied the article "Designs
for Living," in the July
1961 edition of *Playboy*
magazine. From left to
right: George Nelson,
Edward Wormley, Eero
Saarinen, Harry Bertoia,
Charles Eames, and Jens
Risom.

Here is a more realistic image of the
1950s industrial designer [shows a magazine
ad featuring Raymond Loewy in the cabin
of an airplane]. And here's another B.

Women did practice industrial design
in the '50s—Ray Eames is probably the most
famous example—but the group you're looking at is a men's club. In fact, it was photographed for *Playboy* magazine in 1961. And
I'm sad to point out that Charles Eames is
here without his wife. The other designers
are, from your left, George Nelson, Edward
Wormley, Eero Saarinen, Harry Bertoia,
and Jens Risom.

Take away their chairs, and these men
would be indistinguishable from any corporate executive. Industrial design had come of
age in this prosperous postwar decade, and
these designers embodied the subservience
of art and craft to business. Their roots, literal
and aesthetic, are in Modernism, which was
spread to America by refugees from Hitler's
Europe. The message that went with this
abstract, analytical, machine-oriented movement was of deliberation and control. Look at

how they're posed. Trust me, it's not just
their suits. Everyone wore suits in the 1950s,
even artists. Even Abstract Expressionists C.

But the artists are shaggier. And they're
glowering, and they look kind of hung over,
as Abstract Expressionists tended to do.

Look again at the *Playboy* photo. These
men are thinkers as well as makers. Their
chairs are great achievements, but they're
also props, not just emblems of their talents
but tokens of larger accomplishments:
innovative technical processes, streamlined
buildings, world-changing ideas that,
unfortunately, seldom got off the ground.

Maybe Eva Marie Saint doesn't belong
in their company, and yet there's something
apt about this cool, strategic, elegant woman
being associated with a discipline that in the
late 1950s, at the height of the industrial age,
cherished all of those characteristics. And
if Eva Marie Saint's identity is unstable, well,
the same can be said for the industrial designer's identity over the past century or so.

Let me expand that. For decades, a
mixed bag of designers—graphic designers,

Left:
"The Irascibles," a group
of Abstract Expressionist
artists photographed by
Nina Leen for *Life* magazine (January 15, 1951).

Day 2 / Men in White / Julie Lasky

interior designers, industrial designers—have
been as slippery as jellyfish when it comes
to defining who they are. And they've made
attempt after attempt to do so.

American designers have changed their
names, their credos, their activities, and
their uniforms, while, for the most part, their
counterparts in Europe have shrugged their
shoulders and simply done their jobs.

Consider this exchange, a transcript
from a short film based on Charles Eames's
answers to questions posed by the curators
of a 1967 exhibition at the Louvre called
"What Is Design?": [1]

Q What is your definition of design,
   Monsieur Eames?

A One could describe design as a plan
   for arranging elements to accomplish

1/ Quoted in John R.
Berry, *Herman Miller:
The Purpose of Design*
(Rizzoli International
Publications, New York,
2009), 3.

a particular purpose.

Q Is design an expression of art?

A I would rather say it's an expression of purpose. It may, if it is good enough, be later judged as art.

Q Is design a craft for industrial purposes?

A No, but design may be a solution to some industrial problem.

Q What are the boundaries of design?

A What are the boundaries of problems?

What are the boundaries of problems? Limitless, of course, leaving the designer's role and self-definition entirely open ended.

as a strategy to expose his uncle, who he believes has murdered his father. The irony of this line comes from our suspicion that Hamlet may be mad not just north-northwest but in quite a few directions. So *North by Northwest* raises questions about honesty and sincerity from its famous opening title sequence.

Note how the grid behind the titles dissolves into the facade of a modern building. As I said, if one theme is deception, the other is design. This movie is famous for ending on the face of Mount Rushmore, a monumental work of craft, but it makes many references to modern design, not just the glass skyscrap-

"The industrial machine removed designers from their workshops and turned them into the servants of business executives; it furnished them with the expectation to use their minds to solve abstract problems but then deprived them of the chance to be powerful leaders in their own right. Even as the industrial machine is giving way to the postindustrial computer chip, this uncertain status remains the designer's predicament."

In this talk, I will focus on some of the realities and fantasies that have shaped the designer's identity over the past century. I will propose that the marriage in this country between European idealism, embodied by the Modernist movement, and American pragmatism, embodied by free-market capitalism, has made the designer's image—both self-image and public image, as expressed in popular culture—more than a little schizophrenic, a condition that continues to this day.

[Hitchcock's *North by Northwest* plays without sound.] *North by Northwest* has two major themes: deception and design. And I don't think this pairing is an accident.

The movie's title is a reference to Hamlet's line: "I am but mad north-northwest: when the wind is southerly, I know a hawk from a handsaw."[2] Hamlet is explaining that he is sane but that he pretends to be a lunatic

er but also the interior of the United Nations building, which had only recently opened, the sleek Mount Rushmore visitors' center, and a cantilevered contemporary house belonging to the villain and said to be based on the work of Frank Lloyd Wright.

North by Northwest turns on the irony that Cary Grant's character is an advertising executive, in other words, a professional liar. When he meets Eva Marie Saint, he's outclassed by a true master of deception, but he quickly rallies to gain the upper hand. He collaborates with Saint in the spy game, and when she turns out to be a good guy, too, he ultimately saves her life. And I mean upper hand literally if you remember the famous scene of him pulling her up the face of Mount Rushmore.

Hitchcock, a European transplanted to these shores as well as a trained designer, was

2/ William Shakespeare, *Hamlet*, Act II, scene II, lines 272–73.

a master at pitting naive enthusiasm against inscrutable finesse, the innocent against the sophisticate. The quintessential Hitchcock hero isn't Cary Grant so much as he is plain, decent Jimmy Stewart. The quintessential Hitchcock villain is exactly the opposite of Jimmy Stewart: He speaks with a cultivated European accent, has a creepy feline quality, and inspired the central bad guy in every James Bond film. (In this movie, he's played by James Mason and his character is called Phillip *Van Damm*. Names don't get any worse than that.)

North by Northwest, I believe, showcases design as a force of artifice for good as well as for evil. The hero cannot afford to be homespun like Jimmy Stewart. He must have at least a flair for continental panache like Cary Grant. He must wear a suit beautifully. He must learn to play the villain's lethal game of trickery. He must do all this because we are not in Frank Capra's Bedford Falls anymore; we are in a postnuclear age, in the middle of the Cold War, and design is not just the initiative to carve national heroes into mountains but also to smash atoms and destroy Japanese cities in a remote, clinical way. And America in 1959, I would propose, was still very ambivalent about this power.

So death and design go hand and hand in this movie. And you'll find that each of the Modern monuments is the site of a death, real or staged. A diplomat is knifed in the back at the United Nations. Eva Marie Saint pretends to shoot Cary Grant in the Mount Rushmore visitors' center. All hell breaks loose in Philip Van Damm's Modern house on Mount Rushmore in the movie's climactic scene. Adding to this list, let us not forget the movie's most ruthless example of contemporary design: the homicidal crop duster.

Frankly, I first thought the association between murder and Modern design might be a little forced. But then I came across the following quote in a book of conversations between Hitchcock and the French director François Truffaut.

Hitchcock told Truffaut, "I thought up a scene for *North by Northwest*, but we never actually made it. It occurred to me that we were moving in a northwesterly direction from New York, and one of the stops on the way was Detroit, where they make Ford automobiles… I wanted to have a long dialogue between Cary Grant and one of the factory workers as they walk along the assembly line. They might, for instance, be talking about one of the foremen. Behind them a car is being assembled, piece by piece. Finally, the car they've seen being put together from a single nut and bolt is complete, with gas and oil and all ready to drive off the line. The two men look at it and say, 'Isn't it wonderful!' Then they open the door to the car and out drops a corpse!"[3]

I suggested breezily that Mount Rushmore had more to do with craft than design; if so, the old-fashioned values it embodies in the giant heads of revered ex-presidents are treated with something less than respect, as the characters scramble over the faces shooting at one another. And speaking of sacrilege, it should be pointed out that Hitchcock claimed he originally wanted to call this movie *The Man in Lincoln's Nose*. Just as American diplomacy was taking place on a global stage after two world wars, so, of course, was American design; industrialization was making a tremendous impact on global culture, bringing a heightened sense of responsibility.

"As the artisan or craftsman of yesterday created objects of utility and beauty for the few, so the Industrial Designer of today has kept them within the reach of many. Keeping abreast of changes in materials, methods and desires is the responsibility of his art; to its many challenges he must bring ingenuity and taste." –Paul M. Koons, Head of Styling Design, The National Cash Register Co.[4]

This quote—one of a series published by *Industrial Design* (later *I.D.*) magazine in the mid-1950s—precisely defined the designer's role in comparison with that of his professional peers: the artist, engineer, and craftsman. It may seem obvious that the industrial designer was a new breed in the mid 20th century, with the boom in manufacturing capabilities—the sort of character destined to evolve from older craft traditions. But industrial designers weren't the only ones shedding their associations with craft and acquiring

3/ François Truffaut, Alfred Hitchcock, and Helen G. Scott, *Hitchcock* (Simon and Schuster, 1985), 234.

4/ Quoted from *Industrial Design*, October 1956.

Left to right:
Riverside Press, First
Avenue, New York,
c. 1900.

Massimo Vignelli,
ca. 1965.

sleeker identities. With the advent of modernism, the very word "design" was taking on new importance.

A couple of examples: In 1998, I was hired to edit a magazine called *Interiors*. It began its life 110 years before that as a publication known as *The Upholsterer*.

In Victorian times, upholsterers were the men who specified and installed fabric, but they had long done much more than that. According to *The Magazine Antiques*, with reference to Robert Campbell's 1747 book *The London Tradesman*, "By the early 18th century the upholsterer [was] responsible for the complete furnishing of a house. He employed… 'cabinetmakers, glass grinders, looking-glass framers, carvers for chairs, Testers and Posts for Beds, the woolen Draper, the mercer, the Linen Draper and several species of smiths.'"[5]

Note the pronoun: he. Upholsterers were almost exclusively men. Later, the magazine *The Upholsterer* would reflect shifting professional demographics. When I arrived at its descendent in 1998, fully 82 percent of the interior-design workforce was female.

By that time, the magazine had long absorbed changes in the job title, too. In the 1930s, this publication was known as *The Upholsterer and Interior Decorator*. By the end of World War II, the title had settled into the single word *Interiors* to encompass the dividing, but never completely disjointed, worlds of decoration (meaning the arrangement and adornment of environments) and design, meaning a more rigorous construction of space. The age had long passed, of course, when upholsterers could supervise the customized creation of wrought iron railings or hand-ground mirrors. But the age was upon us when designers could carve out enormous corporate or retail environments. Interior decoration was considered superficial; interior design, strategic. Interior decoration was object-oriented, consumed with textiles and furnishings; interior design was systematic and relational, concerned as much, if not more, with space planning and HVAC than with decorative appointments.

Before *Interiors,* I was the managing editor of a magazine called *Print*. *Print* began in 1940 as a journal about printmaking. Its readers were commonly known as commercial artists. Today, *Print* is read by members of a discipline called graphic design, many of whom no longer know their way around a printing press. They may not even have much to do with paper anymore because they're designing websites and videos. Or they're brand strategists, working on everything

5/ Geoffrey Beard,
"Some Eighteenth-
Century English Seats
and Covers Reexamined,"
The Magazine Antiques
(June 1, 1994).

surrounding a product, from the logo to the in-store display to the annual report.

This is what the ancestor of today's graphic designer looked like, a 19th-century job printer ⓓ. Here's a circa-1950 commercial artist. [Shows a designer in a suit.] And here's a graphic designer about 15 years later ⓔ. This is the famed designer Massimo Vignelli who was one of the directors of the international design consultancy Unimark.

Founded in 1964 with 11 offices in 9 different countries, Unimark prided itself on its ability not just to create objects but also to solve problems. Clients included American Airlines, Gillette, Jaguar, and Unilever. Unimark is perhaps best known for its work for the New York City Transit Authority. That project was adulterated from the beginning, but remnants still remain in New York's transportation system ⓕ, and it is considered one of the great unproduced masterpieces of mid-century environmental graphics.

Vignelli was an Italian trained in architecture who relocated to the U.S. to run Unimark's New York office. He led the company with other designers who were either European or who embraced the progressive values of European Modernism. Those values can be summed up in the ideas of analytical approaches to problem solving; timeless solutions expressed with a minimum of material, form, and color; and interdisciplinary practice. If you could work in two dimensions, there was no reason not to extend your talents and principles to three. The Bauhaus, which inspired much of the Modernism transplanted from Europe, trained its students in everything from color theory to paper folding to metalwork, and a former member of the Bauhaus faculty, Herbert Bayer, served on Unimark's board. As for the Modernist emphasis on constraint, Vignelli was famous for limiting his color palette to red and black and for insisting that the world needed no more than six typefaces.

He was also notorious for insisting that Unimark's design staff wear lab coats ⓖ. What I see in these men (and women) in white is a repudiation of the craft-oriented side of design that was their legacy. The printer's cap and apron was protective armor

ⓕ

Top to bottom:
The graphic identity of New York's subway system was designed by Vignelli.

The design team at Unimark Milan, ca. 1965.

ⓖ

to keep clothing from being soiled. [Shows 19th-century job printer again.] But the lab coat is the uniform of detachment. As the body is whited out, the head is more prominently displayed.

According to Jan Conradi, the author of a book about Unimark that is being published in November,[6] Vignelli wanted the white coats to neutralize the designer's personality and focus attention on the work. Conradi also pointed out that white coats are common work garb in Italy, where Vignelli was raised and where another Unimark principal, Bob Noorda, had recently worked—

and is finally just beginning to loosen its death grip .

According to the design historian Steven Heller, the whole story of the shifting identity of designers can be told through fashion. Steve pointed out to me the advantages of bow ties on commercial artists leaning over mid-century drawing boards—nothing to dangle among the ink and X-Acto blades. And he drew my attention to a scene in *Mad Men*, Season 1, where Salvatore, the advertising agency's creative director, demonstrates his status by being the only person in the art department to keep

'Q. What are the boundaries of design?
A. What are the boundaries of problems?'

worn by everyone from butchers to pharmacists to doctors.[7]

The coats may have been self-effacing, but it's hard to argue that, in America at least, they were also clinical. I see them as representing the culmination of the designer's march from artisan to tradesman to corporate cog in a suit to what must have seemed an advanced state in 1964: experimental scientist, or even healer.

Whatever the case, the white coats were an odd blip in 20th-century designer fashion. Unimark went out of business in 1977, a victim, says Conradi, of overexpansion and an evolving design market.[8] Vignelli exchanged his lab coat for a suit of his own design, a variation on the craze for black that seized designers and architects for decades

his jacket on—just like the account guys.[9]

Ah, the suits. Massimo Vignelli tried to speed up the natural process of designer evolution by turning Unimark's staff into brainiacs, and he eventually looked ready to audition for a walk-on part in *Star Trek*.

But he was way ahead of his time. Even now, we haven't caught up to him. The suits remind us that designers' morphing identities have been demonstrated in the accommodation made not between tradesman and scientist but between artist and business executive.

Modernism was a powerful force that converted designers from makers to thinkers, but when it came into its own in 1950s America, it did so on the coattails of corporate culture. The industrial machine removed designers from their workshops and turned them into the servants of business executives; it furnished them with the expectation to use their minds to solve abstract problems but then deprived them of the chance to be powerful leaders in their own right. Even as the industrial machine is giving way to the postindustrial computer chip, this uncertain status remains the designer's predicament.

Which is why for my final film clip, I want to show you a fantasy of the industrial designer every bit as powerful as Eva Marie Saint's little gambit in *North by Northwest*. This scene is from the 1954 movie *Executive*

6/ Jan Conradi, *Unimark International: The Design of Business and the Business of Design* (Lars Müller Publishers, Baden, 2009).

7/ Author interview with Jan Conradi, October 4, 2009.
8/ Ibid.
9/ Author interview with Steven Heller, September 25, 2009.

Suite, directed by Robert Wise. The setting is a Pennsylvania furniture company whose president has died unexpectedly and left no successor. Various executives are vying for the position—the treasurer played by Walter Pidgeon, the controller played by Frederic March, the VP of manufacturing played by Dean Jagger, the VP of sales played by Paul Douglas, and wonder of wonders, the VP of design played by William Holden .

Here's what happens: After a couple of hours of sneaky alliances and backstabbing and some earnest doubts, the board members meet to vote. Holden delivers an impassioned speech about the evils of bottom-line-oriented business and the terrible toll it takes on factory workers who are forced to make lousy merchandise. He smashes a chair. Then he's elected president of the company.

Fifty-five years later, this fantasy of the designer taking a leadership role in business remains largely unfulfilled. Very few designers have positions on executive boards, and I can think of none running a corporation. Designers are continuously teased for their inability to speak the language of business or to negotiate a balance sheet.

By the same token, designers have retained their artistic and craft roots in their desire to be recognized as authors of their creations and to maintain control over them. I could cite dozens of examples, but off the top of my head, I think of George Lois, the legendary ad man who made the art department preeminent in his agency, of Milton Glaser who was a true partner with the editor Clay Felker in founding *New York* magazine, and of the late Tibor Kalman, who positioned himself as an impresario of design and spread his ideas to a wide variety of media.

Meanwhile, designers and business-people are forming new kinds of partnerships. Several business school programs are teaching design-based methodologies focusing not on the creation of products but on systems and strategies: reorganizing operating rooms, inventing banking services, figuring new ways to distribute free bikes in European cities or transport water in third-world countries. These are just some of the projects undertaken recently by design studios.

And designers are even beginning to wear white once again. If we check back in another half century, who knows, they may all be looking like *this* .

Thank you. ✦

Top left to right:
A still from
Executive Suite.

Karim Rashid

Good Design + Good Craft = Good Sense: The Story of Heath Ceramics / Robin Petravic

My name is Robin Petravic, and I'm a co-owner of Heath Ceramics. I'm here representing a company, and it's not a company where I wear a suit to work every day—although that'd be nice. I'm not an artisan, and I'm not really here to talk about artisans, but I am here to talk about a company that uses craft in everything that it does and the importance of craft and craftsmanship. I've been thinking that the word "craftsmanship" might be a word I should use more of today and how we use it in our organization and how important it is to our mission. It's not craft by itself but design and craft are things that are integral to everything that we make. Those values, those disciplines, are the cornerstone of our business, and it comes from a very long legacy of making things at Heath. That makes us still a part of the vision that we have today in 2009.

This year has been an interesting year for businesses, as everybody knows, and for us, it started out with a lot of worry, throwing the master plan out the window and working as hard as you can. Especially for a consumer-products business, a business that manufactures, things have turned out pretty well. Two thousand and nine was a pretty successful year for us. We actually grew our business. We actually added a number of jobs, and we continue to add jobs. We've got a lot of job postings out right now. We had quite a bit of good fortune, and there are a number of reasons for that good fortune, I'm sure—part of it being the hard work I just referenced but also our commitment to this integral vision of design and craft being a main, leading force in everything we do.

I'm sure a lot of you don't know about Heath Ceramics, so I'm happy to tell you about it. I love talking about this place; it's a fantastic place. If you've been there you probably know that. Heath Ceramics is a 60-year-old company based in Sausalito, California Ⓐ.

This is our original factory building that was built for Heath in 1959. We make ceramic dinnerware and architectural tile, and every single product that we make always has been, and is still, designed and made in this building in Sausalito, California.

We've got about 80 employees. This picture was taken a while ago Ⓑ. Approximately 40 to 45 of those employees are in production, on the factory floor, making our products. This picture was taken a while ago, and it's an interesting picture because it also includes a number of alumni. That's why you see all these older folks in the front [laughs], not because we make them work every day, but as you can see, we have some of those, too. It includes a number of alumni people

Top left to right:
Heath Ceramics, small teapot.

The original factory building in Sausalito, CA, built for Heath in 1959, where all Heath ceramics are still designed and produced.

Above:
Heath staff and alumni. Since this photo was taken, Heath's staff has grown from 45 to 80 people, over half of whom work in production.

Right and far right:
Heath Ceramics's
new retail store in
Los Angeles.

that were craftspeople at Heath in the 1950s and are still a part of the family. They come back and visit us on holidays and such things.

We make and design all of our products. We've also got a couple of stores. We've got one store in Sausalito that is part of the building where we make everything, and we have one store in Los Angeles, which is this store here . It's new as of last year. We're opening up another store in San Francisco this spring. And, of course, we have a really fantastic online business that's a big part of what we do as well. I'm going to talk about this a little more, but 87 percent of what we sell we sell direct to the customer (with a little bit of distribution mixed in there)—another important part of who we are and what we do, what we believe in.

I've been at Heath Ceramics for six years, and I don't run the company by myself. If you don't believe me, this woman in the red sweater [pointing to screen] will tell you that. We run the business together. That woman is Cathy Bailey; she's a co-owner, and she's also my wife . She's my partner in life and my partner in work, and that's a topic for a whole other lecture that we'd be happy to give if anybody wants us to. It's interesting, actually, having a child made us realize that working together is a good practice because that's what having kids are about. Cathy and I were both designers and have design backgrounds. She is one of these women designers that are a leading force in design and, as you will see, when we talk a little more about Heath's history, Heath started out that way, too, being led by a woman.

We're both designers. Cathy is a more traditional industrial designer and was trained as an industrial designer. I was trained as a product-design engineer. The way things work at Heath is that Cathy is the creative director—that's her title. She's more focused on the design, on the making, on the brand image, and all those aspects of the business. Because of my background and love for systems and engineering, I focus a little bit more on managing the operations. I like to say I run the business, the operations, overseeing production and finances, but together, we set the vision. We also set the culture and make sure that design and craft are at the forefront of that culture, from our employees on out to our customers. That's what we do.

We haven't always been at Heath, as I said. In our previous life, we were design consultants; we worked for a lot of big-name corporations. Last time I was in Minneapolis, I was flying through because of one of those consulting jobs. About ten years ago, we started to realize that the design work we were doing was missing some elements. It wasn't really what we had bargained for, and it wasn't really why we got interested in design in the first place. Design had really become, or design consulting rather, was not so much about designing products. Eighty percent of it was designing presentations for internal concept pitches—never any kind of focus on the final product itself, which is what we got so excited about when we said we were going to go to design school. We felt like we needed to make some kind of change. The kind of design process that I was involved in on a day-to-day basis was not working in real materials but working in things like foam core and doing ergonomic studies. I have seen people rip foam core apart and be a real craftsperson in foam core—you can be a real craftsperson or not in foam core—but there was something lacking in what we were doing. We were also missing that connection with the making part of everything—especially with more and more making happening overseas, not happening where the design is happening—which became more and more something we felt was lacking, something we were missing.

[Shows picture of a factory.] This is not Heath. This is a sewing factory in Asia that Cathy used to spend a lot of time in when she was working at Nike. But with that process, she would design something and then the design would be sent over to the factory. And if the budget was there, maybe they'd send her, too, but usually they'd only send her if there was a problem after somebody tried to interpret the design. She'd go over there and try to fix it, and in the meantime, she'd learn a lot of things about how she might have designed something differently if she'd been working with the person that was actually going to try and put that piece together. The person that was trying to put that piece together would have learned something as well about her design intent—what was trying to be achieved—if they'd had that communication right from the get-go. That kind of connection was really missing for us in what we thought would be a better process of coming up with better results. What was missing was working in real materials and that feedback loop of understanding materials and understanding the processes of design.

Since you saw it already, I'm going to skip ahead to the picture of Charles and Ray [Eames]. The reason we have this in here is because, in the thinking about what kind of design life Cathy and I wanted to have, this is our inspiration for why we got into design. There are all these images that we saw of Charles and Ray Eames working with real materials. Whether or not much of it was real, I don't really know, I wasn't there, but that was our impression: Designers working in real materials, being hands-on, having a lot of fun doing it, and having a blast. If there were pictures of Charles and Ray sitting in a focus group with a bunch of executives, I didn't see it, and I wouldn't be here if I had. I certainly never saw pictures of them hunched over a computer monitor. It was always them

working in steel and wood and being hands-on, and that's what we wanted to get back to. We wanted to again be able to focus on good products, not just ideas. We wanted to focus on the *process* and really give that process room to breathe.

That's what we were looking for back in about 2002 or 2003, and that's when we stumbled across Heath. Even though we really did literally stumble across Heath—we happened to have just moved to town and didn't really know it was there; we just came across it—it really doesn't appear like an accident toward the end, because Heath is a place that was always about designing and making, and we were two designers that felt like we needed to become designer/makers. We thought that would be, for us at least, a better way of achieving the results we wanted to do and would be a much more satisfying design process. So, really, no accident.

There were a lot of things at Heath that resonated with us when we first came across it. Something about the building itself not being a factory. It has this feel of an oversize Case Study House—nice geometric form, simple materials augmented by all these wonderful, rich, beautiful tiles scattered around in nooks and crannies on the exterior and interior of the building Ⓔ. Then, of course, peering in the windows, we would see all this old machinery and these well used tools and clay on the floor and this feeling that you really make things here. These are the things that go into making things. There was that tangibility that was just so exciting to us as designers that we had always been kept away from

Left:
Cathy Bailey and Robin Petravic, owners of Heath Ceramics since 2003.

Below:
The simplicity of the Heath building resonated with the future owners.

when we were working as designers. Those things always appealed to us.

Then, finally, there was the product itself when we first picked it up. When I first picked it up, it felt different. You pick up the bowl, and a Heath bowl is a little heavier. It's got a little bit more of a warmth in your hand, at the same time, along with that heaviness. It also had real, obvious craftsmanship and obvious consideration and detail going into how that piece was made. That was intrinsic in picking up that piece with your eyes closed. We'll talk a little bit about that later. Because at first, in 2003, looking at the pieces, it's not

up at 2 a.m. every morning. He's been doing this for a long time. We have a lot of people who have been here for over 30 years, and they're people who are not trained artisans or trained potters necessarily. They are people that have smart hands—people who pick up a piece of material, and their hands know what to do with it, and it makes them satisfied. They are very satisfied and have a lot of pride in that kind of work, and they'd be sad if that's not the work that they did. I should also tell you a story about the longest-serving employee that has been here for 45 years now, this year. Last year, I was rummaging around

"There was a very simple design vision that Edith Heath had that really helped us stay focused and keep things consistent. What she wanted to do was to create what she called 'simple good things for good people for everyday use,' and that's the ethos that kept it all going."

something you got; you got more from just handling something with your eyes closed, just feeling that piece and what it meant.

The other thing that was really appealing, that resonated with us at Heath, was the people. Long-term employees/craftspeople that had been there for a long time and had a lot of pride in their work and loved what they did. This is Lawrence **F**, who has been glazing for 37 years. He says he's going to retire in January, but he said that last year as well. He still goes for a run every lunchtime and gets

some old cabinets and found his appointment book from about 1968. Heath is kind of like that: You find all these things like in your grandmother's house, like a really cool grandmother's house. I took it down the stairs and said, "John, look, it's your appointment book from 1968. You want to know what you were doing on the day that I was born?" [Laughter]

There's no doubt that Heath has been around for a long time. One of the reasons that we know that is that you can't buy a five-piece place setting for $12 any more. Maybe not even at IKEA, or maybe you can, but certainly not at Heath; it's been a while. Heath has been around for 60 years. It was born out of the mid-century, and it wasn't the only pottery of its kind at the time, at least on the surface level. But when we found it in 2003 (and it still is today), it was one of the last potteries in the country. It's the last pottery in California of that era, and so, of course, it begs the question: Why is that? What is it about Heath that allowed it to endure for so long when all these other businesses went away?

It's a very multifaceted question; it's a fascinating question. One of the main reasons, of course, being because of this lady **G**. This is Edith Heath, the driving force behind Heath Ceramics. It's her legacy that continues on and inspires the work that we continue to do. Edith Heath was a potter. She's not just posing in that picture. She taught herself how to throw pots. She taught herself a lot of things. She started out as a potter doing production on her own wheel, a wheel that was made by hand out of an old sewing machine. This is how she learned her craft, and Heath Ceramics wouldn't be around today, I don't believe (and it certainly wouldn't be as it is), if Edith Heath had been, say, a businessperson who had an idea to start a pottery. It is what it is today because she started out as a potter, and she had that innate understanding of all the integrated parts that go into making a piece. She knew what the relationship was between the raw materials and the final piece. After it came out of the kiln, she had that depth of understanding. A lot of potters tend to have that level of understanding.

She was really interested in materials. That was a starting point for her as a designer, as a craftsperson. She taught herself chemistry. She always focused on a lot of experimentation—experimentation with glazes, experimentation with clay bodies. The clay bodies that we use right now are ones that she designed back in the '40s. She designed them because she wanted a certain aesthetic out of her piece. She designed them because she wanted a certain functionality out of her piece. I find that remarkable—a designer wanting to achieve an aesthetic starting out not with a sketchpad but with the chemistry of the raw materials that are going to build that final piece. I think that is quite rare. I think maybe it was quite rare even then. This is where all of that comes from, that real depth of holistic knowledge of what it takes to make something and design something. That was evident in her hand-thrown pieces, her early hand-thrown pieces, that understanding of the clay and of the glazes.

Our clay happens to not be very easy to throw; it happens to slump a little bit. It doesn't stand up straight, and every clay is different. That's the kind of thing I think you need to understand when you are designing. Every raw material reacts a little bit differently even in the same shapes and in the same forms. That potter's understanding and that attention to the materials as being such an aspect of design is something that was integral to these pieces. Even when the Heath pieces go to a production piece—more of a production method in this case, slip casting, or in some cases, jiggering or even pressing—that consideration for the choice of materials and how the materials are used, how the materials are manipulated, still comes through in those production pieces. Because they're part of the original design vision, they're not lost

Top to bottom:
Edith Heath, potter, founder, and driving force of Heath Ceramics.

A selection of Edith Heath's original ceramic designs.

when something is handed over to a mold, at least not in the case of Heath. That's the real part of it.

These are beautiful pieces by the designer Eva Zeisel, and they are wonderful. We have quite a few of them in our house, back in our closet, but now they've been replaced by Heath. The reason that I show Eva's pieces is because this is a different kind of pottery to me. This is much more about the forms, this is much more about the sculptural elements, whereas at Heath it is so much about the raw materials and the craftsmanship that go into those pieces as part of the design, part of the consideration that goes into it. For me, those are the reasons that Heath continues to endure, because the design is taken to such a depth of a beginning level with the material choices.

Heath moved to production pottery in the '50s, and this is very interesting, I know Edith Heath caught a lot of flack for no longer hand-throwing her pieces. However, she moved into production molds and jigger machines and all those things. I think it's very interesting to take a close look at how that transformation happened. Heath and her team, they were really craftspeople, and they didn't just look at production pottery as a means to hand over a shape or a form and just have it be made more efficiently. They were true experimenters. She was a true experimenter and a creative force, so these tools were other tools for her to explore. She was looking at industry as: "This is interesting stuff. How can I use this in my work, as a

designer, as a craftsperson?" The same kind of consideration for her went into designing a tool or designing a mold. It's just a little bit less spontaneity than you get out of hand-throwing but the same amount of consideration. Consideration is something that has to go into all craft elements, all design elements. This transformation was industry's tool in the quiver for Edith Heath, in not allowing industry to become the master of the process but just another tool or another partner.

Design and craft have this really long history at Heath Ceramics. Design is really there to create that context for the pieces. Design is there to recognize a cultural relevance for a certain moment in time, to recognize what qualities in products really resonate with people at the time, and by doing so, then allowing the craftsmanship to shine. There was a very simple design vision that Edith Heath had that really helped us stay focused and keep things consistent. What she wanted to do was to create what she called "simple good things for good people for everyday use," and that's the ethos that kept it all going. Very clear, very simple, very straightforward.

We still make the same pieces that we always did Ⓗ. These are not pieces that were brought back. These are not pieces that ever went out of production. A lot of these shapes are from the 1940s; this set here is from the 1940s. This is an original glaze from the 1940s. The Heath aesthetic will always maintain a very simple aesthetic, very much drawn from the beauty of the materials themselves, not swayed by trends. It's that simple functionality that they were after: "simple good things for good people for everyday use."

One of the real pleasures that I had when I first came to Heath in 2003 was hanging out in our store on the weekends. It seemed like every weekend we would have another lady, probably in her fifties or sixties come in and say, "I'm the oldest Heath customer." It happened every weekend. I'd think, I've met about ten of the oldest Heath customers, and they were so proud to tell the story of how they registered at Heath 40 years ago and how they still have all their pieces. And they were in there to replace the first piece that broke, or they'd just given the whole set to their daughter or son and they were there to buy something new for themselves. That thrill has been replaced these days by a different kind of thrill, of hanging out in our store and meeting three generations of people that are shopping together—grandmothers, mothers, daughters—and it

Far left top and bottom:
There is a high level of skill in the craftsmanship of Heath's products.

Glazes are not just specified or selected but experimented with to see what happens from an aesthetic standpoint.

Left:
These espresso cups are new shapes in the winter 2009 collection.

makes me aware of how few things there are that are so intergenerationally appreciated.

Then there's the skill and the execution and the craftsmanship that really makes sure that the design intent, the quality, and the functionality is still there ⓘ. There's a skill in that execution that's really important to this whole equation. What's really important here with the way that we do things is that design and production all happen in the same building, on the same floor. That elevates production and making to another level of respect, putting them on an equal level with design. That's very important that these two are partners, and equal partners in that.

Heath was always very good at craftsmanship, they were always very good at design and putting things in context: everyday dishes for the northern California lifestyle. There was a space in time when design kind of left the building and for about 10 to 20 years, when Edith Heath was in her older years, there was nobody there to guide that and put design in a leading position, in guiding the company. [Refers to slideshow.] This is the store in 2003 as we found it. This is what I was talking about, about seeing the value of these pieces maybe with your eyes closed, maybe a little bit more than with your eyes open. The same craftsmanship and the

same materials and the same craftspeople were making all these pieces. These are really well-made pieces, but design puts that in context. Design makes them relevant for a certain moment in time. Our store now, in 2009: same materials; same pieces; same molds; same tools; same clay bodies; in some cases, the same glazes in different combinations; and made by the same people. Lawrence sprayed a lot of these pieces; he sprayed a lot of the other pieces in the other picture as well. That's what design does: It brings a cultural relevance to a certain moment in time and recognizes what really resonates.

These are the things that we make today: simple shapes. Tiles that we used to make 40 years ago have inspired cousins—even though we still make the ones from 40 years ago—for 2009. This is a new line of dishes [showing product slides in rapid succession]. This is a new line of dishes that we did with Alice Waters for her restaurant Chez Panisse, in Berkeley—simple functionality for serving food, still part of that vision. We've always made this kind of serving bowls; we continue to make them. We love to experiment with rich colors and glazes. Experimenting with glaze is a process in order to get the aesthetic. Here, we're layering glazes to see what happens from an aesthetic standpoint ⓙ. The aesthetics are coming from experimentation and not just from selection or specification—new functionalities and different shapes. These espresso cups are also new. I didn't mean to show a lot of new things, but these are new shapes ⓚ.

We continue to make the old things we make because, in my mind, they're still good. That's why they're not nostalgic; they're just still good. The tiles we make—tile is a big part of our business—even though there's a lot less handwork in the tiles, they still have this feel of the hand coming through. There's a little bit of imperfection in every piece. No two are the

Above:
Tile is a big part of
Heath's business.

same . There's an intrinsic variation, that lack of flatness or straightness in every piece that we do, with a lot of the aesthetic coming from the way we lay our materials together and the things that we do with glazes.

We think of ourselves as designer/makers. At least I think of myself as a designer/maker/enabler because I'm not on the floor every day. I've actually never thrown a pot successfully.

I'm going to talk a little bit about process. These are line blends that we do to develop glazes. We do a glaze and we mix and do different levels of the formula to see what kind of results we get. One of the things that I'm most proud of is one of the designers that we hired five years ago as an intern. Her name is Christina Zamora. She's our main designer now, and she works with Cathy on all of our new product development. She came out of an industrial design school with traditional industrial design skills. She learned how to sketch, do production drawings, do CAD drawings, renderings, choose materials, all those things. She's really interested in what we do at Heath. She's interested in being more hands-on, and the way that she designs now is very different from the way that she designed five years ago and from the way that we designed five years ago. She works with a team of technicians, and she's the lead designer. She knows now how to design the way Edith Heath did—maybe not as well, I shouldn't say "as well," but she knows how to design with chemistry. She understands what happens when you change that formula. She's designing with raw materials. It's something you don't learn in design school, something she really had to learn on the job.

If you look at the pieces, the new products that we did five years ago and the new products that we do today, the pieces that we do today blow them away . It is because of

on a glaze or if you dip a glaze. They know that if you layer one glaze on top of the other, as opposed to the other glaze on top of the first one, you're going get a very different effect as well. That's all part of the design process as much as it is the production. The process of designing and making is focused on raw materials and on process. It is designers working with the people on the floor who are actually going to make these final pieces, keeping that feedback loop tight and keeping that understanding integrated.

The other important component is that we do all of this on a human scale. We have about 45 people in production. When I say "doing that on a human scale," I mean that all the elements of craftsmanship and design become tangible. They're all understood in our process, and they're understood in the final pieces. What we do right now is come to work every day with the express priority of making good products that express the full range of values that go into making products. There are a lot of components of it, and we want them all to come out when we do that.

The other thing that we do, making things in Sausalito, California, as we continue to do, is reconnect making things with our community so that people understand what it takes to make things or that things are even made. We have a lot of weird questions from customers. Sometimes they'll just be peeking around the corner of the plant and asking, "You really make everything back there?" and we say, "Yeah, everything." Because they think that, No, you must make some of it somewhere else. No, we make absolutely every piece back there. We give tours of our factory on weekends, and we get a lot of weird questions out of that, too. We had someone a couple of weeks ago say, "I never thought that you actually had to make a plate." People really did! She thought pieces

"Heath was always very good at craftsmanship, they were always very good at design and putting things in context: everyday dishes for the northern California lifestyle."

that depth of understanding and that change in the process. This image could either show production of tile or it could show design of tile. It could've shown design process because they are one and the same. We're putting on a glaze here, but we know and our designers know that if you pour on a glaze, you are going to get a different effect than if you spray

just showed up on the shelves of stores. A lot of people don't think about these things.

That's what I mean when I talk about reconnecting with that physical act in our communities and adding to that. Telling that story is really important. We make a big effort to communicate that to all of our customers—where we make everything, how

we make it, who makes it, what we care about in this whole process. Shoppers are very wary. They come into a big store, and they think, Somebody's going to try to sell me something. The first thing that we say to that person is, "Heath has been around for 60 years, and we make everything in Sausalito, California." Immediately, when we say that, this barrier just drops. All of a sudden, from a wary shopper you get a very curious person who wants to know more, because there's a lot in that story.

In our Los Angeles store, we actually have a pottery studio in the back . Our studio director, Adam Silverman, runs that location, and he's got throwing wheels and kilns in the back of that store. And he's making back there, and his pieces come up to the store once they're fired, mixed in with all the other pieces we make from Sausalito. Of course, all of our materials, our website, etc. go to a lot of length to tell that story about where we make it, how we make it, how long Lawrence has been there, and how his run was that day at lunchtime.

We've had Heath for about six years, and our business is about five to six times the scale of what it was six years ago. Obviously, that sounds like a lot of success, and you're kind of making a lot more pieces, you're making a lot more money. We had 24 employees, and we have about 80 now. It's not about the size or about the money you're making. What it does for us is that it enables us and affords us to be able to focus on our process—that process we believe in of integrated design and making. Even more so, it allows us to

do it even better. It allows us to have more resources that we can put toward everything, and it allows us to educate more people and more customers about what we do, how we do it, and the way we feel this is a better way of doing things and maybe an adjustment that could be made in the way that we approach making things in society.

Six years ago, this was kind of an experiment for Cathy and myself to prove that we could do this, that we could be designers who are also makers and that we could get better results out of it that way. It's not just another opportunity for us to continue to do that, but what excites us now is that there is also the potential example for other people—particularly designers, manufacturers, craftspeople—for how you can make products in our society and do it domestically in the U.S. and be successful. The final thought that I want to leave you with is that you can do a successful craft-based business, but it has to be very tightly integrated with design on a holistic level. That's what we're hoping that more people are going to give a try at.

Thank you. ✦

Left to right:
When designing new products for Heath, designers focus on raw materials and process. They work directly with the people on the floor who will be making the final pieces.

Above:
The pottery studio in the back of Heath's Los Angeles store.

New Models of Marketplace / Lydia Matthews

Let's imagine that this glass represents your personal experience of these first few years of the 21st century. The optimists in the room perceive the glass to be half full, while the pessimists believe it is definitely half empty. How do you characterize your ability as an individual to feel a sense of agency in a world as complex and problematic as ours? What about as a member of something larger than yourself, some kind of collective movement or community—do you feel a stronger sense of agency then? Regardless of whether your answer points to a half-full or a half-empty scenario, there is no question that we're all facing our lion's share of urgent circumstances brought on by a range of major catastrophes. As makers and global citizens, we cannot help but be affected by them in our daily lives.

Those of us who focus on the half-empty glass can easily point to monumental and often overwhelming crises, wicked problems including the escalating, massive violence of both 9/11 and its aftermath, including ongoing military activities drawing blood as we speak in the Middle East and throughout the world; the plundering of environmental natural resources generated by an excessive petroleum-based consumer lifestyle, one leading to cata-

strive to increase levels of material consumption regardless of the associated costs. In fact, most of those ethical and physical catastrophes that I've included in my dirty-laundry list can be traced back to particularly problematic aspects within our current economic structure. These aspects include valorizing competition over cooperation, and personal financial gain over a more complex understanding of what "success" might actually entail. There is always a bottom line, but more and more people are wondering: What factors are we putting into the equation that allows it to add up to these kinds of disastrous results? If our current economic logic and accounting methods have failed us, then how might we develop other models now and in the future that could help ameliorate our current crises?

On September 14, 2009, on the one-year anniversary of Lehman Brothers' shocking declaration of bankruptcy, French President Nicolas Sarkozy spoke to a packed hall at the Sorbonne, in Paris, and made international front-page news by challenging the world's political and financial leaders to radically rethink how we structure and measure our capitalist economic system. He delivered

"In the face of this [economic] crisis, many artists… are looking for new economic means and models that will help sustain and gratify them in a globalized arena as confounding as ours."

strophic levels of climate change and global warming; increasing health problems brought on by poor nutrition, environmental hazards, and anxiety-provoking lifestyles as well as new global pandemics, biological challenges that defy our existing (or nonexistent) health-care system; the expanding injustice and tremendous financial and social costs associated with incarcerating an inordinate number of black and brown youth and adults in U.S. prisons; the neglect of our city's marginalized communities as well as the physical infrastructures meant to support them, leaving populations vulnerable to natural disasters like Hurricane Katrina; and last but certainly not least, perhaps the mother of them all—the global economic crisis that has become so palpable.

Plummeting financial markets indicate the failure of capitalist systems operating on Wall Street and beyond that perpetually

his impassioned speech beneath Puvis de Chavannes's "The Sacred Grove," a late-19th-century painting depicting the rebirth of all things that people once believed in and now desire again in modern life. He called on the world to join him in an economic overhaul that would bring about progressive social change, namely, the Gross National Happiness movement.

President Sarkozy referenced the study he commissioned by two Nobel Prize–winning economists: Joseph Stiglitz, of Columbia University, and Amartya Sen, of Harvard University. Their radical proposal recommends complicating the bottom line of the Gross Domestic Product (GDP) by factoring in metrics that account for people's median income in relation to their expenses as well as a quotient for good health in daily life. If issues surrounding human and environmental well-being were literally measured and given

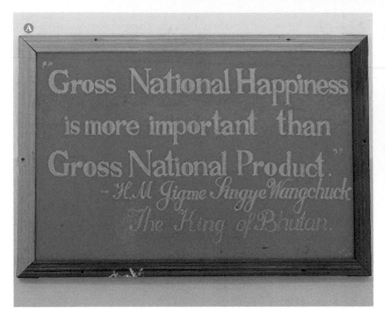

Top left to right:
Gross National
Happiness sign in
Bhutan.

His Majesty Jigme
Khesar Namgyel
Wangchuck at his
coronation ceremony.

real credence, the Gross National Happiness quotient, or GNH, would greatly impact the GDP's bottom line. Some countries that seem rich, like ours, would suddenly appear more impoverished, and vice versa.

In the words of Stiglitz, "What we measure affects what we do. If we have the wrong metrics, we will strive for the wrong things. In the quest to increase GDP, we may end up with a society in which most citizens have become worse off. We care, moreover, not just for how well off we are today but how well off we will be in the future."[1]

Stiglitz and Sen's report suggests that we need to design GNH systems for measuring our quality of life, our levels of joy and anxiety, our short-term versus long-term satisfaction, the impact of the taxes we pay, the vitality of our ecological environment, our access to health care and leisure time spent caring for friends and family, and so on. The goal of proposing such metrics is to foster social initiatives and financial exchanges that would prove more sustainable, ethical, and desirable in the long run. As President Sarkozy proclaimed, "A great revolution is waiting for us…. The current financial crisis doesn't only make us free to imagine other models, another future, another world. It obliges us to do so."[2]

A few days after Sarkozy's speech, Facebook invited its 180 million users to co-produce the United States' own GNH.[3] This site will now data mine the emotional quality of the words people use to represent how they feel that day. Amateurs have offered up this social-networking technology as a crude metrics-gathering prototype, inviting both Facebook users and professional economists to continually refine it in the future—Wikipedia style.

Of course, Sarkozy, Stiglitz, and Sen did not originate this timely vision. They borrowed and expanded upon the Gross National Happiness movement that was born during the 1970s in the little Himalayan country of Bhutan. Adhering to traditional Buddhist principles, then King Wangchuck vehemently criticized the impact of First World economic systems on indigenous cultures and vowed to protect Bhutan's ornate, handcrafted visual culture, which so eloquently conveys its belief systems, by launching the GNH movement to interrupt globalization's logic Ⓐ. He maintained that capitalist economic models had disregarded deeper values of spiritual comfort, proper human ethics, and community integrity within a pure, indigenous culture. This resulted in a ban on, among other things, advertising, smoking, wrestling

1/ Joseph Stiglitz, "Towards a Better Measure of Well-Being," *Financial Times*, September 13, 2009. www.ft.com/cms/ s/0/95b492a8-a095-11dc

b9ef-00144feabdc0.html. 2/ Telegraph.co.uk, September 14, 2009. www.telegraph.co.uk/ news/worldnews/ europe/france/6189530/ Nicolas-Sarkozy-wants-

to-measure-economic-success-in-happiness.html. 3/ http://apps.facebook. com/usa_GNH.

channels, plastic bags, and traffic lights. Sound and look like Shangri-la to you? Well, GNH also took the form of culturally repressing and ultimately banishing from the south many Nepalese-speaking Hindu peoples, who comprised 35 percent of Bhutan's citizenry. Because their sensibilities and clothing styles did not contribute to the GNH from the king's perspective, despite centuries of peaceful cohabitation, most were ostracized and have been suffering in refugee camps for more than 15 years. Clearly, crafting the systems and conditions to produce more beauty or happiness are not simple, uncritical matters.

His successor and son, the 28-year-old Oxford-educated King Khesar Ⓑ, was crowned the same week Barack Obama was elected president and has vowed to uphold his father's GNH Movement in this, the world's youngest democratic country, while opening the country to more controlled global exchange. Bhutan is poised to join the World Trade Organization this year, so time will tell how the new king negotiates and manages the change brought on by globalization's complex economic and cultural forces.

I'd venture to say that every one of us in this room has struggled to varying degrees

gies and tactics, as I will soon illuminate through several case studies. But the larger argument I'd like to make is that for many people around the world the desire to return to "business as usual"—and continue investing exclusively in more familiar economic models that privilege the individual at the cost of the collective—no longer seems like a viable, long-term solution.

To craft new modes of exchange from the bottom up for craft communities, we need to do some cross-disciplinary, cross-generational, peer-to-peer teaching and learning, as well as some rigorous research. We must turn to artists and crafters who are developing new models but also to people outside the craft community whose knowledge and resources can enhance our practices: namely, community activists, design theorists—especially those who practice strategic and service design—and social scientists, whose work is now essential reading.

New economic models do not only focus on financial capital (which includes employment, savings, household income, credit, investment, etc.) but also generate other kinds of capital—for example, those that the French sociologist Pierre Bourdieu so bril-

"We must understand that the things we imagine and craft today will cumulatively generate the template of our collective future. And with that deep recognition comes a sense of responsibility."

with fallout from the mismanagement of top-down globalization—either we are pinching pennies in our own households right now or feeling that squeeze within our schools, or both. In the face of this crisis, many artists are looking for new ways of restructuring both their personal lives and professional practices. Or, perhaps more accurately, many are looking for new economic means and models that will help sustain and gratify them in a globalized arena as confounding as ours.

But what does developing a more sustainable creative practice actually involve? It may, in fact, involve not one but many strate-

liantly identified in the 1980s.[4] Along with financial capital, we need to recognize the value of social capital (including personal relationships, various human networks, and forms of reciprocity within and across groups) and cultural capital (forms of knowledge, skill sets—craft skills included—and education that offer a person advantages for a higher status in society). We have the ability to actively generate and exchange social and cultural capital—not just highbrow culture but everything from actively participating in sports and hobbies, attending evening courses, visiting a gallery exhibition, planting a

4/ Pierre Bourdieu, *Distinction: A Social Critique of the Judgement of Taste* (London: Routledge, 1984).

garden, storytelling, etc. These activities, Bourdieu suggested, signal what is important to you and what sort of person you are. Securing access to cultural resources and experiences that nurture one's psychological existence becomes just as important as holding onto property. In fact, this combination of human, social, and cultural capital is essential in creating sustainable local communities, and it is in these zones where craftspeople can have real currency.

Lest we forget the image of the polar bear on the melting ice cap or the victims of Hurricane Katrina, there are two more critical forms of capital that we need to factor into any new economic model: namely, ecological capital (forest, flora and fauna, sources of fresh water, mineral resources, clean air, biodiversity) and physical capital (which includes infrastructure such as equipment and machinery, roads, railways, markets, clinics, schools, etc.).

In his new book, *Design Futuring*, the Australian design theorist Tony Fry synthesizes these various forms of capital and suggests that we exchange them ethically.[5] While we all know that people have ethics, Fry's brilliant insight is that *things* also have ethics. Each thing harbors the capacity to passively generate additional things required to negotiate that thing's existence in this world, all of which carry real financial, human, and ecological costs. Just imagine the invention of the automobile and all the things it spawned that are necessary to create and support it (the oil rigs, the freeway systems, the factories, the advertising, etc.). Anything we make has an ethics that can be measured at every stage of its life cycle, from the moment its materials are harvested to its demise as a waste product. This is why Fry advocates that we popularize the practice of "design futuring": We must understand that the things we imagine and craft today will cumulatively generate the template of our collective future. And with that deep recognition comes a sense of responsibility.

In relating Fry's ideas to craft-studio practices, you may be provoked to reevaluate how you source materials or to question if other people's lives have been unnecessarily burdened or harmed through the materials, tools, or production methods you choose to employ. You may scrutinize your price points, considering how, where, and for whom your work will circulate beyond the studio. You may reconsider what conversations you want your work to inspire, or how to make a more deliberate contribution to your local, social, and natural environments in ways that go beyond the kind of cultural work craft can achieve through exhibitions, fairs, online sales, or specialized journals alone. I believe we have a great opportunity to be more adventurous in how we situate and contextualize craft practices, whether they are studio-based, critical, curatorial, or commercial in nature.

How are new economic models that privilege GNH (i.e., collective happiness) actually taking shape in the world? Let's explore some case studies and begin to map out a broad field of thinkers, makers, and collaborative ventures that may have particularly valuable implications for us within our craft communities as we try to envision new economic models and more sustainable, globally conscious lifestyles and professional practices.

Ethical Metalsmiths is an organization cofounded by Christina Miller, Susan Kingsley, and Jennifer Horning five years ago. It aims to reconcile membership in a community of metalsmiths and jewelers who take pride in their craft with knowledge of the human and environmental costs of the metals they use. They work to "stimulate demand for responsibly sourced materials as an investment in the future."[6] The Ethical Metalsmiths website describes their various projects and details the gory aftereffects of metals mining. For example, a single gold ring leaves in its wake at least 20 tons of mine waste. Staggering as that is, the devastating effects of gold mines are proportionally even worse in Third World countries, where nearly half the world's gold has or will come from. To add insult to injury, there are unethical gemstones: namely, "blood diamonds" that fund civil wars and human-rights abuses. In recent years, an estimated 3.7 million people died in conflicts fueled by diamonds in Angola, the

5/ Tony Fry, *Design Futuring: Sustainability, Ethics and New Practice* (London: Berg Publishers, 2008).
6/ www.ethicalmetal smiths.com.

Congo, Liberia, and Sierra Leone. Ironically, these tainted diamonds make their way back onto gold bands in order to ensure matrimonial well-being for their wearers. So, as was the case in Bhutan, one person's GNH experience might be another person's worst nightmare.

To disrupt these deeply disturbing circuits, Ethical Metalsmiths launched their Radical Jewelry Makeovers. These are one- or two-weeklong intensive workshops offered within art and design schools and craft centers across the country. The workshops challenge young jewelers to start thinking early in their careers about the ethics of things—first and foremost, mined metals, but also the potential value of stuff at the back of people's drawers that would otherwise become landfill.

The first step in a Radical Jewelry Makeover involves soliciting donations of used or discarded fine and costume jewelry "mined" from the local community, with the promise of transforming them into original new works . Trading in social capital, donors are invited to share personal stories about where these objects came from and are given a dollar discount that can be used toward purchasing a made-over piece. Workshop participants acquire cultural capital by learning a variety of traditional craft techniques used to transform these found materials into bold and unusual designs. They generate ecological capital by studying how to melt down gold and silver for reuse and become familiar with the fair-trade movement and the

kinds of microeconomic models funding artisanal and small-scale mines operating abroad. They also learn about activist efforts to create an official certification scheme to support artisanal miners around the world and give consumers a way to know that the gems and metals they buy are ethical.

During the workshops, students generate art jewelry through a collaborative, cooperative effort, with the final step being a gallery exhibition and sale. At Penland School of Crafts this past summer, they also learned how to distinguish between precious materials and fakes in order to maximize their profits. This project does many things, not the least of which (speaking with my teacher's cap on now) is that it points to our urgent need to overhaul contemporary craft curricula to provide students with more contexts for understanding their practice, including

Left to right:
Workshop participants sort donated jewelry at a Radical Jewelry Makeover event at Virginia Commonwealth University.

Radical Jewelry Makeover creation by Shabnam Bahmanian.

Top to bottom:
Harvesting bamboo in
New Jersey.

One of the Bamboo Bike
Studio's custom bikes.

A workshop student
builds a bamboo frame.

frameworks in economics, ecology, and cultural systems, so they are better equipped to challenge taste and tradition in truly compelling ways.

Thoughtfully linking First World and Third World is also the goal of the Bamboo Bike Project ⓓ. Cofounded by David Ho and John Mutter of the Earth Institute at Columbia University, it pairs scientists, engineers, UN policymakers, bicycle enthusiasts, and crafters to co-create inexpensive, handmade cargo bikes manufactured from local bamboo, a plentiful and renewable resource in many parts of the world. The bamboo bike prototype was invented in Santa Cruz, California, by Craig Calfee in his bike shop. David Ho, an avid bicyclist was looking to buy a custom bike and ran across Craig's model on the Internet. They soon joined forces with a unique goal—not to export the bicycles but rather to export inexpensive DIY production methods as well as an indie economic model that will enable people in sub-Saharan Africa to create locally owned and managed bamboo bicycle factories to address their transportation infrastructure needs and generate financial income for their local communities.

The bikes are prototyped and tested locally in their Brooklyn studio, where they can draw on an abundance of yet another renewable resource: laborers from the DIY craft community as well as devoted bicycle enthusiasts who form their own pro-am subculture. What do I mean by "pro-am subculture"?

Pro-ams are "professional amateurs"— people who passionately practice something in their spare time without getting paid for it and yet perform up to professional standards. The pro-am movement is being taken seriously by business theorists like Charles Leadbeater and Paul Miller, because pro-ams do things previously thought possible only through a large business model: namely, they voluntarily do research and development that innovates new exchange systems and products.[7] Pro-ams substantially invest in the cultural capital associated with their passion, thus challenging the whole notion of how we categorize leisure versus work, professional versus amateur. They demonstrate the kind of "craft" sensibility that Richard Sennett

7/ Charles Leadbeater and Paul Miller, *The Pro-Am Revolution* (London: Demos, 2004). Download available at www.demos.co.uk/publications/proameconomy.

spoke so eloquently about yesterday; in fact, the Linux operating system was invented through a pro-am community of impassioned amateur as well as professional computer geeks who write code.

In their Brooklyn studio, pro-am bicyclists and crafters gathered to become the labor force of the Bamboo Bicycle Project. With the goal of making their own bike in one weekend, they learned how to select, harvest, treat, and miter the bamboo stalks, track, fill the joints, carefully wrap the frame to secure it, attach the component parts, and produce the instant community of bike riders who have bonded through the hands-on, peer-to-peer learning experience.

For the past three years, the Bamboo Bike Project has done workshops with local craftspeople in Kenya and Ghana, learning craft techniques from each other in order to design the best possible *boda-boda* bike taxi . Until now, they only had access to relatively expensive but poor quality aluminum bikes imported from China and India—knockoffs designed to mimic the British colonial models originally meant for the amusement of the wealthy class in well-paved cities, not for the critical transportation needs of rural people in areas that lack basic physical or infrastructure capital.

Today, they are trying to co-design with the local businessmen an effective factory model that is capable of producing a larger number of bicycles in order to more significantly contribute to the local economy. Although they still have to import metal components to assemble the bikes, making

bamboo bike frames that are durable and affordable would stimulate more economic opportunities, since they allow for a much larger radius in which to develop new markets and trade opportunities. It is a model where locals are empowered through craft to make a necessary item using sustainable local materials to create it.

The Bay Area–based artist Stephanie Syjuco also banks on pro-ams to create her work, the Counterfeit Crochet Project .[8] Recognizing the global proliferation of knockoffs of luxury goods—those made in Asian sweatshop factories and then exported illegally to cities worldwide—Syjuco began to think of the black market as an alternative economic system, one that challenges corporate capitalism while also replicating many of its technological modes of production, distribution, and consumption. Fascinated by the creative potential of the knockoff while wanting to critique sweatshop practices, she turned to the pro-am crochet community to co-produce her project. What would a pro-am black-market enterprise look like?

She put a call out on the Internet soliciting interest from crocheters, asking them if they would be willing to create a crocheted replica of their favorite luxury purse. Dozens

Top left:
A village elder test-riding a bamboo cargo bike outside Accra, Ghana.

Bottom right:
The Counterfeit Crochet project, 2006.

Top to bottom:
The Unswoosher,
designed by John
Fluevog and produced
by Vegetarian Shoes.

The Classic Blackspot
Sneaker.

of people from around the world replied, and Syjuco suggested they download and work from low-res Internet images. The technical limitations imposed by trying to create detail with fiber from basic images took advantage of the individual maker's ingenuity and problem-solving skills.

The makers were instructed to conform to the exact dimensions of the actual object, but their choices of materials and crafting methods were their own to determine. She also asked that after they completed their knockoff, they keep and use it themselves, out in their local hometowns. She did, however, ask each producer to send her a digital photograph of the work. She explained that these images and the bags would be understood as part of her own art project, and that if the counterfeit crocheted handbags were ever exhibited, she would borrow the purses temporarily for the duration of a

specific exhibition, crediting their makers by name. The works have, in fact, been exhibited in many cities worldwide, including Beijing, China—home to many of the actual sweatshops responsible for the proliferation of knockoffs internationally.

In 2003, the editor of *Adbusters* magazine, which Rob Walker has called "one of the noisiest and least compromising contemporary critics of the commercial persuasion industry," announced they were going to sell their own brand of sneaker called Blackspot ©. This was to be an "experiment in grassroots capitalism."[9] Adbusters basically replicated the manufacturing structures of transnational capitalism. They outsourced their factory production, but instead of being motivated by profit, they aimed to prototype what it takes to produce an ethical yet high-quality item of clothing at a minimal price.

Designed by John Fluevog—now there's some cultural capital!—the shoes are crafted with hemp sourced from Romania, recycled tires, and vegan leather, and produced in fair-trade or unionized factories in Pakistan and Portugal. They sell only to independent retailers worldwide in order to cycle money back into local economies. Blackspot is also an open-source brand, which means that it can be used by anyone for any purpose at no cost. On their website, they state: "Our hope is that people with similar philosophies will be inspired by our experiment and start their own business ventures, spreading indie culture and providing ever more alternatives to buying from megacorporations. Blackspot is about more than marketing a brand or deconstructing the meaning of cool—it's about changing the way the world does business."

Essentially, the shoes become a vehicle for getting an anti-Nike message out into the world. For $75, you can snag the boots, and the sneakers cost $47.50 when purchased off of their website. Or you can reduce your cost by another 25 percent if you sign up at no charge to become a member of the Blackspot network, thus receiving regular emails that include megacorporate news alerts and invitations to other "antipreneurial" activities. Adbusters funnels all Blackspot financial proceeds back into their nonprofit campaigns, but they encourage their Blackspot indie retail shops to benefit from the customary markup from wholesale that enables the shops to survive as small local businesses.

Adbusters does its culture jamming by adopting and adapting a globalized economic model, but other artists, like Otto von Busch, focus on local knowledge production as the site of change. Von Busch is an artist, designer, curator, and PhD in critical fashion design. Dale Sko Hack 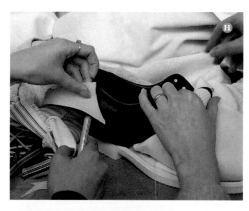, a three-day project in April 2006, challenged the global fashion system's model of mass production by hacking within a local business site, the small-scale shoe factory in the bucolic town of Dale, Norway.[10]

Von Busch handpicked a team of fashion designers, who met the shoe-factory workers and began to exchange skills and ideas, often experimenting with how to use industrial machinery in new ways. Von Busch employed collaborative design practices, which include: conducting ethnographic interviews of the factory members (or "storytelling," as the innovative design team IDEO calls it), spontaneous brainstorming sessions, one-on-one peer learning that evolved into the creation of new shoe prototypes or spin-off products like a shoe that has cleverly been transformed into a small purse.

Sponsored by the Nordic Artist Centre, the Dale Sko Hack project aimed to revolutionize the working methods of the factory's labor force, shifting from a linear Fordist assembly line churning out specific models for retail to one where laborers recognize their capacity to produce unique customized shoes rather than merely replicating the same shoe model over and over. The shoe hackers' tactics involved temporarily hijacking the factory labor force and machinery in order to put it to new use—or creative or subversive misuse—much like Michel de Certeau theorizes in his influential book *The Practice of Everyday Life*.[11] De Certeau examines the ways in which people individualize mass culture, altering things from utilitarian objects to street plans to rituals, laws, and language in order to make them their own.

In essence, the project inspired shoe-factory employees to work more like tradi-

tional creative cobblers again and allowed the young designers to learn craft techniques from their older counterparts, often imagining new uses for discarded materials. Through their intergenerational collaboration, they imagined together what might be possible in shoe design, testing and prototyping a new economic exchange that involved social, cultural, physical, and ecological capital. As a result of the project, this small shoe business not only maintained the mass production of their standard shoes; they also became more open to product innovation and began to understand their factory workers as co-designers as well as co-producers.

The shoes created during the project were "modeled" in a series of surrealistic high-gloss fashion photographs and incorporated into London Fashion Week in 2006. The photographs and the shoes have also functioned as artifacts of Otto von Busch's work as an artist practicing relational aesthet-

Top and bottom: Fashion designers worked with shoe-factory employees in Dale, Norway, to create new shoe designs and spin-offs.

10/ www.kulturservern. se/wronsov/selfpassage/ daleSkoHack/dale SkoHack.htm

11/ Michel de Certeau, *The Practice of Everyday Life* (Berkeley: University of California Press, 1984).

Left to right:
The Dutch fashion collective Painted worked in collaboration with New York fashion design students and Native American artists to decorate a cottage on Governors Island.

The Pioneers of Change "LAND!" sign on Governors Island.

ics and, as such, can be exhibited online and in contemporary-art venues worldwide, thus generating more cultural capital and commissions.

Tony Fry's understanding of a thing having ethics, Ethical Metalsmiths' radical jewelry, Blackspot shoes' antipreneurial enterprise, Otto von Busch's shoe hacking, and Stephanie Syjuco's embrace of the black market all make things that help restore the original historical meaning of the word "thing."[12] The Old Norse and Old English etymological roots of "thing" meant an assembly of free people overseen by lawmakers—an act, a deed, an event. A "thing" was a gathering of people where ideas and experiences were exchanged, policies crafted and then acted upon in a specific place. It wasn't until the 14th century that a "thing" became synonymous with an autonomous object or a possession. So perhaps, as is often the case, it is high time we return to the past to reclaim some "thing" that has currency now and bodes well for our collective future.

This year marks the 400th anniversary of Henry Hudson's arrival into New York, so the city and the Dutch government have been busy creating a series of commemorative events. One entitled "Pioneers of Change" took place recently on Governors Island overlooking lower Manhattan and Brooklyn ❶.[13] Curated by Renny Ramakers, cofounder and director of Droog, it featured projects by Dutch artists, architects, and designers with the common theme of envisioning a more responsible and sustainable approach to living. They emphasized things that are hard to

come by these days in a city like New York, such as space, fresh air, care, silence, slowness, and time. These are the "luxuries" of our moment, as opposed to the spices transported by the Dutch East India Company when Hudson sailed in under its flag. Based on what Ramakers called "a new movement in design and architecture," the event encouraged interactive involvement on the part of visitors, celebrating the value of handcraft and one's local context.

Inhabiting a naval cottage on the island, the Dutch fashion collective called Painted collaborated with Dutch-born, New York–based artist Pascale Gatzen to re-envision Hudson's original colonial encounter and imagine what a more respectful cultural exchange could have produced ❶. Creating what they called "slow garments growing out of many hands in fellowship," the Dutch contingent invited the Native American artists Joyce, Juanita, and Jessica Growing Thunder, a three-generation Sioux family known to be some of the most accomplished beadworkers in the country; Marie Rose Delahaye, a Bulgarian lacemaker; and young students from Parsons the New School for Design to collaborate with them over a six-day period. Together with the local furniture company Nightwood, which designs recycled furniture, they furnished and decorated the cottage, producing a series of improvisational couture doilies.

They focused on sharing their unique traditional craft practices, preserving bygone skills and witnessing them change over the course of the project under one another's

12/ www.etymonline.com/index.php?search=thing&searchmode=none.
13/ www.pioneersofchange.com.

influence. Playing the Surrealist game of Exquisite Corpse, one artist would begin embroidering, lacing, or beading on a piece and then pass it to the next person, who would improvise according to his or her own sensibility, creating a palimpsest of sorts. Ultimately, they cut up their work and distributed it amongst the participants as a souvenir of their place making, to be recycled into future clothing designs.

The Pioneers of Change project demonstrates what Robert D. Putnam, a political scientist and professor of public policy at Harvard, has argued is most necessary for the health of a city or region: namely, the ability of people to interact constructively around mutual interests, thus creating two types of "social capital": bonding (in which people already know one another) and bridging (between communities that are either unaware or antagonistic toward each other). Putnam says, "Bonding social capital constitutes a kind of sociological superglue, whereas bridging social capital provides a sociological WD-40." It provides social lubrication by allowing people from different backgrounds to share common experiences. As is well known amongst champions of the creative communities movement, a growing school of economists sees a cause-and-effect relationship between social capital and economic development. Putnam argues that "active cultural events that help people better share their cultures and stories is one of the best ways people develop their capacity to cooperate and build social and civic connections."[14]

Another fascinating project on Governors Island was the Go Slow Café 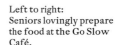, conceived by Marije Vogelzang and Hansje van Halem to reference the values of the Slow Food movement.[15] It reacts to an accelerated society in which people consume at a pace that doesn't allow for the appreciation of details and processes. At Go Slow Café, the menus are embroidered. Seniors prepare food with attention and serve it slowly. Tea bags are sewn on the spot. The menu visualizes the transport of food. Food with ingredients from distant places are served in tiny portions, food from the local garden is served in generous portions. Café visitors are provided with both a communal table and rocking chairs with foot massagers and slippers if they feel like they want to relax as the food is being slowly prepared.

The kind of care and attention to slow food that we see in this café and heard about yesterday [in Kristin Tombers's presentation] can also be linked to another important contemporary cultural phenomenon: the locavore, or the local food, movement. Attempting to lessen the carbon footprint by minimizing the transport of food, it simultaneously aims to financially support a region's small-scale agricultural enterprises by advocating that we should ideally only eat what is available to us in a 100-mile radius.

In 2007, the artist Kelly Cobb tried to imagine what the locavore movement would look like if it were applied to clothing. To create her project "100 Mile Suit: Costume as an Exercise in Regionalism," she began to break down all the component parts of a suit and research local makers and ethical material

Left to right:
Seniors lovingly prepare the food at the Go Slow Café.

Droog designed plates for the Go Slow Café that allow patrons to visualize the distance each ingredient traveled.

14/ Robert D. Putnam, cited in Tom Borrup with Partners for Livable Communities, *The Creative Community Builder's Handbook: How to Transform Communities* *Using Local Assets, Art and Culture* (CITY: Fieldstone Alliance, 2006), 7.
15/ www.pioneersof change.com/ bloomingdale.html.

Top to bottom:
Mary Smull weaving
cloth for the 100-Mile
Suit.

Curator Aaron Igler
models the 100-Mile Suit.

sources in a 100-mile radius of Philadelphia ①.[16] Through intensive Internet research, she found the sheep on Ewe Can Do It farm, which provided the wool; found spinners, dyers, and weavers like the artist Mary Smull who transformed the raw wool into cloth; leather makers and cobblers; knitters; hunters who could transform animal horns into buttons—all of whom were willing to participate in the project, many meeting one another for the first time. In total, 23 farmers and craftspeople worked over 506 collective hours to complete the 100-mile suit. Each donated time, skills, and energy. The suit reflected a growing structure and social capital that developed between these individuals, a physical signature of a collective effort at a specific moment in time.

The final product was exhibited at the Institute of Contemporary Art, in Philadelphia—transforming the gallery into a production space during a "demo day" when the community could view the process of making, talk to the artists, and touch the materials. [Shows a photograph of the suit being worn by the show's curator.] And, OK, never mind that it didn't fit—this is a proposal, not a glamorous finished product! It is iterative and meant to be improved, expanded, multiplied, just as was the case with Ethical Metalsmiths, Blackspot antipreneurship, Syjuco's black-market enterprise, or von Bush's hacked shoes. By making the 100-Mile Suit's activities into an occasion for regenerating traditional heritage, bringing it into contact with the most advanced technological and organizational possibilities, encouraging barter

exchanges and gifting, Cobb and her team of co-producers turn the project into the seed of a new local culture and economic model.

In the Bay Area writer Rebecca Solnit's inspiring new book, *A Paradise Built in Hell: The Extraordinary Communities That Arise in Disaster*, she argues that we are so conditioned to believe we live in a Hobbsian dog-eat-dog world that we ignore the multitude of examples of how people actually abandon individualist orientation under dire circumstances and focus instead on collective needs.[17] In fact, Solnit argues, we tend to deny the many ways in which we live outside of that competitive capitalist model in our ordinary daily lives. She cites the radical economists J. K. Gibson-Graham (two women writing under one name), who portray our society as an iceberg, with competitive capitalist practices visible above the waterline and below all kinds of relations of aid and cooperation within families, friends, neighbors, churches, cooperatives, volunteers, and voluntary organizations, from softball leagues to labor unions, along with activities outside the market, under the table, bartered labor and goods—a truly bustling network of uncommercial enterprise.

As a marine veteran who lived through the first Gulf War, the artist Ehren Tool speaks to Solnit's poignant ideas through his work ⓜ. He throws ceramic cups and occasionally plates, often as a public performance, not to create a splashy spectacle of technical bravura but rather to entice people to ask him questions about his disturbing yet fantastically crafted work, which depicts images of war or the insignia of our military complex: bullets, explosions, cartoons, hydrogen bombs, caskets. By speaking about his traumatic and sometimes amusing war experiences while throwing his pots, Tool makes viewers aware of the ritual repetition and discipline involved in both making ceramics and being a soldier ⓝ.

Tool not only relives harrowing experiences while he performs (unscripted), but he is also eager to make connections to what he sees occurring in our social systems today, engaging his viewers in an insightful conversation about the current political realities we

16/ http://100-milesuit.
blogspot.com.

17/ Rebecca Solnit,
*A Paradise Built in Hell:
The Extraordinary
Communities That Arise
in Disaster* (New York:
Viking, 2009).

share. At the end of the conversation, Tool invites you to choose one of his finished cups as his gift to you, no charge. Or, conversely, you can go to his San Francisco gallery and buy a similar cup for $75–$150 or a larger installation, like "Platoon," with its carefully constructed hierarchy of cups. You can actively choose what kind of exchange defines your patronage: Will you trade in financial or social capital today, or both?

Because I've attended Ehren's performances, I have several of his cups in my kitchen cupboard and catch myself deliberately reaching for or actively avoiding them as I start each day, reminded that we are at war through their presence. It is an uncanny experience to drink from that cup, haunted again by his words, aware of my privileged civilian status, and conscious of my tax dollars at work funding violence in the Middle East and elsewhere. His imagery forces me to slow down and consider something I would rather shy away from in the same way that Garth Clark has described his interaction with a Betty Woodman teacup—its flared lip and wide mouth simply would not allow Garth to rush around while drinking his tea, because if he moved too fast, he ran the risk of spilling it all over his computer. Erhen Tool's cup, like Betty Woodman's, demonstrates what I would call the ethics of the slow movement— it becomes dysfunctional if you simply opt to move about as if it were fast-paced business as usual. Hello! Its dysfunctionality confirms your own.

The examples I have shown you are by no means exhaustive: They point toward a myriad of other projects, from the extraordinary creative-community building happening in North Carolina through Handmade in America's efforts to link entrepreneurs and artisans to scientists and the local tourist industry, to the Berlin-based weaver Travis Meinolf, who is out to make the act of weaving both accessible and deeply meaningful to mass culture through wildly divergent price points, diverse display venues, and an imaginative and effective use of open-source technologies.[18]

All of these projects align with and harness the insights of timely grassroots social movements, some of which remain under the radar while others are quickly entering mainstream culture. Craft can be understood to exist in a much broader field, and I, for one, think traveling across borders is one of the most enriching experiences possible. Through a spectrum of strategies and tactics, these examples demonstrate what a galvanizing role craft can play in reshaping capital exchanges to gain a greater sense of satisfaction and purpose in life by actually producing, co-producing, or proactively consuming with some global awareness.

In fact, much of the optimism of the "glass half full" comes from directly confronting our monumental obstacles head-on and finding pleasure in the process of navigating through and around them by virtue of our own insurgent imaginations. Do you know what Dr. Felton Earls, professor of public health at Harvard, discovered through a 15-year study to be the single-most important factor differentiating levels of health and well-being—or GNH—from one community's neighborhood to the next? It was not wealth, gender, or ethnic makeup. It wasn't even health-care access or crime levels. Those were just the usual suspects. The factor that made that qualitative difference between neighborhoods was actually something more elusive called "collective efficacy"—namely, the capacity of people to act together on matters of common interest.[19] So, crafters, roll up your sleeves and go look for some new allies! ✦

Bottom left:
Ehren Tool, *One of Thousands*, 2005, stoneware and decals.

Below:
Ehren Tool demonstrating at the Berkeley Art Museum in 2007.

18/ See Handmadeinamerica.org and Actionweaver.com
19/ Dr. Felton Earls, cited in Tom Borrup, *The Creative Community Builder's Handbook*, 73.

Palace and Cottage
/ Garth Clark

This is not a paper but the presentation of some talking points, as it strikes me that more good can be done by turning most of my hour over to discussion.

I believe in a Craft Nation, something vast, unquestionably real and yet deeply mystical, much of it transient but beguiling, driven by an atavistic urge to make, some of it professional, some of it hobbyist, some of it pure catharsis.

Regarding the latter, I recently spent some time at Burning Man. I have been wanting to go for almost 20 years and finally got there this year. What met me was an expression of craft that was so powerful, so celebratory that I am still trying to fathom how much it has changed my life, my feelings about making, about materials, and about community. It was craft made out of joy and without agenda, arguments over status, or careerism. I think I must have lost about ten pounds while I was there, not fat but discarded cynicism.

But I feel little of that magic in this room. This is not the Craft Nation but the remnants of the American Craft Council–based ruling party. During its reign, the craft brand has been severely damaged, maybe fatally so. In private discussion with delegates

impossibility, by the way) was remarkable in many ways. It was like being beamed down onto Planet ZoZo. If one stumbled into the conference by accident, I am not sure one would not have realized it was a craft conference. A young curator from Yale, one of a handful of attendees who was not AARP fodder, suggested that one might think that it was "a conference about stuff that was almost good enough to be art."

By the time we gathered in the Hilton's unpleasantly chilly auditorium, it was already clear that the craft market was in free fall, that its "brand" was being abandoned by one institution after the other. One could almost make a living chipping off the word "craft" from portals. Was that crisis addressed? No, it was skillfully avoided almost as adroitly as the "c" word. Those who had removed craft from their title were featured speakers. No one speaking at that conference was described as a craftsperson, craftsman, or craftswoman, or the word I prefer, crafter—compact, specific, and genderless without straining for correctness.

What was worse was that not once, and I mean *not once*, did a full-time, self-defining crafter stand on stage. It was wall-to-wall aca-

"Caring about the cottages was Aileen Osborn Webb's mission when she founded the American Craft Council in 1943. This gutsy New England bluestocking was not an aesthete but a social activist."

and some trustees, I find an unhappy festering tone as *your* craft world grows smaller and smaller, more and more culturally irrelevant, while you remain in denial of that fact.

The American Craft Council conferences have been revealing of the institutional position of craft leadership. They remind me of Christo's first job in his native Bulgaria. One summer, he was hired to paint haystacks, cows, huge piles of wheat on large boards. These were then cut out in silhouette and mounted on hills some distance from train tracks so that, when the Orient Express came racing through, its passengers from the free world would see signs of agricultural abundance that did not in fact exist. Change the word "agricultural" to "cultural," and I see the same device being presented at these conferences.

Your previous conference in Houston, "Shaping the Future of Craft" (a metaphysical

demics or crafts organizers who I presume were the architects for craft's tomorrow.

Up until that point I had not been aware of the class schism that existed between the American Craft Council and the Craft Nation. Innocently, I approached a trustee of the Council and asked why the rank and file was not represented. The reply surprised me. "Just as well," she growled, "those people are always trying to take control." Another said patronizingly, "My dear, you know that they do not make our kind of craft."

The elitism of these remarks should not have surprised me, but they did. It was then that I realized that the conference was only for palace crafters—the stars, the aristocrats of our nation. The mentality was still that of a trickle-down economy in which all the resources were given to the top 5 percent with the justification that some of it would flow down. Remember how that played out?

Middle-class and working-class incomes first became stagnant, then they began to decline. The top 5 percent, the tricklers, made out like bandits. They saw their wealth soar by 40 percent. Craft in the last quarter of the 20th century mirrored this, with 90 percent of craft's limited resources lavished on the top 5 percent.

And with this, craft entered its Versailles period, lasting roughly from 1980 to 1995. Prices soared to unimaginable heights, admittedly more in glass than in any other media, but all the materials benefited. Craftsmanship responded to the mood of greed,

> "And with this, craft entered its Versailles period, lasting roughly from 1980 to 1995. Prices soared to unimaginable heights, admittedly more in glass than in any other media, but all the materials benefited. Craftsmanship responded to the mood of greed, becoming bloated and pointlessly virtuosic, and excess was the dominant aesthetic."

becoming bloated and pointlessly virtuosic, and excess was the dominant aesthetic.

Then there was that bogus, hubristic veneer of pretension that craft had become fine art. Ordinary little craft objects groaned under the weight of quotes from Foucault and footnotes from H. W. Janson's *History of Art*. In amongst all the vulgarity, some remarkable craft was made.

Meanwhile, what was happening in the cottages? Most of American craft is cottage craft—small-scale, rural. This is the bulk of our community—the 500,000 makers not invited to the Houston conference. Let me give you a brief snapshot of their world. Some of you, particularly those who work on a local or state level, are well aware of this, but the higher levels of craft leadership seem either unaware or disinterested.

The only data I could find (the American Craft Council has no data on its own world) comes from a superb study in western North Carolina by DESS Business Research. The average crafter has sales of $62,181.67. Studio-running costs average $37,842, leaving a take-home of $24,339.46. Total household income is an average of $45,000, suggesting that there is other income, maybe from teaching, odd jobs, or a spouse's income. The market is dependent upon tourist traffic and craft buyers, not "collectors" in the sense of the gilded age. The median purchase price for an individual craft object is around $198, and the annual total is $984.

This is a pretty marginal lifestyle, and it looks grim. But it gets a little brighter once one totals it up. The collective cottage craft power of western North Carolina contributes $206 million to the state's economy. I then extrapolated these figures to reach a national number, roughly but conservatively. The total cottage craft world represents a national professional activity of at least $16 billion to $20 billion. The number is impressive, but remember the figure to keep in mind is that crafters take home $24,339.46 annually. That is living on the edge of extinction, not just for crafters but for craft as well.

While the palace craft period may be over, at least as a movement, cottage craft is still alive. But it's getting dicey at the bottom of the pyramid. They need so many things. They need a national organization that does more than sell magazine subscriptions. They need a lobbying arm, something they have never had, to advocate on their behalf, so they can get favorable tax codes, money for apprenticeship programs, money to set up craft zones in rural areas with co-ops to sell their work and bulk-buy materials. They need a national website that allows a traveler to type in their itinerary and find all the open craft studios on their route. They need state-based handbooks and guides to that craft community. They need to have the craft brand given dignity and a little luster.

So, then, one may ask why are we here looking for a "new" craft culture. And what does that mean? More glamorous, less country? Or are we just asking how we can bring the palace back? I have no idea whatsoever, and I suspect that might be one of the things that the American Craft Council and I have in common. But it seems ludicrous to be looking

are likely to be a very difficult five years.

Craft is vast. It is many things. It has at times been a political movement, an anti-industry movement, and, at the end of the last century, an aesthetic movement. Now the moment has come to be an instrument of social change in which aesthetics are far less important than brute survival. It's about keeping the rice bowl filled.

I am sure you can tell from the tenor of this missive that I feel very deeply about this, and my belief is that the new craft culture will be a socially activist one, a return to grassroots, a concern with preserving a profession. Just as palace craft reflected the character of trickle-down economics, the crafts movement today needs to approach its field exactly the way nonpartisan economists tell us we need to rebuild our economy—from the bottom up, one crafter at a time.

Craft employment fills a special role in the economy because the profession is mainly in rural or semirural areas where job blight is at its most intractable. That means that when a studio closes there are no employment opportunities in the region to replace this loss. And half a million studios are at risk.

Caring about the cottages was Aileen Osborn Webb's mission when she founded the American Craft Council in 1943. This gutsy New England bluestocking was not an aesthete but a social activist. She was concerned with creating income in rural areas, particularly for women. Her moment has returned, and the times demand a return to her mission. If craft's contribution to American culture in the next decade is rebuilding and growing the cottage-craft industry from $16 billion to $32 billion, or $64 billion, that, more than anything else, will vindicate the power of the handmade. ✢

"I believe in a Craft Nation, something vast, unquestionably real and yet deeply mystical, much of it transient but beguiling, driven by an atavistic urge to make, some of it professional, some of it hobbyist, some of it pure catharsis."

for something over the hill when on one's own doorstop there is a vast professional group of crafters, the very core of the Craft Nation, crying out for attention, for a parent body to organize their collective power, desires, and needs, to see them through what

Day 2
Saturday, October 17, 2009
4:30—5:30 pm
Conference Conclusion

Craft as Subject, Verb, and Object

Moderator

/ Sonya Clark

With

/ Stefano Catalani,
/ Jean McLaughlin,
/ Lacey Jane Roberts,
/ Andy Brayman,
/ Garth Johnson,
/ Brent Skidmore

I am grateful for this opportunity, and I know that everyone's head is spinning. There is a lot that has been going on. But let me start by saying that one of the things that I really treasure about being here with this group of people is that you all feel like family. The good, the bad, the ugly of family, but often the good as well.

There is a saying in Nigeria, where some of my ancestors are from, that you don't know who you are unless you know ten generations of your ancestors. Now if you think about that, there are about 512 people that you are accountable to. That's a lot of people, just

gone before us, we are also uniquely individual. So there is this struggle between trying to find our voice as crafters, craftspeople, artists, whatever one chooses to call themselves, and to find the connections between others. No one *is* us, and so it is that we evolve. Natalie Chanin talked about this sort of succession of slow progression in her line of clothing, this notion that nothing is ever quite out, but there is this evolution as well. And so, in that moment, when someone clapped with the connection between DIY, or the indie movement, and studio craft—and, I should say, as a 42-year-old, I feel

"There's strength in both the shared community that we have as craft, and there's strength in the diversity of our community." / Sonya Clark

you, yourself. That's two to the power of ten for those mathematicians in the house. Today at lunch, a friend of mine showed me an image of her granddaughter, and what's most interesting is that this four- or five-month-old, this precious bit of her next generation and that lineage, looks just like [my friend] did as a baby. In my friend's face I saw this sort of joy and discovery in what it means to see something of yourself reflected in the next generation, and it made me think of the parallel between this moment that occurred when we spontaneously clapped when someone [earlier] said that the studio movement and the DIY movement are actually connected.

There was a moment three years ago [referencing the 2006 American Craft Council conference "Shaping the Future of Craft"] when there was a sort of disconnect. I felt it. But today when someone said that, there was a sense of seeing a little bit of oneself, whoever made that comment, in the next generation. We are, any individual one of us, a composite of all those who have gone before us, and that's a responsibility.

I worry that one of the things that we do is that when we think about craft we only go as far as the history of the studio craft movement. We don't go much further. If we really went back ten generations, each one of us, we'd be practically on another planet. We'd practically be in the sludge. We tend to just trace ourselves back to a very short lineage. So that's one charge that I feel that we have before us.

At the same time, being responsible also as composites of all those who have

rooted between these two generations—that if there are, in fact, generational things that are taking place, it's nice to know that this is a slow progression that is evolving.

This play between individuality and community is really essential to us. We at once seek our commonality. We try to find things that hold us together. That's one of the reasons why I annoyed you with green sheets [holding up green survey]—to find something of our commonality, this play between our commonality. I wanted to seek the nexus and find the slippage, to find the places where we're connected and then to find the places where we are uniquely different.

It's one of the things that I do personally when I meet someone who looks like me, is to find out what we have in common and, more importantly, what we don't have in common. When I find someone who doesn't look like me, or doesn't seem to have something apparently in common with me, I try and find what we have in common and then find out what we have that's different between us.

There's strength in both the shared community that we have as craft, and there's strength in the diversity of our community. And I'm sorry that the brown girl has to stand up here and say this [laughs]. In one sense, I went to Cranbrook, and that doesn't make me particularly diverse in this community. I went to the Art Institute of Chicago, so I'm connected to many of you in those kinds of ways. In other ways, in heritage ways, the African heritage, I'm not so connected. I wonder, What are we doing wrong that there aren't more people who evidently seem more diverse in this group? You could fit us at a table here. That shouldn't happen at a conference with 300 people. And I'm sorry to be the one to have to say that, but I suspect you noticed before.

I want to move quickly to talk about this survey and how it came about. But, first, the other thing that I want to share with you is that I want to tell you that I believe strongly in this notion of collective wisdom. When I discussed the opportunity to close with you at this conference, I'm smart enough to know that I'm not very smart. And I also know that I believe very strongly in this notion of collective wisdom. This image that I'm sharing with you not only refers to this notion of all those generations of ancestors that have gone before us but this notion of collective wisdom. It's an image of a hand of someone who is 102 years old. It's always been inspiring to me because in it I feel as if every one of those wrinkles—and perhaps this is where palmistry comes from—has a story. Every one of those wrinkles has something to do with use, has something to do with action, something to do with a verb. Perhaps if this was the hand of a craftsperson, and it wasn't as far as I know, it would be a mark of the ingenuity and creativity of this person, their wisdom.

In compiling this survey, what I did was ask people from many, many constituents—I asked students, I asked faculty, I asked the conveners who were here pre-conference—to come up with questions. There were about 150 questions. Then we culled them down to this 35 with the great help of my colleagues who joined me from the Virginia Commonwealth University, as well as a graduate student by the name of Aaron McIntosh, who has been dutifully, dutifully collecting this information. It made me think of this notion of the democratic process. Whether these questions are good or bad is a reflection of us as a whole, but perhaps we need more expertise as well to come up with good questions. Lydia Matthews was talking about collective efficacy, and I'm hoping that some of that is contained in this as well.

What I'm going to do is move very quickly through the survey results, then I'm going to collect my posse of people, because, as I said, I'm smart enough to know not to stay up here on my own. I know that there are wise heads among us, and I like their company.

I believe the questions are generative. I believe that there is something to be said about a generation that I live in, and yet I see reflected in my generation of students who are in their twenties and early thirties, who grew up making declarative statements that sound like questions. "Making declarative statements that sound like questions?" [Laughter] Now you laugh, and, in fact, I had my graduate students in a class that I was teaching give artist presentations, and a lot of them gave "artist presentations?" And the person who was evaluating them on this said, "You know, you sound like you're undermining yourself on this." I understood the criticism, but I also understood that one of the things that might be happening in this generation, and I do it myself, I might do it in this talk as well, the "upspeak" thing, as we call it, is that, in fact, you are inviting someone into the conversation by changing a declarative statement into a question. And there's something powerful about the difference between going, "Oh, really" and "Oh, really?" You hear how one invites you in and one closes you off. That someone might be using a declarative statement and posing it as a question to invite you into the dialogue.

What we have is an attempt at finding the pulse of this group. Here are the questions and here are your answers, and we will move through them very quickly. I should let you know that the green questions are the ones that you voted to be most relevant, and the blue questions are the ones that you voted to be least relevant.[1]

The ubiquity of craft media in the world. Is that a hindrance to its market value? We were pretty much split on that [41 percent said yes, 59 percent said no]. I would say that's an issue of slippage, and that one might be worth spending more time with. But you all said it wasn't so relevant to our issue.

Is the interface between craft, design, and

1 / For full survey results, visit the BlogBeat on our conference website: http://www.craftcouncil.org/conference09.

> "If we had an engagement with design that was similar to what's going on in Europe right now, and if those lines became a little bit more blurry, I think this world would be a little more interesting." / Garth Johnson

art moving in a positive direction?
When we get 89 percent yes, that's a general head nod. We're sort of bored on that question, to make a little *Star Trek* reference. We tend to think that we are moving forward in a good direction in terms of those three coming together.

Should craft become the example of critical making, parallel to critical thinking, in our culture?
Now I thought that was a difficult and perhaps scholarly question, but those of you who answered the survey, which I have to say was more than half of you, answered yes to that, at 84 percent.

Do you find *American Craft* magazine relevant to you personally?
Most of you said yes [71 percent] but said that it's not really that relevant a question.

Have you witnessed a change in the way craft is taught?
The answer to this was 82 percent [yes]. That not many of you found it relevant was interesting to me personally.

Has the academic craft community abandoned the traditionally educated craft community?
You see how we're split on that one [50 percent yes, 50 percent no]? I think where there's slippage there's actually more discussion to be had.

Is the craft community invested in broader notions of crafts that come from diverse communities?
Yes, [72 percent said] we're invested.

Do you value the contributions of traditionally or non-academically trained artists in the field?
Split on that one [50 percent yes, 50 percent no]. Slippage there.

Are traditional artists in the field well represented in our galleries, museums, and/or magazines?
We're saying yes [76 percent].

Do you have any formal education in craft history?
Ninety-two percent of you said yes, which I found really amazing, because I am thrilled that the Center for Craft, Creativity and Design and lots of other institutions and presses have come up with all these books that finally can be used in terms of craft history and, in relevance to the next question, craft theory.

Do you see the preservation of craft traditions as a forward-looking strategy?
Split on that one [45 percent yes, 55 percent no]. So there's something about our history that's kind of interesting to this group in the way that we value it.

Is there a difference between the way you use the word "craft" and the way you define it?
[Eighty-one percent said yes.] That's kind of shocking, isn't it? So you use the word differently than the way you would define it.

Should we curate, collect, and exhibit DIY in museums?
This was deemed *not an important question*, and yet almost everybody [96 percent] said yes we should. I think that makes it an important question somehow.

Have we reached a point in which we can say we have codified studio craft as a movement?

And that one is 62 percent saying yes and 38 percent saying no. Those last two questions were coming straight from the convenings group for curators, so I thank you for that.

Do you value craft that embraces its history and then challenges it?
A resounding 72 percent said yes, which is curious compared to some of the other history questions that we had.

Would craft be better off if it more actively and directly engaged societal needs?
The answer to that is 76 percent saying yes, and I think that we've seen in the talks that we've had presented in this conference that there is definitely a move in that direction—thankfully, in my opinion.

Does DIY present a threat to craft taught in academia?
This is a resounding no [88 percent no, 12 percent yes]. So I feel like this divisiveness doesn't exist as it did as few as three years ago.

Do you think of craft as a field?
Eighty-one percent said yes.

Do you think of craft as a set of fields?
Eighty percent said yes.

Do you use "craft" to describe technique?
Almost 90 percent said yes.

Do you use "craft" to describe skill?
Ninety percent said yes.

Do you use "craft" to describe conceptual approaches?
Here it starts going down a little bit, but still a majority saying 74 percent yes.

Do you use "craft" to describe historical precedents evident in work?
Eighty-one percent said yes.

Do you describe something as craft depending on the narrative of the object?
I realize this is a difficult question, but here is the story in the object that was talked about so fully by some of our presenters. This is one of those places where there is a little bit of slippage [52 percent yes, 48 percent no]. I, personally, am interested in those questions where we are at a 50/50 split more or less.

Do you use the word "craft" based on the training or academic pedigree of the artist?

[Sixty-six percent said] no. So it doesn't matter where someone went to school or what they studied there—you're not determining it that way.

Do you define objects, ideas, and techniques as craft, regardless of the maker's definition?
Seventy-eight percent of us said yes.

Has the word "craft" acquired any new meanings in the last ten years?
Eighty-five percent say yes. So there's something really interesting in terms of the ways we're defining this word that we've been throwing around with abandon in the past couple of days and over many decades.

Does the field need to embrace new technologies as a whole?
Seventy-nine percent say yes.

Does "craft" mean too many things to be useful?
Given that all of those were definitions, now we're at slippage again [46 percent yes, 54 percent no].

Does craft need to expand its definition to be more inclusive?
Again, a little slippage there [58 percent yes, 42 percent no]. So I would say this notion of "Are we overdefining craft?"—get over it already! A lot of the questions that I got in from those 150-some questions were about defining craft, and we're still having issues over that.

Does the democratization of making add to the value of craft in the marketplace?
Sixty-nine percent of the people said yes to that.

These are just the questions you found most relevant and least relevant, so you can see those together.

The Wisdom of the Crowd

There is a wonderful quote, and I believe Richard Sennett quotes it as well in *The Craftsman*, in which Emmanuel Kant says, in French, of course, that the hand is the visible part of the brain.

I'm going to bring my posse of brains up to the stage. I want to let you know that the reason I'm inviting everyone up is that one of the things I was trying to do, again, is to bring this conversation, the questionnaire is generated from a group of people. Your answers are obviously generated from you. I wanted to reflect, as best I could, something of this group that's here, and I couldn't make it less than six people. And I won't tell you why I brought each one of them to the stage, but I'm hoping that everyone feels at least somewhat connected to the group that we have gathered here. If you can just raise your hand, I'll tell everyone who you are.

Lacey Jane Roberts holds an MFA in fine arts and an MA in visual and critical studies, which she received in 2007 from the California College of Arts. She completed her BA in studio art and English from the University of Vermont. Her studio practice consists of large-scale, site-specific knitted installations. Lacey Jane also maintains a critical-writing practice that bridges craft and queer theory. She currently lives in Brooklyn, New York.

Brent Skidmore, director of the University of North Carolina, Asheville, Craft Campus Initiative. Brent's background is in sculpture, though he primarily makes studio furniture these days. I'm assuming everyone in this room is familiar with the Asheville Craft Campus Initiative.

Garth Johnson and I said that if we got together, then we'd make a Garth Clark, but I'm not sure if that's true. [Laughter] Garth Johnson is a writer, artist, and an educator who lives in Eureka, California. He is currently an assistant professor at the College of the Redwoods, and he is best known for his weblog Extreme Craft. He also writes widely. He's writing a blog for *ReadyMade* magazine and does a lot of other things as well.

Stefano Catalani did classic studies in Italy, which he says provided him with a theoretical background in art history and philosophy. He is now the curator at the Bellevue Arts Museum and has been there for the past four years. Stefano says his curatorial practice seeks to explore the fields of art, craft, and design beyond their traditional definitions and distinctions.

Andy Brayman has a BA in sociology, a BFA in ceramics from the University of Kansas, and an MFA from Alfred University. His work is a combination of traditional craft, industrial processes, and contemporary art strategies. In 2005, Andy founded the Matter Factory, in Kansas City, which is part studio, part laboratory, and part factory. It produces objects of his design, and the company contains a collaborative design element as well.

Jean McLaughlin is the director of the Penland School of Crafts. Prior to 1998, Jean worked with the North Carolina Arts Council for 16 years. She holds a master's degree in liberal studies from North Carolina State.

What I asked this posse of people to do was to make my task a little lighter, because it's a heavy burden to sum up, especially when time is short. I asked them to answer four questions that you have before you. These four questions are: What reactions do you have to the results of the survey? What two wishes do you have for the future of craft? What have we learned from the past or should we have learned from our past to carry us into the future? And what question do we need to address in the future?

I'm going to ask each person to address the first question: <u>What reactions do you have to the results of the survey?</u>

Stefano Catalani

I want to make a motion to have the next American Craft Council meeting at Burning Man. That's my first thought. That's what I learned from this survey. In

"I'm trying to figure out what craft is, honestly. I think after 90 years of encroachment of art into the field of the object, from the collage and Duchamp and Brillo boxes to making objects part of the vocabulary of art, I think the craft field has lost a lot of territory, a lot of land." / Stefano Catalani

> "I'm interested in the humanities but also just the breadth of ways that craft is a part of learning and life. There are so many ways that the idea of touch and material could be so much more broadly understood." / Jean McLaughlin

August, September, Liberty Weekend, so the museum will let me go. It will look like vacation [laughs]. I think [my reactions to this survey], actually, were pretty predictable in a way. I think all of the old contradictions in the field of craft came through in the survey.

Jean McLaughlin

I thought it was a great idea to poll everybody just so that we were checking our assumptions. I think that research is a really important thing for us to do, and that is what I was going to talk about. The idea of coming up with what kinds of questions we all would like to have answered and consistently, over time, ask those questions, so that we're not just asking it today of this group but we're asking and gathering information about our field and ourselves and weighing in on it over time. Questions can change, but have some questions be very similar that arise as important questions that we then consistently ask over time.

Lacey Jane Roberts

I'm stuck on a question: Should craft be an example of critical making, parallel to critical thinking, in our culture? Why isn't there one thing where we are all critically thinking about our making? That seems like a really important thing to me. I want to combine that question and say that every time you make something you should be critically thinking about it. And every time you think about it, make your practice an example of an object that functions in the world that demonstrates what you are thinking about. That's my reaction to that question. I felt really strongly about it.

Andy Brayman

I thought the example of looking for slippage, the points that were really divided—in some of those cases, it was surprising to me that it was divided so evenly. But when I think about it, that's fine for a lot of the issues. Consensus is not necessarily the objective. This conference is a really great example of how diverse people's interests are in the field. The areas where there is slippage are, as you said, worth talking about, because there could be really interesting stuff there.

But allowing that divergence to remain that way is totally fine in my mind.

Garth Johnson

I think a lot of these questions are important to me, and a lot of the things we've addressed this weekend have been important to me, but I guess we keep coming back to and getting stuck on the DIY issues. On the one hand, I'm someone who comes out of the DIY world. I've had great conversations and have been very engaged by a broad population of people who have been here. And, on the other hand, the entire weekend I've heard people making passive-aggressive comments and grumbling behind me. During Garth Clark's discussion, a gentleman behind me, when Garth raised a question about DIY, just flat-out said, "Because it sucks." So I think this is a very interesting survey to me because it's telling me that it's a very vocal minority, and that sometimes distorts the way we think about things, the vocality of the minority.

Brent Skidmore

Believe it or not, I would totally agree with that. But I really want to be in Lacey Jane's posse, because I think what's missing on the survey, and what's missing in any conversation continually that we have as a group, is the power of transformation in the human. That could be a student. That could be someone who will never be a potter but is throwing a pot. That could be anyone you know that is going to be any number of things, coming at this from many different angles. But where is the conversation about the transformative moment and the power that exists in that moment to move us forward, as a field, as a society? I would challenge this group in forming the next conference, because I'm hopeful that there will be a next conference, that we could address that issue as our thematic topic and move from there. I think by doing that we'll be a lot more inclusive globally and our diversity will increase greatly, because we'll be looking at it, as we did this weekend, either from an economic vantage point, a cultural vantage point (although I think that one could be greatly increased), but a scientific human-health vantage point would add to our discourse here. For me, there were questions that still were missing, that aspect in the survey—what takes place in me, it's a very personal stance, but I know it exists. Even in historians who are looking at the work and looking at how it was used and where it is placed in history. It exists in every aspect that we touch on in craft, but we never address that. One person said it over the course of the whole weekend, and then Rob [Walker] addressed it this weekend in two ways: I stay sane when I make things. Let's all give it up, you do. And Robin [Petravic] said, "Those people," he was referring to the people who work at Heath Ceramics, "would be sad if they weren't doing what they are doing."

Sonya Clark

I want to say one other thing that I felt about putting this survey together. The survey was problematized by a decision that I made, frankly, to come up with questions that had "yes" and "no" answers. I think the really rich questions are "why" questions and "how" questions, and that sort of thing. But in the interest of time and being able to take your pulse, it meant taking on that limitation.

BS

This gets us beyond talking about craft as a word and how many ways we use it. Does the act of transforming materials through techniques and processes into an object that we define as craft change you?

SCLARK

Me, personally? Yes!

BS

We would have had at least one question that I bet we'd have 100 percent on. Then we could say there's at least one. I think in these questions, sometimes we're talking to ourselves too much.

SCLARK

I also think there's another thing to be said—and this speaks to what you mentioned, Jean, and a little bit of what Lydia Matthews was saying earlier—there are all these people who have expertise out there. We could have someone come into this conference who puts together these kinds of surveys and puts the questions to us, and then we could say, "Here are 150 questions not generated by us but generated by someone whose expertise is to listen well" and see what it is that we might be trying to figure out about ourselves, and then have us choose which are the questions we feel are most relevant, that we want to know about ourselves. So that would be an interesting move.

Let me move on to what two wishes you would have for the future of craft. Just two!

SCATALANI

What is craft? That's the first question. That's the real problem here.

SCLARK

OK. That's one of the reasons you're up on the stage.

SCATALANI

I see my job as a practice. I'm trying to figure out what craft is, honestly. I think after 90 years of encroachment of art into the field of the object, from the collage and Duchamp and Brillo boxes to making objects part of the vocabulary of art, I think the craft field has lost a lot of territory, a lot of land. That has to definitely be addressed. So is craft something that is made out of one of the five traditional materials? In the Lee Nordness "Object: USA" show, 1969, plastic made it into the book, but somehow plastic didn't make the cut here. I don't know why. I think we're spinning around this question. We're trying to figure it out. That would be my first question. I think a lot of the questions in the survey deal with how you use the word "craft." In the end, they all underline the fact that we're still trying to figure out what is craft.

SCLARK

So you've actually answered: What question do we need to address in the future? We're going backward.

SCATALANI

Oh, what two wishes. I'd like to have wishes for the present of craft. To have more of these conferences or discussion around whether or not we have to be more inclusive. How do we expand the conversation without feeling passive-aggressive about whether DIY gets more attention in the press and on blogs and in cyberspace and why other traditional craft media don't. So I think my two wishes would be: Can we be grounded in the present and forget about the future?

SCLARK

So just to figure out who we are?

SCATALANI

Yeah, I think before we start to talk about a new craft culture. Like Garth [Clark], I feel that I don't know what it means, a new craft culture, if we don't know who we are now. I don't know if that answered two wishes, but I think as one wish it can be pretty big, honestly.

JM

So mine's somewhat similar. I was thinking about discourse and civil discourse and how that as a topic has been coming up a lot politically. How do we, as a culture, move

"Does the act of transforming materials through techniques and processes into an object that we define as craft change you?" / Brent Skidmore

forward and have civil discourse be a part of what we're all about? And how comfortable are we with the idea of debate? And how do we have debate and have a chance to explore our own intellectual inquiry and our own emotions? To be able to do that together as a group. I've been so blown away by the minds that are here and the conversations that I've had. I'm just so delighted and proud to be a part of this group of people. I was thinking about that in contrast to the [2006] Houston conference, because I wanted to be a part of the anime folks that were in the elevators and doing performance in the lobby, for those of you who were in Houston. I didn't feel connected to our group at all. I thought, These guys are having a much more creative time than we are, but then we were saved today by the dogs.

SCLARK
Animals do humanize.

JM
Yes. So that's one wish. And the other wish I've heard a lot in the conversations that I've had, and it is certainly always with me, is the desire for more time for reflection and the desire for the wonder and the spirit of joy and wonder that comes. I have to say, in all the intellectual and fabulous thinking and engagement that these two days have been, I just breathed a huge sigh of relief when we actually saw some objects and got to have a conversation about materiality—making and touching with wonder.

LJR
I have a lot of wishes. I was lucky to be educated in a palace that dropped the word "crafts" from its name. I went to CCA [California College of the Arts]. At CCA, I was part of the textiles department, so I was part of a very fierce, craft-dedicated, driven community that will defend craft and textiles down to the last penny. It's there. I also was part of the visual and critical studies department. I'm also queer. Since we're family, I'll just come out to you. I was able to immerse myself in queer theory at CCA and make all the time, while they were in concert with each other, constantly bouncing off of each other. My practice is like a pinball machine. I fire a ball, it hits a trigger, it lights up the making, that bounces off and hits the theory, and

then it comes back again and hits the triggers repeatedly, over and over again. Craft has been a vehicle for me to practice theory, and queer theory is completely informed by craft at the same time. So my wish is to expand craft into the humanities. It's already in a bunch of visual and material culture. Take it into other realms, to other places in your universities and schools, invade the humanities, and inform your making that way. By that, you're going to increase the diversity. You're going to get more queer kids. You're going to get more people who are combining craft with critical race theory, with poststructuralist theory. I'm a theory-head, I admit it, but I'm in my studio five days a week, if not more. So that's my wish.

AB
Well, I think, like you, I love the idea of expanding. When I thought about the different possible wishes for the field, it's a difficult question because it's so many fields. To come up with a wish for the whole field, it has to be very broad.

SCLARK
You can be selfish.

AB
So I will. The first one is broad. It sounds cliché, but really to allow and celebrate the diversity in the field and really not insult our pioneers, in the sense that there are so many people before us who have done really amazing things. A lot of that stuff really needs to be mined by us. There are a lot of really good solutions that people have already come to, and then there are these sort of half solutions that could be finished. Well, that happens naturally. We all do that, but it would be nice to do that even better. The second wish is much more specific. I think that the areas of sustainability coupled with material science are a dynamite combination for people working in crafts. These two things just pair up perfectly together. To take that pairing from a craft perspective, I think that there is a ton of really exciting work that could be done in that area.

GJ
My first wish can't be more wishes? [Laughter] My first wish, I think, actually dovetails with Andy's nicely and is very influenced by knowing him and having him sitting

next to me. Today, with Julie [Lasky] and Robin [Petravic], we paid a little bit of lip service to design in this room. We spent our whole weekend gnashing our teeth about DIY when we all sort of think the same thing. I've heard very little engagement about design. My point is that in Europe right now it's not DIY craft that has all of the energy and the young people; it's the field of design. If we had an engagement with design that was similar to what's going on in Europe right now, and if those lines became a little bit more blurry, I think this world would be a little more interesting. Which leads into my second hope, and kind of going against Stefano, hoping fervently that the word "craft" doesn't get defined more strictly. If craft can't encompass toothpick sculptures and people who make butter sculptures at the state fair, I'm really screwed with my writing. So I'm really rooting for a fuzzy interpretation of craft, not that we can't talk about it.

BS

I knew theirs would be complicated and the best! Going last again and I'm going to keep mine simple: That we will never entertain the question of our field being dead. That's one. And that as a result of never entertaining that, we will always have an active and engaged American Craft Council.

SCLARK

I'm actually going to skip the next question and go to the last one, which is:

What question do we need to address in the future?

SCATALANI

I think what we need to address for the future is the idea that craft is sort of like a romantic mental space, which is also, though, a community. And so, how to keep this space active and expanding. I see this community here, and it's torn by difficulties of understanding or defining each other: "I'm working with process. I'm working with technique. No, I'm working with material. Just because I'm working with clay doesn't make me a craftsman. No, but I'm making sculpture." We all feel like we all belong, including me,

coming back as a prodigal son to this community. The question—What do we need to address?—is to keep working on this idea of a community, which is a network of people who are all engaged in discussing around what craft is and how craft expresses the times in which we are living, from ethical, social, political, humanitarian, and environmental aspects, everything that informs our daily life. That's what I think is important.

JM

I have a practical one and maybe one that's not so practical. I think that we need to do a lot more research. Part of that research has to do with continuing to really understand the pulse of the artists that make up our field, in emerging, mid-career, and later-career times. I think the needs somewhat stay the same, but they also vary. Right now, I'm particularly thinking, not that this is more important than mid-career or early-career people, but, in fact, there was a huge upsurge in the number of people making work in the '60s. So that means that there are a lot of folks that are going to be at an age where they really need to be thinking about where their work is going to go, and what's going to happen to those artist estates, and what's going to happen to all of that work. I think it's a wonderful and serious issue for us as a field to think about. How are we going to revere—and not just make video tapes and fill archives with material, collect letters? That's really important, but I think the work itself is also important. We need to think where that work is going to go, what's going to happen to that. At Penland, we have conversations a lot about intergenerational engagement and how the classes are intergenerational and the living community is as well. Sometimes people suggest that maybe we ought to be thinking about what's going to happen to the artists who will need someone to be helping them in those senior years. All of a sudden I'm thinking about this. I don't want to be taking on a retirement community idea for the field of craft [laughs], but we need to be thinking about what's going to happen to our friends and mentors. I wake

"Every time you make something you should be critically thinking about it. And every time you think about it, make your practice an example of an object that functions in the world that demonstrates what you are thinking about." / Lacey Jane Roberts

> "I think that the areas of sustainability coupled with material science are a dynamite combination for people working in crafts. To take that pairing from a craft perspective, I think that there is a ton of really exciting work that could be done in that area." / Andy Brayman

up and all of a sudden I say, "Oh, my god, I'm not 20 anymore." I would love for others to help us think about this.

The other thing is that I, too, am interested in the humanities but also in just the breadth of ways that craft is a part of learning and life. I was having a conversation with Stoney Lamar about how our feet know things, that there are parts of our body that know things, that don't just come through our head. There's neurological information that we could be connecting to. There's historical, there's scientific, and humanities. There are so many ways that the idea of touch and material could be so much more broadly understood. Those are parts of what I'd like to be part of our future.

LJR

I think I want to go back to something I said with that survey, which is how objects function in the world and how what you are making is existing not only as an object but as a material thing, and what kind of circles is it entering and what is the thought behind it. When we're producing, who is it engaging and why, and how does it live these multiple lives? I think craft is a goldmine. I think that these objects that have been put into the world live multiple lives, and that this can be studied over and over and over again. I also am really interested in craft becoming its own field. But also, like I said before, becoming its own field by taking from other places to enrich itself. I'm curious to see how that might happen. I know that there are textbooks coming out, but I think that there needs to be this kind of really wide breadth of what we're taking from in terms of making and thinking.

AB

I guess the question is, What's the question we're going to address in the future? It's difficult to answer, because why not just do that now? [Laughter] I think the question seems to be about looking further than yourself. It goes to how you spoke about generations. It does seem cliché, but it seems like trying to reflect on the way we're all working and how we spend our time and energy from

the standpoint of after we're gone—and beyond legacy. I mean, everybody has ego. Legacy is really important, and I don't want to disregard that. I just assume that will be fine for people. Other than that, how are we spending our time? What is truly important? The bigger questions that go beyond craft and are about humanity.

GJ

I get to trim my little planned rant here. I think the question that we need to ask is one of inclusivity. I'm totally heartened by the results of the poll. I felt the grad student from New Paltz had her questions danced around. Maybe I've got a couple of quick observations that can help answer those questions and heal the divide. The first question was one about quality in the DIY movement. People act like there aren't people who show at ACC shows and who are ACC members who don't show at DIY shows. I know tons of them who do. I went to the Renegade Craft Fair in San Francisco. I've been with this DIY craft movement since the beginning, and I walked around with my jaw dropped, seeing couture-quality stuff, things with high price points, things that show at ACC shows. So don't make those observations if you don't have anything to back them up, if you don't know what you're talking about. The second thing is a question about having so much DIY work out there and does that cheapen or lessen the effect of the work that the craftspeople here make, which I think is an incredibly ridiculous statement because it's one of connoisseurship. Did all of you spring from the womb buying thousand-dollar silk scarves and expensive jewelry? You should be turning cartwheels that there are people out there buying $20 skull-and-crossbone iPod cozies, because I've got news for you, the DIY generation is getting older. If you go to any of these shows, they are filled with families and babies. I just bought my first $1,000-plus piece of craft this year, and so will plenty of the people who are buying things at DIY fairs. [Applause]

BS

Succinctly, where are we going to host

the next American Craft Council conference? Will it be on a university campus, will it be in rural America, will it be a group of regional conferences, as it has been in the past in other incarnations? The other one is: How will we get 10 times to 100 times to 1,000 times the amount of what I and Sonya are marking ourselves as a bridge between—the younger generation, and some will refer to that as the students? That, for me, has been the light of this conference and a major jolt and power.

SCLARK

That's a great place to end because that's one of the things that's made me really thrilled in the differences between the last ACC conference and this one, which is that I'm not the youngest person here. I was 39 at the time of the Houston conference, and I thought, "That's not young. Thanks for the compliment."

Can you join me in thanking the collective wisdom? [Applause] I also want to let you know that the questions that you felt have been missing from the survey have been recorded for future consideration, so thank you very much. A round of applause to yourself as well. ✦

Top:
Conference sessions were held in the Scandinavian Ballroom of the Downtown Minneapolis Radisson.

Below:
Current and past recipients of the Aileen Osborn Webb Awards, photographed after the awards luncheon on Friday, October 16.

Top:
The Friday Night Craft Tour brought conference attendees to the Northern Clay Center.

Below:
Attendees collaborated on an on-site weaving project masterminded by the Philadelphia artist Kathryn Pannepacker.

/ Speaker Biographies
/ Photo Credits
/ Thanks and Acknowledgements

Speaker Biographies

Sandra Alfoldy is associate professor of craft history at NSCAD University and associate curator of fine craft at the Art Gallery of Nova Scotia, in Halifax. She has a doctorate from Concordia University, Montreal (2001), and completed postdoctoral research at the University of Rochester (2002). Her books include *Crafting Identity: The Development of Professional Fine Craft in Canada* (2005), *NeoCraft: Modernity and the Crafts* (2007), and *Craft, Space and Interior Design, 1855–2005* (2008). She convened the 2007 NeoCraft international conference and is chief curator of the Canadian Fine Craft exhibition for the 2009 Cheongju Craft Biennale, in South Korea, and the Canadian Fine Craft exhibition for the 2010 Winter Olympics in Vancouver.

Elissa Auther is assistant professor of contemporary art in the visual and performing arts department at the University of Colorado, Colorado Springs. Her forthcoming book, *String, Felt, Thread and the Hierarchy of Art and Craft, 1960–1980* (University of Minnesota Press, 2009) focuses on the innovative use of fiber in American art. She is the coeditor of the April 2007 special issue on feminist activist art for the *National Women's Studies Association Journal* and director of Feminism & Co.: Art, Sex, Politics, a public program that explores issues of women and gender through creative forms of pedagogy. Currently, she is working on a book and exhibition about the counterculture in the American West titled *The Countercultural Object: Consciousness and Encounters at the Edge of Art, 1965–1975*.

Lisa Bayne is CEO of the Guild and Artful Home, a print and online resource for both artists seeking buyers for their work and consumers seeking access to a broad selection of original art in a variety of media. This position has allowed her to merge her training as a textile artist and her personal passion for art with her professional 25-year career in specialty multichannel retailing for brands such as J. Jill, Gymboree, and Eddie Bauer. Helping hundreds of supremely talented artists market their work to a greater art-loving public in a changing retail environment is her daily mission. Bayne is also a self-described serial knitter.

Natalie "Alabama" Chanin is best known as the cofounder of the American couture line Project Alabama and now for her company Alabama Chanin, launched in 2006. Her designs for hand-sewn garments constructed using quilting and stitching techniques from the Depression-era South have been lauded for their beauty and sustainability. Using a mixture of recycled and organic materials, Chanin creates limited-edition jewelry, clothing, home furnishings, and textiles handmade by artisans located near her home in Florence, Alabama. Firmly believing that good design should be a part of everyday living, Chanin provides a modern context to techniques that have been passed down through many generations. She is the author of *Alabama Stitch Book* (2008) and is at work on *Alabama Studio Style*.

Garth Clark is a leading writer and commentator on modern and contemporary ceramic art and an increasingly outspoken critic of the craft movement. He has written, edited, and contributed to nearly 50 books on ceramic art and authored more than 200 essays, reviews, and monographs. Among the touring museum exhibitions he has curated internationally are "A Century of Ceramics in the United States" and "The Artful Teapot." Clark was the coowner, with Mark Del Vecchio, of the Garth Clark Gallery, in New York and Los Angeles from 1981 to 2008, and since 1979, has been the founding director of the nonprofit group Ceramic Arts Foundation. He has received numerous awards and honors for his scholarship, several lifetime achievement awards, honorary doctorates, and book awards. Now a resident of Santa Fe, he is at work on several books.

Sonya Clark is the chair of craft and material studies at Virginia Commonwealth University School of the Arts. Under her leadership and alongside a world-class faculty, the department—which teaches technical and conceptual approaches to glass, fiber, metal, clay, and wood—has received high rankings from *U.S. News & World Report*. She is the recipient of numerous grants and awards, including a Virginia Commission for the Arts Fellowship, a Pollock-Krasner Foundation Grant, a Ruth Chenven Foundation Grant, and a Lillian Elliott Award. Her work has been exhibited nationally and internationally in more than 150 museums and galleries. Clark holds degrees from Cranbrook Academy of Art, the Art Institute of Chicago, and Amherst College.

Claudia Crisan attended the University of the Arts in Philadelphia, where she received a double bachelor's degree in metals and fibers, and got her master's degree in jewelry and metalwork from the Royal College of Art, in London, under the noted jewelry artist David Watkins. The Romanian-born artist's work ranges from small-scale gold chasings to large sculptural body pieces for catwalks, elaborate sugar sculptures, and jewelry for private parties. She currently co-owns and operates (with her husband) a small bakery and edible-art gallery called Crisan, in Albany, New York.

Julie Lasky is editor of *Change Observer,* a recently launched online magazine devoted to design for social impact that is affiliated with the popular website *Design Observer.* Prior to that, she was editor-in-chief of *I.D.,* the award-winning magazine of international design. A widely published writer and critic, she has contributed to *The New York Times, Metropolis, Dwell, Architecture, Slate, Surface, The National Scholar,* and NPR. She is the author of two books: *Borrowed Design: Use and Abuse of Historical Form* (written with Steven Heller, 1993) and *Some People Can't Surf: The Graphic Design of Art Chantry* (2001).

Adam Lerner is the director of the Museum of Contemporary Art Denver and chief animator in its department of structures and fictions. He was the founder and executive director of the Laboratory of Art and Ideas at Belmar until the Lab merged with the MCA Denver in 2009. Lerner was the master teacher for modern and contemporary art at the Denver Art Museum (2001–3) and, before coming to Colorado, was the curator of the Contemporary Museum, Baltimore. Lerner received his PhD from the Johns Hopkins University and his MA from Cambridge University. A pre-doctoral fellow at the Smithsonian American Art Museum during 1997–98, he is currently a Livingston Fellow of the Bonfils-Stanton Foundation, awarded to emerging leaders in the nonprofit sector.

Faythe Levine is an artist, a curator, an author, and a filmmaker currently based in Milwaukee, Wisconsin, where she produces the indie market Art vs. Craft and until recently owned Paper Boat Boutique & Gallery. Levine is the director and producer of *Handmade Nation,* an independent documentary about the rise of do-it-yourself art, craft, and design, and the co-author, with Cortney Heimerl, of a companion book of the same title (Princeton

Architectural Press, 2008). Her work has been reviewed and featured in many publications, including *The New York Times, Los Angeles Times, Modern Painters, ReadyMade,* and *American Craft.*

Lydia Matthews currently serves as academic dean and professor of visual culture at Parsons the New School for Design, in New York. Her work focuses on the intersection of contemporary art/craft/design practices, diverse local cultures, and global economies. She taught for 17 years at the California College of the Arts (formerly CCAC), in San Francisco, where she cofounded the graduate program in visual criticism and directed the MFA program in fine arts. An adviser for numerous institutions, ranging from small artist-run spaces to international art residencies and major museums, Matthews was commissioned to curate the U.S. section of the 2005, 2007, and 2008 Art Caucasus International Biennial, in Tbilisi, Georgia.

Jennifer Komar Olivarez is associate curator of architecture, design, decorative arts, craft, and sculpture at the Minneapolis Institute of Arts. Since she joined the MIA staff in 1991, she has organized numerous exhibitions on 20th-century architecture, design, and craft. Since 1994, Olivarez has been curator of MIA's Prairie School–style Purcell-Cutts House, and in 2000, she authored *Progressive Design in the Midwest: The Purcell-Cutts House and the Prairie School Collection at the Minneapolis Institute of Arts.* She attended St. Louis University, the University of Minnesota, and the University of Glasgow.

Thomas Patti, an artist who trained as an industrial designer and sculptor, is known for his innovative use of glass and plastics to create visionary architectural systems, small-scale sculptures, and large architectural commissions. His work, which spans four decades, has been widely exhibited and can be found in collections worldwide, including those of the Museum of Modern Art and the Metropolitan Museum of Art, in New York, and the Louvre, in Paris.

Robin Petravic manages operations, manufacturing, and business development for Heath Ceramics, a 60-year-old dinnerware and tile company located in Sausalito, California, with a new design studio and store in Los Angeles. After receiving a master's degree in product design from Stanford University, Petravic spent six years as an independent consultant for companies ranging from makers of electronics to sporting goods. In addition to stints at the Silicon Valley think-tank Interval Research, he also managed design and engineering teams at LightSurf Technologies. In the culmination of a quest to build a more satisfying and tangible life that would bring together designing and making, Petravic and his wife, the industrial designer Catherine Bailey, purchased Heath Ceramics in 2003. Since that time, the company has gained recognition as a design leader and model for bringing together manufacturing, design, and responsible business practices as a combination leading to long-term business viability.

Richard Sennett, sociologist and writer, received a BA from the University of Chicago (1964) and a PhD from Harvard University (1969). In the 1970s, he cofounded, with Susan Sontag and Joseph Brodsky, the New York Institute for the Humanities at New York University. In the mid-1990s, Sennett began to divide his time between NYU and the London School of Economics. His recent book, *The Craftsman,* names a basic human impulse: the desire to do a job well for its own sake. Although the word may suggest a way of life that waned with the advent of industrial society, Sennett argues that the craftsman's realm is far broader than skilled manual labor; the computer programmer, the doctor, the parent, and the citizen need to learn the values of good craftsmanship today.

Amy Shaw is a writer, blogger, and independent curator in Brooklyn, New York. In 2005, after working for many years in the art world, Shaw and her husband founded Greenjeans, a store, online market, and blog where they put their values and ideas about craftsmanship, sustainability, and conscientious living into action. Always on the lookout for new work by the next generation of craft practitioners, Shaw designed the 2009 Searchlight Artists exhibition at the American Craft Council Show, in Baltimore, and in 2008, organized a festival for Brooklyn-based furniture makers. Though the Greenjeans store closed in 2008, Shaw continues to find the craft world a fertile place for putting her ideals and values into action. She blogs about art, craft, design, and sustainability on her new site, Found Curve.

Michael Sherrill moved from Charlotte, North Carolina, to the western North Carolina mountains in 1974. His primary influences have come from his proximity to the North Carolina folk pottery tradition and to the surrounding community. He is a frequent instructor at Penland School of Crafts and has taught at craft schools and workshops across the country and in Canada. Sherrill has always been a bit of an inventor, and in 1995, he designed a line of tools for potters and sculptors called Mudtools. In 2003, Sherrill was honored as Artist of the Year by the Mint Museum of Craft + Design. His work has been widely exhibited throughout the United States and internationally. As part of the 2004 International Ceramics Symposium/WOCEF, Sherrill was one of ten artists invited to build outdoor sculptures to be placed permanently at the International Ceramic Museum, in Inchon, South Korea.

Maria Thomas, CEO of Etsy.com, the dynamic online marketplace for the handmade, leads a team of 60 staff members in helping to connect unique people, stories, and products in a playful and meaningful way. Etsy celebrates individual creativity in design, craftsmanship, and the feel of hand through its role as an innovator in the interactive marketplace. Prior to Etsy, Thomas was, for six and a half years, senior vice president and general manager of NPR Digital Media, where she built and managed NPR's online, podcasting, and mobile operations. She was also instrumental in launching NPR Music, a music discovery destination. Thomas began managing Internet-based businesses at Amazon.com, where she played a key role in the launch and management of Amazon's camera and photo store. Thomas's first career was in banking and finance.

Kristin Marie Tombers is a Minnesota native and has been the owner/operator of Clancey's Meats, in Minneapolis, since 2003. After an advertising career in Los Angeles, she moved away from the corporate structure and relocated to New York and then Philadelphia before finally settling back in Minneapolis. Not knowing where to buy food outside of farmers' markets or the farm itself, Tombers founded Clancey's Meats to bring passions together over the politics of food in a real meat market focusing on the butchery of humanely and sustainably raised animals.

Rob Walker is the author of *Buying In: The Secret Dialogue Between What We Buy and Who We Are* (2008) and a contributing writer and columnist for *The New York Times Magazine*. His column, "Consumed," has assessed consumer culture, design, marketing, and related topics since January 2004. Michael Pollan has called him "the most trenchant psychoanalyst of our consumer selves." Walker also writes for his own site, Murketing.com. He lives in Savannah, Georgia, with his wife, the photographer Ellen Susan, and their dog, El Rey de los Perros.

Namita Gupta Wiggers is curator at the Museum of Contemporary Craft, Portland, Oregon, where she directs the exhibition, collection, and public programming. Wiggers recently co-authored *Unpacking the Collection: Selections from the Museum of Contemporary Craft,* with contributions by Janet Koplos and Glenn Adamson. She served as a panelist for the Pew Charitable Trust (2007, 2009) and the Bush Foundation (2008) and has written for *The Journal of Museum Education, Art Lies,* and *Metalsmith.* Wiggers is currently guiding the museum's curatorial vision through a second transition—the museum's integration with Pacific Northwest College of Art. Combining experience and training as an art historian, museum educator, ethnographer, teacher, and studio artist, she is committed to a program that considers both craft and design in new ways. Wiggers holds a bachelor's from Rice University, Houston, and a master's from the University of Chicago.

Photo Credits

59 **bottom**/ Courtesy of Adam Lerner.

60 **top right**/ Library of Congress, Prints & Photographs Division, HABS. Reproduction number: HABS ILL, 16-CHIG, 88-1.

61 **middle**/ Library of Congress, Prints & Photographs Division, HABS. Reproduction number: HABS ILL, 16-CHIG, 39-75.

61 **bottom middle**/ Library of Congress, Prints & Photographs Division, HABS. Reproduction number: HABS ILL, 16-CHIG, 39-89.

61 **bottom**/ Chicago Architectural Photographing Co., July 1899. Sullivaniana Collection, Ryerson and Burnham Archives, The Art Institute of Chicago. Digital File #193101. C33914 © The Art Institute of Chicago.

62 **top left**/ Library of Congress, Prints & Photographs Division, HABS. Reproduction number: HABS ILL, 16-CHIG, 36-1.

62 **top right**/ Minneapolis Institute of Arts, the John R. Van Derlip Fund.

62 **middle** (detail of capital)/ Library of Congress, Prints & Photographs Division, HABS. Reproduction number: HABS ILL, 16-CHIG, 36-6.

62 **bottom** (lobby)/ Library of Congress, Prints & Photographs Division, HABS. Reproduction number: HABS MINN, 74-OWAT, 1-28.

62 **bottom** (detail of lamp)/ Library of Congress, Prints & Photographs Division, HABS. Reproduction number: HABS MINN, 74-OWAT, 1-26.

63 **top**/ Minneapolis Institute of Arts, gift of Kenneth and Judy Dayton.

63 **bottom**/ Minneapolis Institute of Arts, gift of Ruth L. and Walter Swardenski.

64 **top**/ Library of Congress, Prints & Photographs Division, HABS. Reproduction number: HABS ILL, 16-CHIG, 33-8.

64 **second from top**/ Library of Congress, Prints & Photographs Division, HABS. Reproduction number: HABS ILL, 16-CHIG, 33-2.

64 **side** (chair)/ Minneapolis Institute of Arts, gift of Susan Decker Barrows.

64 **bottom two photos**/ Courtesy of the Northwest Architectural Archives, University of Minnesota.

65 **top two photos**/ Minneapolis Institute of Arts, bequest of Anson Cutts.

65 **bottom left and right**/ Courtesy of Jennifer Komar Olivarez.

66/ Minneapolis Institute of Arts, gift of Ruth and Bruce Dayton in honor of Russell A. Plimpton.

67–70/ All images courtesy of Clancey's Meats.

77–83/ All images courtesy of Alabama Chanin.

85 **top**/ Courtesy of Faythe Levine.

85 **bottom**/ Courtesy of Kate Bingaman-Burt.

87/ Courtesy of the Little Friends of Printmaking.

88 **top and bottom**/ Courtesy of Jennifer Marsh.

89 **top**/ Courtesy of Faythe Levine.

89 **middle and bottom**/ Courtesy of Kate Bingaman-Burt.

90 **top**/ Courtesy of Faythe Levine.

90 **bottom** (portrait)/ Courtesy of Robyn Twomey.

90 **bottom** (two purses)/ Courtesy of Stephanie Syjuco.

91 **top**/ Courtesy of Faythe Levine.

91 **bottom two photos**/ Courtesy of Faythe Levine.

92 **top left**/ Courtesy of Bergere de France.

92 **top right**/ Courtesy of Lacey Jane Roberts.

92 **bottom**/ Courtesy of Mallory Whitfield.

93/ Courtesy of Whitney Lee.

96/ Courtesy of Vignelli Associates.

97/ Courtesy of *American Craft* magazine. Photo by Laurie Frankel.

98/ Courtesy of Ethical Metalsmiths.

99/ Courtesy of Droog.

122/ Originally published in *Playboy* magazine, July 1961.

123/ Photo by Nina Leen/Time Life Pictures/Getty Images.

126 **left**/ Photo by Lewis Wickes Hine. Library of Congress Prints & Photographs Division. Reproduction number: LC-DIG-NCLC-05626.

126 **right**/ Courtesy of Vignelli Associates.

127 **top**/ Photo by Paul Songco.

127 **bottom**/ Courtesy of Vignelli Associates.

128/ Photo by A. Sue Weisler/RIT

129 **right**/ Courtesy of Karim Rashid Studios. Photo by Milovan Knezevic.

131–139/ All images courtesy of Heath Ceramics.

142 **right**/ Photo by Gelay Jamtsho, Bhutan-360.

145 **left and right**/ Courtesy of Ethical Metalsmiths.

146 **top**/ Courtesy of Bamboo Bike Studio. Photo by Joe Zorilla.

146 **middle**/ Courtesy of Bamboo Bike Studio.

146 **bottom**/ Courtesy of Bamboo Bike Studio. Photo by Jesse Huffman.

147 **top**/ Courtesy of Bamboo Bike Studio. Photo by Marty Odlin.

147 bottom/ Courtesy of Stephanie Syjuco.
Photo by Nicole Stowe.
148 top and bottom/ Courtesy of
www.adbusters.org.
149 top and bottom/ Courtesy of
Otto Von Busch.
150 left/ Courtesy of Droog.
Photo by Experimental Jetset.
150 right/ Courtesy of Droog.
Photo by Isauro Cairo.
151 left and right/ Photos by Raphael Brion,
www.eatmedaily.com.
152 top and bottom/ Courtesy of
Kelly Cobb.
153 top and bottom/ Courtesy of
Ehren Tool.
170-171/ Copyright American Craft Council.
Photos by Greg Hegelson.

178 / 179

Thanks and Acknowledgements

"Creating a New Craft Culture"
is generously sponsored by:
Marlin Miller
Sara S. Morgan
Rotasa Foundation
Ron and Anita Wornick

NATIONAL
ENDOWMENT
FOR THE ARTS

Both the Dido Smith Award and the Carole Stupell Award for promising artists supported scholarships for this conference.

We would like to thank the Windgate Charitable Foundation for sponsoring the American Craft Council conference intern through the UNC Center for Craft, Creativity and Design.

Sponsors
Tote bags / Etsy.com and the Society of North American Goldsmiths (SNAG)
Print materials / NSO Press, Inc.
Friday luncheon program and signs / Spyglass Creative
Music for closing party / The Grand Hand Gallery

Additional Thanks
Jenny Gill/ conference assistant
Haberman & Associates / conference public relations
Belinda Lanks / copy editor for conference book
Meetings à la Carte / Kate Lichter, Shefali Kubavat, and Sara Martinez
Kathryn Pannepacker / craft installation artist
Rational Beauty / conference identity and print collateral
Rumors / conference website
And to all the volunteers who donated their time to make the conference a success.

All conference attendees who made donations for student scholarships. Your tax-deductible contribution helps the American Craft Council encourage and support professional excellence, education, and the public's understanding of American craft.

Monica Hampton / Director of Education
American Craft Council,
New York, NY

Committee Members
Stoney Lamar / Council Trustee
Sculptor, Saluda, NC

Sara S. Morgan / Council Trustee
Cofounder and former President, Houston
Center for Contemporary Craft
Board Member, Museum of Fine Arts
Houston, TX

Tina Oldknow / Council Trustee
Curator, the Corning Museum of Glass
Corning, NY

Warren Seelig / Former Council Trustee
Visiting Professor, University of the Arts
Philadelphia, PA

Cindi Strauss / Council Trustee
Curator, Museum of Fine Arts
Houston, TX

Lydia Matthews
Academic Dean and Professor of Visual Culture, Parsons the New School for Design
New York, NY

Sienna Patti
Owner, Sienna Gallery
Lenox, MA

Ann Pifer
Owner, The Grand Hand Gallery
St. Paul, MN

On the Ground Committee, Tour Hosts
Marcia Anderson
Senior Curator, Minnesota Historical Society

Emily Galusha
Executive Director, Northern Clay Center

Lin Nelson-Mayson
Director, Goldstein Museum of Design

Jennifer Komar Olivarez
Associate Curator, Architecture, Design,
Decorative Arts, Craft, and Sculpture,
Minneapolis Institute of Arts

Ann Pifer
Owner, The Grand Hand Gallery

For audio podcasts, photos from the conference, and continuing conversation, visit the "Creating a New Craft Culture" website: www.craftcouncil.org/conference09.

The "Creating a New Craft Culture" weaving now hangs in our offices on Spring Street in New York.